Learning {Re}imagined

How the connected
society is
transforming
learning

Graham Brown-Martin
Photographs by
Newsha Tavakolian

Contents

Software

This book is digitally enabled with
an optional app that is free to download.

The app provides you with access
to exclusive additional material including
video interviews and discussion groups.

To learn more and download the app
please visit

learning-reimagined.com/app

Stavros N. Yiannouka,
Chief Executive Officer
of the World Innovation
Summit for Education (WISE)

Since its establishment in 2009 under the patronage of Qatar Foundation's Chairperson, Her Highness Sheikha Moza bint Nasser, the World Innovation Summit for Education has been a thriving platform for debate and collaboration in education. WISE has also carried forward Her Highness's commitment to high-quality education for all by mobilising skills and resources which can empower individuals and transform communities.

In our ever-changing and increasingly interconnected world, education faces new challenges, and the needs of learners are increasingly complex and varied. As noted by the Chairman of WISE, HE Sheikh Abdulla bin Ali Al-Thani, PhD, 'When you take a look at what is going on in the world today it is clear that the need for innovation in education has never been so urgent. This means we need to think bigger and show more determination in our quest to bring innovation to the field of education. We also need to ensure that best practices in education are shared and adapted to different regions and cultures in the most effective ways.'

This latest WISE book seeks to respond to this situation in an original way. Part travelogue, the book takes us on a journey around the globe to visit schools and educators. The tales that emerge illustrate a wide range of learning environments, each with its own needs and unique approaches to the role of technology. Through interviews, case studies and essays, you will learn about the schools and projects that are engaging students – and teachers – in new ways. You will meet some of the most innovative, energetic and effective educators whose ideas and practices are shaping the connected world in all its diversity.

The book also treats technology as a touchstone for a wider exploration of the role of education systems: What is education for? In what ways do contemporary technologies merely reinforce outmoded teaching practices? Is there a danger that technology might erode or displace the cultural values of communities? Can the use of technology in learning spaces benefit societies and, at the same time, help individuals nurture their creativity and achieve their personal goals? What emerges is not a full endorsement of all that technology offers, but a considered look at the role of the teacher, assessment practices and access to high-quality education in both tech-enabled and underserved communities. The book includes portraits of education visionaries and dialogues with thinkers whose ideas have sparked new projects and innovative approaches to unique situations. These exchanges demonstrate the optimism of those who are reflecting deeply on, and confronting, the day-to-day challenges of bringing high-quality education to their communities and beyond.

WISE will continue to support the work of such innovators based on the conviction that education is our most powerful tool to improve lives. We very much hope that this book will provide food for thought to readers and inspire them to continue asking the important questions that will guide our progress.

Foreword

Bloomsbury Qatar Foundation Publishing

17th Floor

Tornado Tower

PO Box 5825 - Doha, Qatar

www.bqfp.com.qa

—

Bloomsbury Academic

An imprint of Bloomsbury Publishing Plc

50 Bedford Square - London – WC1B 3DP - UK

1385 Broadway, Fifth floor, New York, 10018 USA

www.bloomsbury.com

—

First published 2014

© Qatar Foundation, 2014

—

BQFP Hardback ISBN 978-99271-01-94-6

BQFP Paperback ISBN 978-99271-01-93-9

Bloomsbury Academic Paperback ISBN 978-14742-22-73-0

—

Cover and design by

DES SIGNES studio Muchir Desclouds

—

Printed in China

Reprinted once 2013

—

Front image

Adeiso Presbyterian Junior High School,

Ghana (Worldreader)

Back image

Himalayas (Taken from Flight CA437 Chengdu

to Kathmandu *en route* to New Delhi)

Bloomsbury is a trademark of Bloomsbury Publishing Plc

MIX

Paper from
responsible sources

FSC® C008047

www.fsc.org

Acknowledgements

I want to acknowledge the support, diligence and effort of the World Innovation Summit for Education team in making this project a reality. This book and related media would not have been possible without the support, ideas, participation, patience and resilience of many who were as passionate as I about this publication. You can't create something like this on your own and it would be impoverished if you tried. As with the spirit of this journey, it is through sharing and collaboration that we progress.

I thank all of those who were so generous in giving me their time and putting up with the endless questions that I have attempted to capture here. I also want to thank the legion of people who worked hard in the background to help me schedule meetings and visits as well as the drivers, fixers, airline crews and hotels who showed kindness and helped to make such an intense journey much more enjoyable.

I thank Newsha Tavakolian, whose photographs illustrate this book, and Raphael Yaghobzadeh, who made sure everything worked. Without your good spirits, humour and hard work this journey would not have been so incredible. I will always have happy memories of you both.

I thank my wife, Ren, and my children, Joshua, Jessica, Forest, and Phoenix, for being patient when I was travelling and putting up with me when I was home.

I would also like to acknowledge my father, Vincent, who died whilst I was making this book. Like all of us he wasn't perfect, but he did teach me to reach further. I miss him.

And I would like to thank Her Highness Sheikha Moza bint Nasser, Chairperson of Qatar Foundation, and Dr Abdulla bin Ali Al-Thani, Chairman of WISE, for their commitment to education and their support. The World Innovation Summit for Education is an initiative of Qatar Foundation, launched in 2009 with the guidance of Her Highness. Ultimately, it is her vision of a better world through innovation in learning that has made this project possible. And it is through initiatives such as WISE that we understand each other better.

Graham Brown-Martin

I would like to thank my assistants, Elie Domit and Neda Jahanbani, who helped me to organise everything. Special thanks to my husband, Thomas Erdbrink, for all his support and love.

Newsha Tavakolian

The programmes featured in this book

Map

Quest to Learn
New York
United States of America
High Tech High
San Diego
United States of America
NAVE School
Rio de Janeiro, Brazil
Porvir
São Paulo, Brazil

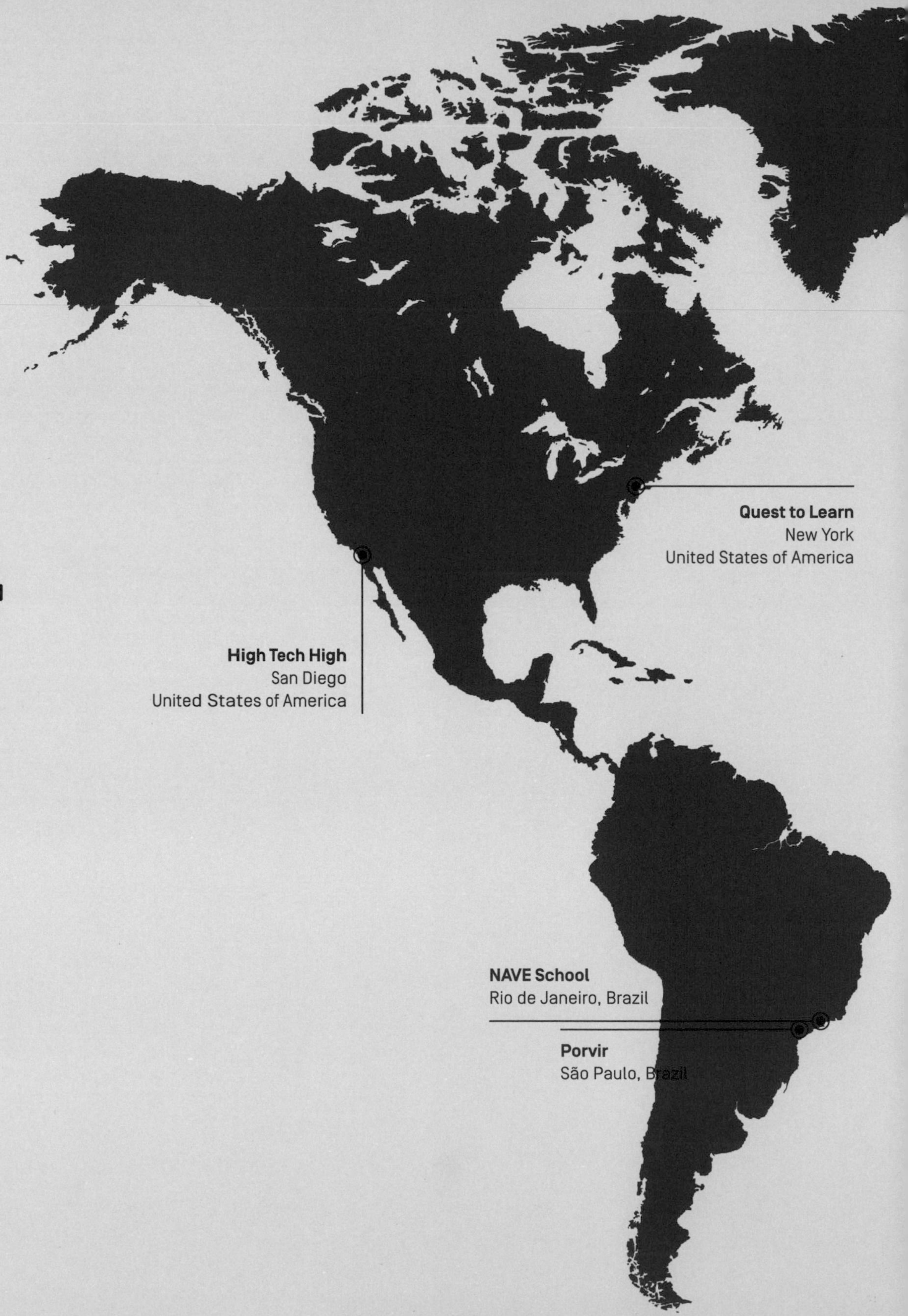

Essa Academy
Bolton, United Kingdom

Raspberry Pi
Cambridge, United Kingdom

Eastwood College
Beirut, Lebanon

RDFZ Xishan School
Free Lunch for Children
Beijing, China

Awsaj Academy
Doha, Qatar

GEMS Education
Dubai, United Arab Emirates

Jordan Education Initiative
Amman, Jordan

Mobile Web Ghana
Accra, Ghana

Worldreader
Adeiso, Ghana

XSEED
BBC Media Action
India

National Institute of Education
Singapore

Introduction

I recently backed a project on Kickstarter, an online crowd-funding site, for the creation of an inexpensive computer kit that children could make themselves and learn how to code. It was an impulse investment of around $150 just before the winter holidays in England, soon after I returned to London following the adventure that I will be taking you on in this book. There was something about it that reminded me of my youth, when I experienced adventure after adventure taking things, anything, apart to see how they worked, before eventually being rewarded with a computer kit of my own. One way or another, the homemade computer of my childhood determined the career and life choices that brought me here writing this book.

Walking my eight-year-old daughter to school on that chilly winter morning, I asked her, 'Would you like to make a computer?' She pondered the question for a while before replying, 'I'd rather make pancakes.' Suddenly my imaginary bubble of sitting around the kitchen table with my daughter, soldering iron in hand, whiling away an afternoon building the first of many devices that would see her becoming a thrusting entrepreneur to challenge any of those in Silicon Valley was burst. The reality was that I'd really bought the kit for myself in a fit of nostalgia while demonstrating the difference between how my daughter and I valued what people of my generation call 'technology'.

To paraphrase educational technologist Alan Kay, technology is something that happens after you were born. I was born in 1964 to a world of black and white television with three channels to choose from, when the BBC began its first broadcasts to target children and the only music radio stations worth listening to were run by pirates. By contrast, my daughter was born in 2005 to a world of mobile connectivity, the iPhone, the Internet, video on demand, near-photo-realistic computer animation, interactive entertainment, YouTube and social media. Whilst academics, educators and policy-makers consider what it is to be a 21st-century learner, this is the only century that my daughter and her generation have ever known.

It's this difference, I believe, that produces a 'So what?' response from my millennial child where for her there's no contest between making pancakes and making a computer. She could, in fact, do either and it's just not a big deal in her world. That's not to say that she's not agile or interested in the digital tools and toys that to her are part of the landscape she was born into. Far from it.

Rather, her relationship with technology and the connected world will always be different from mine.

This isn't without precedent either. My father was an automotive engineer from a long line of engineers. I was supposed to continue the family business but, to his dismay, as my teenage years coincided with the birth of the personal computer, I couldn't have been less interested in being a grease monkey. And so we return to coda.

It's this generational shift that is at the crux of the story and the journey that will unfold in the pages you are holding in your hands. For several generations up to my father, and even my older brother, it was assumed that the family business of industrial engineering would continue father-to-son *ad infinitum*. But as we know, the invention of the microprocessor and its convergence with mass communications technology are driving seismic change in our society with largely unpredictable outcomes within structures that are designed to resist change.

The role of digital technology in learning remains a fertile area for debate, ranging from discussions around technology as a learning outcome in itself to whether memory recall assessments are relevant in an age where, for many, information is available at their fingertips. There are debates about what a school or university should now be and even if we still need teachers. But these discussions invariably arrive at the same destination of what we think, as a society, education is for. Perhaps when we can answer that it will be easier to determine the role that technology can play.

In a society shaped around the Industrial Revolution we often deploy technology to reduce costs, increase quality and automate standard processes to achieve a predictable and standardised output. Is this what we want when we deploy technology within a learning context?

Had I written this book even ten years ago, it would have been a carefully curated collection of essays and stories that presented a watertight case that digital technology was the silver bullet for the transformation of the world's ills, including education. Indeed, I already have a bookshelf full of tomes that promise digital nirvana in various flavours. Today, however, I'm a little more circumspect and wonder if some of the things we think are transformational aren't really; to quote my late father at a car auction, '...Nothing more than a bodykit on an old engine.'

'Transformation', like many words that suddenly become fashionable and begin appearing on countless Powerpoint slides, is becoming harder to define, along with its bedfellow 'disruption'. Both words are also context-sensitive in that their definition and correct use will be subject to the context in which they are used. A light bulb in a village without electricity could be described as transformative, whereas an interactive whiteboard used in an affluent neighbourhood to replace a chalkboard or projection screen may be less so.

For me, what makes the *Learning {Re}imagined* project – as well as the WISE initiative – unique is its global view. This project has given me the opportunity to review my thinking around transformation in learning through many contextual lenses and, like education itself, there is no 'one size fits all'. What I have learned is that there are a great many voices, thinkers, doers and practitioners who are all tackling the challenges of making teaching, learning and education as engaging and as relevant as they can for what is an uncertain future.

My journey took me across five continents with official visits to ten countries and several other trips that coincided with this project and included speaking engagements. I participated in a high-profile think tank to create a blueprint for learning in the year 2030.[1] I listened to many well-known voices but far more less-heard voices. I visited remote villages in developing countries as well as some of the most technologically advanced places of learning. Without exception, what I found were passionate people, real-life heroes and innovators determined to meet the challenges of a changing world head-on. From a macro perspective, what I saw were people in different parts of the world all working on different parts of a big picture and, whilst technology is a part of this, I discovered that it's not the most important part.

The visits and meetings documented in this book took place from July to November 2013 following a number of months of research and complex logistical planning to determine how myself – accompanied by photographer Newsha Tavakolian and our technical assistant, Raphael Yaghobzedah – would be able to fulfil such an ambitious schedule. Inevitably there are numerous individuals and organisations that could be included in such a journey and their absence from this collection of stories should not be taken either as an oversight or lack of regard for the part they play in what is a global movement to improve education.

The research for this work is therefore qualitative, based on authentic experience and being there in the field. It's about what people think and feel as much as what they are doing. As a result, it's much more difficult to subject to analysis than quantitative research that would be full of things that are easy to measure. Thus we once again arrive at the nub of the dialogue around learning and education. Do we measure what is easy or what is important? Industrial systems favour the former and there is a risk that digital implementations of education will do the same.

I should take a moment here to outline my credentials. I completed an automotive apprenticeship under my father at the age of 12 and left full-time education at 15, teaching myself from then onwards. I was an unschooler before the term existed, an autodidact who tutored himself from shoplifted books before seeking out some of the most inspiring mentors I could muster to help me answer the questions I felt were important. I am still doing this today – seeking out mentors that is – for my lifelong learning and questions. I have built and sold educational publishing and digital entertainment businesses. I have been penniless, wealthy and penniless again. I have experienced pain and joy. I am a socialist, or at least a free-market one. I am passionate about the endless creativity of the human species and optimistic about its chances for survival.

Part travelogue, part diary, part commentary, this book takes you on a journey in the form of essays, interviews, case studies and thought pieces, illustrated with beautiful photography and an evolving library of digital resources that documents how a more connected world is changing and how educators and learners are responding to these changes.

Some may ask, 'Why in this digital age am I holding a printed book?'

I would say because it's beautiful and because there is still a place in our society for a tangible artefact. Whilst the digital economy continues to disrupt and displace the physical, the story isn't over yet. There are signs that the physical economy, whether it be retail, the handcrafting of objects or artisan farmers, will undergo a renaissance – a re-imagining, if you like – in response to the digital takeover.

Such a renaissance flies in the face of the techno-utopian vision of Silicon Valley solutionists where everything is but a click away.

Where once we thought atoms would be converted to bits, the new story is that bits are now converting to atoms as we see the emergence of the maker movement. This is partly driven by new digital platforms such as 3D printing, Arduino and Raspberry Pi, where individuals are taking a new interest in making technology and tangible objects rather than simply using technology as a passive consumer.

In keeping with the theme of the story, this book is an example of how the printed media and authors might re-imagine themselves. The eBook format is a fine example of what digital technologies are good at: taking something that is standard and then digitising and distributing it cheaply with minimal loss to the experience. But digital technologies are inevitably lossy, whether it is the miscommunication we experience with a carelessly worded email or the compression of music in an mp3 file. This got me wondering about what we could do to create a physical experience that weaved in a digital one, given that the either/or argument seemed like a false dichotomy. Having been a digital kid for much of my life, it now felt like there was room for both.

In authoring and designing this book I've tried to create something that you as the reader can jump into wherever you like. If you wish, you can traverse it from cover to cover, but if you're like me you may prefer to browse the visuals, flip the pages and then dive in when you feel the urge. There is no right or wrong way to read this book. I haven't designed it as a linear journey. There is no grand conclusion other than the one you make and share with your friends and colleagues. I will tell you what I think but it will just be an opinion, no more valid than yours. But to be honest this journey isn't random either.

What I discovered by travelling the planet at an impossible speed is that challenges and solutions began to blend as a result of sleep deprivation and cultural dissonance. In a perverse way, I hope that this will happen to you as you travel through these pages.

I hope you enjoy this journey and that you'll let me know your thoughts as you navigate your way through it.

You know where to find me.

@GrahamBM

'...there are a great many voices, thinkers, doers and practitioners that are all tackling the challenges of making teaching, learning and education as engaging and as relevant as they can for what is an uncertain future.'

'Technological determinism is the religion of Silicon Valley, a reductionist theory that presumes that society's technology drives the development of its social structure and cultural values...'

Followers of Ray Kurzweil and the Singularity will be aware that it is anticipated that by around the year 2030, give or take, computers will become sentient. That is, they will think like you or me, make decisions and be self-aware. It is beyond the scope of this book to consider the implications of such a prophecy but it is worth considering what the world might look like in 2030.

Why 2030?

Well, because a child entering formal education today (2014) will emerge from university, should universities still exist, in 2030.

Futurists are always good value at a conference, especially those who are technological determinists and ignore all of the social implications of what they are saying. Technological determinism is the religion of Silicon Valley, a reductionist theory that presumes that a society's technology drives the development of its social structure and cultural values. Bless them, of course they do.

Technological determinism is matched only by economic determinism, which gifts economic structure over politics in the development of human history, usually touted as a misunderstanding of the works of Marx or in the sound bite 'It's the economy, stupid'. I would however argue that economic determinism has the edge over technological, given that most of the proletariat are consumed by their pursuit of food, clothing and shelter. Anyway, I digress.

Technological determinism seeks to convince you that technical developments, media or technology as a whole are the key movers in history and social change. Indeed this is quite convincing when one considers the invention of the steam engine as the trigger for the Industrial Revolution. So let's stick with this for a while.

All this said, there are probably some things that we can predict in regard to technology, assuming we follow current trajectories. The most obvious first base is raw computing power. Futurists will always show you a set of graphs that demonstrate the ever-increasing processing power of computers, whether they are based on silicon or something else. They are probably right in this regard, and if they are, it shows that by 2020 we will arrive at what they call 'exascale', computing power which is roughly comparable to human brains, or at least some of them. That will probably be in a laboratory but give it a few years and it will be in your mobile phone. By 2030 it is suggested that we will arrive at 'zettascale', computing which is 1,000 times more powerful or faster than the human brain. Who knows what this really means?

Let's ignore this notion of 'machine consciousness' on the basis that it is just too difficult to comprehend. What could a zettascale computer do?

Well, it could accurately predict global weather patterns at least two weeks in advance. That doesn't mean a sort of rough guess that it might rain in London two weeks from now, but rather that it will know with complete accuracy when, how long and how much. It could do this for every location on the planet. This could be useful for travel agents or umbrella sales. But this sort of computing power could mean that your personal DNA could be sequenced in a matter of seconds, or that every single digital interaction you've had with anyone could be profiled in the blink of an eye, or that what you'll do next is almost 100 percent predictable.

This could be great news if you find yourself struck with a life-threatening cancer. Rather than the crude and primitive broad spectrum poison of chemotherapy used today to treat cancer patients, you could have something that is designed to search and destroy the unique cancer cells in your body. On the flipside, there is very little you could do without someone knowing it first. But if you haven't done anything wrong you've got nothing to worry about, right?

Well, wrong, actually.

The wrong is about who is in control and who we trust to make decisions about ethics, morality and our ability to think for ourselves. I'm writing this in 2014 and the world is currently in a primitive dialogue about ideology, theology and morality. To be honest, I couldn't tell you what will happen by 2020, let alone 2030, but I'm sure that I don't want to outsource this to a computer farm coded by Silicon Valley reductionists.

So let's look at this from another point of view. You are the mentor or a teacher of a five-year-old child entering full-time education today in 2014. What are the skills that you should equip that child with to navigate this future?

Being able to code in Python probably won't cut it.

'By 2030 it is suggested that we will arrive at *zettascale* computing which is 1,000 times more powerful or faster than the human brain.'

photo credit: Joi Ito

In 2012, US author and entrepreneur Seth Godin published his manifesto for changing the way we educate our children. Entitled 'Stop Stealing Dreams'[2], his publication made a strong case that Western economies had changed significantly but their education systems had not. I caught up with Seth to ask him to explain some of his thinking.

Graham Brown-Martin: Seth, tell me what you think school and education are for.

Seth Godin: Public education is only 150 years old and we built it with a specific function in mind. We built the educational system to train kids to sit still long enough to work in the factory. That's what it's for, to create compliant, obedient factory workers, so the question we need to ask is: What is school for now? We're not asking that question. Parents, administrators, taxpayers are not asking: What is school for? I have an opinion. I think what it's *not* for is to create more factory workers because we don't need more factory workers.

I think what we need to do is teach two things. One, how to solve interesting problems, and two, how to lead. If you look at just about any public school in North America or Europe, we're not teaching that. We're teaching kids how to do well on the test.

Graham: Why do you think our industrialised schooling systems are resistant to the sort of changes we've seen in other parts of society?

Seth: What we built when we built the school system is an institution insulated from the outside world. We built a bureaucracy that is designed to maintain structure year after year. We built the system based on professionals doing some professional work based on some decisions that were taken 100 years ago. I'm not surprised at all that the school system doesn't wake up every morning, look at the outside world and say, 'Oh, let's reinvent ourselves so that we can create better graduates for a different kind of world.'

We don't live in an industrial-driven economy any more. We don't make the things we used to make the way we used to make them. What we have now is an economy where value is created by connections. Value is created when we work with people we trust, when expectations are high, when we innovate. All of those things come from human beings doing art, doing something without a map, doing something that matters to them. None of them come from following instructions and yet from the time you're in first grade, what you are graded on — what you are rewarded for — is following instructions. That has to change.

Graham: How do you think creativity can be valued more within our education systems?

Seth: School is a factory, a box, a building that produces an output. That output is the educated student. What they learned in Detroit in the 1980s when they were making lousy cars is that if you measure the quality of what you're making, the quality will go up. Detroit figured out how to cut down defects but of course Japan figured it out faster than they did. Factories in the industrial world all embrace scientific management, they all embrace this idea of measuring every single detail. We took that and we handed it to the factory we call school and we say, if you can measure, make it better.

If you can't measure it, it doesn't matter. Why are we surprised that the people who work in schools, the people who we are rewarding for measurement, are choosing not to teach things they can't measure?

The mistake is ours. The mistake is that, as the people who are paying for the factory, we are demanding the wrong thing. Instead of demanding things that can be tested by the ACT or the SAT, or some other standardised test, we should be demanding enlightened human beings who desire to make a difference.

If we start measuring how many of those are getting made and how big a difference is getting made, schools are going to start making something different as well. There's a little computer called an Arduino. You can buy it for $29, probably wholesale half that. And on it is the entire Linux operating system and everything you need to build and operate a new kind of computer. The question I want to understand is: Why aren't we giving that to eight-year-olds and saying, 'Here, figure it out.'?

Why aren't we going to nine-year-olds and saying, 'Here is a problem. No one knows the answer. Come up with your best approach.'? Why aren't we teaching kids that it's OK to say, 'This might not work.'? Because we're about to enter an era of innovation where the only successful people and the only people who do work that matters are the ones who wake up in the morning saying, 'This might not work.' And yet all we're teaching kids to do is stuff that they're sure is going to work.

Graham: What would you say to critics in the education profession who say it's one thing to state the problem but an entirely different one to implement change?

Seth: You want a map? You say to people like Sir Ken Robinson and even me, 'Tell me step by step what to do.' You want instructions, you want the dummy's guide? Sorry, that's not what I do. I'm in the compass business, not the map business.

I'm not the person who can tell you step by step by step how to create art. What I'm trying to tell you is that there's a huge disconnect which is that the world needs something from you, the school organiser, the school teacher. We need something from you and you're not even trying to give it to us.

I have no doubt that the brains and the passion in the education industrial complex are smart enough and focused enough to solve this problem 100 different ways if they choose to. Right now, before we start arguing about the tactics, we have to agree on the strategy. We have to agree that there is a problem that isn't being solved and we have to stop trying to solve a problem from 1950 and 1962 and start acknowledging that the number on the table is a different one.

Graham: What do you think the role of technology can be in the transformation of our school systems?

Seth: If it's worth memorising, it's worth looking up. Everybody has access to everything they'd ever need if they have a smartphone that can find you every fact, every figure, every mathematical calculation done for you. So why are we spending all of our time in classroom – extremely expensive time, extremely valuable time – getting kids to memorise something as opposed to giving them the incentive and the desire to look it up?

The role of the classroom, as Sal Khan has pointed out, is to do homework. At night we'll watch lectures by the best and the brightest teaching with passion online. When I come back to school the next day, I'll say, 'Work with me. Coach me. Put me into an uncomfortable position.'

School is for problem solving. School is for mentoring and coaching and teaching me where my fear is and getting me to befriend it so I can figure out how to be in the business of leading and connecting and solving interesting problems. I don't need you to test me on whether I know the capital of Alaska. It doesn't matter.

>   **Graham:** With the introduction of Massive Open Online Courses and other online learning platforms, how do you see the role of the university changing?

Seth: What's a university for? What's a college for? It seems like a silly question until we realise that now we can take all the courses in MIT [the Massachusetts Institute of Technology] and all the courses in Stanford and set them free.

Suddenly, there's no scarcity. There's an abundance. So if college is just access to lectures, college is over because you can't keep the lectures inside the building any more. We set them free. Not only that, but I can get a better lecture than you can offer me at your local institution because I can take the best lecture from anywhere in the world.

Now that the college lecture is set free from the building, now that I can take a Stanford course or an MIT course for free anywhere in the world, we need to ask a new question: What is college for? What has college ever been for? If college

is a scarce resource where we control access so that only a few people get to see the lecture, then university is over. I think college is more important than that.

I think college has always been about three things. First, sure access to lectures. This is no longer relevant because the best lectures in the world are going to be done online. If I live in Manchester or Berlin, I don't have to take the course from Manchester or Berlin, I can take the course from the very best teacher on that topic in the world.

Now I think we get two other things from college and university. Second, who am I in school with? Who am I sitting next to? Who are my mentors? Who are my teachers who care about me, because that's a formative force in our life. Third, we get accreditation. What label do I get to put on myself when I'm done? How do I prove I'm a Harvard man or an Oxford man?

The scarcity is no longer going to be about who got to see the lecture. The scarcity is going to be about who you sit next to and how you prove that you finished, so it's not like the record industry where all the record industry had was some file that was liberated from the vinyl LP then put on the CD and now, anywhere you want, whenever you want for free.

Now that we have removed the classroom, we've got to figure out what colleges and universities offer that makes them worth the time and worth the money so that someone will go through the hoops to get that label. Because all you've got is some *faux* scarcity that comes from the fact that you're accredited and the online course isn't. That's not enough to make me pay you $200,000, sorry.

>   **Graham:** It's been suggested that our education systems are about to be disrupted in a similar way to how the music industry was disrupted by Napster. What's your take on this?

Seth: If we're really serious about education, this is a chance of a lifetime. If you talk to people from the music industry, there are two

camps. There's the camp that loves the industry part of the music industry and they miss the limos, and they miss the big parties, and they miss the A&R guys. Then there are the people who like the music part and they can't believe how amazing it is that an act can go from being unsigned to being known worldwide in three days. That if you care about music, the Internet is the best thing that ever happened. More music made by more people listened to more often than ever before. The same is happening right this minute to education.

The institutions –a lot of them– are going to fall by the wayside. But the amount of education that we can create is greater and faster, with more leverage than anyone ever imagined, and how dare we settle for mediocre, how dare we settle for good enough? We have this opportunity to lower our standards while we lower our cost. I would rather raise our standards. I would rather create something that's ridiculous, something that's impossible, something that when people look at it five years from now they'll say, 'I can't believe we were able to teach this many people this much smartness.'

'...we should
be demanding
enlightened
human beings
who desire
to make
a difference.'

Adeiso

Accra

Ghana

Ghana

Our journey begins in Ghana.

Ghana is located on the Atlantic Ocean and the Gulf of Guinea in West Africa; on its borders lie the Ivory Coast to the west, Togo to the east and Burkina Faso to the north. Only a few degrees north of the equator, it enjoys a year-round warm climate and lies on the Greenwich Meridian that by coincidence crosses my home town in South London.

Married to a Ghanaian myself, it is a country that I know well and have been visiting for 15 years, noting the rapid change that has been taking place. It would be fair to say that I have more than just a passing interest in the fortunes of what is essentially my second home.

In 1957 Ghana became the first nation to declare independence from colonial rule in Sub-Saharan Africa after colonisation from the 15th century by successive European traders that included the Portuguese, Dutch, German, Swedish, Danish and finally the British. Today, Ghana functions as a stable parliamentary democracy with a rapidly growing economy. Once known as the Gold Coast, Ghana has an abundance of natural resources including gold, oil, gas and agriculture. It is the second largest exporter of cocoa beans in the world after its Ivory Coast neighbour. It has a growing population of 25 million.

In 1996 the Ghanaian government prepared a policy framework directed at the transformation of Ghana 'from a poor undeveloped, low-income country into a vibrant, prosperous, middle-income country within a generation'. This blueprint was later renamed Ghana Vision 2020 and bears a striking resemblance to the plan devised by Lee Kuan Yew for the transformation of Singapore when he came to power in 1959. We'll be visiting Singapore during our journey but for now let's put a pin in this one because we'll come back to it later.

It is beyond the remit of this book to delve into the intricacies of national politics and policy, but the macro/micro viewing lenses that this journey afforded me certainly laid out a series of dots that, correctly or incorrectly, one couldn't help connecting. This is particularly relevant when one considers the potential of education as a key driver in a nation's economy. When determining education policy one might ask what economy we want to have in 15 or 20 years' time. Indeed, I'll argue later that this is, in fact, what successful education leaders do.

Some Ghanaian commentators suggest the objectives set out in the Vision 2020 document are unattainable or have even been forgotten. Nevertheless, aspects of growth, certainly within Ghana's middle classes, are visible at least within its major cities such as the capital, Accra, and Kumasi.

In March 2013 the Ghanaian government under President John Mahama launched a three-year, $10 billion project to build an advanced digital hub with offices and housing for technology companies and their employees just outside Accra. Called Hope City, this project reflects Ghana's ambition to compete in the global market and digital economy.

Beyond being one the friendliest countries I've had the pleasure to visit, I've also found it to be one of the safest. Every time I return to Ghana I am surprised by its development. It's like visiting a family member once a year and, like an embarrassing uncle, remarking on how everyone has grown. Visible material wealth and growth are happening from the centre of these cities outwards. I am struck by Ghana's potential to resemble the growth patterns of Brazil, where sharp differences between the rich and poor encourage *favela* districts where the have-nots look inwards at the haves. There are parts of Accra that remind me of visits that I made to Seoul in South Korea in the mid-1980s, so it is not hard to imagine a 'gradually then suddenly' style growth. The objective of the 2020 plan was to eradicate poverty by expanding the middle classes and one wonders if Ghana can embrace modernity whilst maintaining its unique cultural identity and way of life.

Whilst in Ghana, I had the opportunity to visit a school in Accra for digital entrepreneurs and a rural primary school using 1:1 (one-to-one) tablet computing. I also made an informal drop-in to a school on a beach in Jamestown. It goes without saying that my team and I enjoyed our stay in Ghana and came away inspired by what we learned.

Ghana

'In March 2013 the Ghanaian government under President John Mahama launched a three-year, $10 billion project to build an advanced digital hub...'

Ghana

Ghana

'Worldreader
had distributed over
800,000 books
into the hands
of more than 12,000
children in nine
African countries.'

Worldreader is a global non-profit organisation on a mission to eradicate illiteracy among the world's poorest people. They use e-readers such as the Amazon Kindle or mobile applications that work on low-cost feature phones to provide access to a vast library of books.

By curating thousands of local stories, together with a collection of leading international books, Worldreader provides a programme that starts with primary school children then extends to their families when they take their e-readers home.

Worldreader was conceived by former Amazon.com executive David Risher and ESADE Business School Marketing Director Colin McElwee, and launched in Ghana in 2010.

By the end of 2013 Worldreader had distributed over 800,000 books into the hands of more than 12,000 children in nine African countries.

The programme operates on a donor-supported basis where individuals or organisations can sponsor schools or classrooms, starting from $10,000 to receive a kit that includes technology, training and support. The Worldreader initiative seeks to ensure that such developments are sustainable and scalable by working with donor organisations to reduce the cost of devices and books to a price that local communities can afford, whilst also capacity building at a community level with pedagogical and technical training for project managers and local teachers. Local businesses, already servicing feature phones, are supported in repair of the e-readers by the Worldreader team. The result is an ecosystem that supports reading in developing communities.

We visited Adeiso Presbyterian Junior High School in Ghana's Eastern Region to learn more about Worldreader, spending time with children, teachers, project managers and Worldreader Co-founder Colin McElwee.

Adeiso is a small rural village about three hours' drive from Accra where agriculture is the principal activity. The bustle of city life and Accra's impossible traffic give way to lush countryside as we travel towards our destination, arriving just before the start of the school day.

The children are excited by the presence of the camera team and myself but settle into their class quite quickly. It is the summer school period for them, and the school provides a safe place during the holidays while their parents work. The climate is warm all year round so the class is designed to keep the children as cool as possible while they learn. It has shutters that open the windows wide to allow the flow of air, while providing shade to avoid direct sunlight that is fierce by noon.

While back in London the debate rages about whether children should be allowed to use tablet computers in class, here in this Ghanaian village every child has one.

Through a Western lens, the transformation here may not seem immediately apparent. After all, these base-level Kindle e-readers don't offer children the opportunity to surf the Internet, Skype their friends or learn how to write computer code. But within the context of this location they are a vitally important step into the digital world.

A post-colonial nation, Ghana deploys an education system that is firmly rooted within literacy and the provision of books. The cost, distribution and maintenance expenses for printed books are beyond the resources of the less affluent. As a result, libraries of current books are rare, homes may not enjoy the luxury of book ownership and schools rely on the sharing of texts within classes. Inevitably this hampers the everyday work of rural teachers whose endeavour it is to educate children within a curriculum whilst encouraging curiosity and the love of reading.

An e-reader provides each child with a library's worth of books. The Worldreader programme typically provides access to more than 5,000 local and international stories and books. The limited functionality of the e-reader compared to that of an iPad, for example, contributes to the success of the programme and its national scalability. There is very little governmental resistance to a programme that seeks to provide books within an existing teaching practice. One could argue that this isn't transforming teaching practice but simply making it possible – and for this school and many like it that is transformative.

The same features that made these devices successful as Western consumer electronic products have made them successful in this setting. Low power consumption, robust build, sunlight readable screens, low skills threshold to usage, negligible e-safety concerns and low cost have colluded to the advantage of these children. One could debate the advantages of a fully featured tablet computer as an alternative but without affordable Internet and a raft of pedagogical and technical support issues it's unlikely that the project would have got beyond a pilot, whereas Worldreader has created a programme that is now scaling across the African continent and benefiting children and their families today.

The initiative is achieving collateral benefits too. Initial government concerns were that the electronic distribution of books would harm domestic or pan-African publishers and their authors. As a result of domestic publishers partnering with Worldreader, not only are more people within the region gaining access to their work but also authors have gained access to an international audience and export market. Young people and Worldreader alumni are also now beginning to create and publish in the ePub format favoured by the Kindle and the Worldreader mobile app format.

www.worldreader.org

Ghana

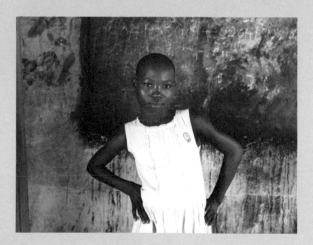

Ghana

Colin McElwee

co-founder, Worldreader, Adeiso

Interview

Colin McElwee is Co-founder of Worldreader and focuses on business development, putting to good use his for-profit and non-profit experience across the globe. Most recently, Colin was the first Director of Marketing at ESADE Business School in Barcelona, where he helped establish the school's reputation as a world-class business education provider. Prior to that, he started his career as an economist for several Brussels-based lobbies to the European Commission, and later worked in global marketing in the consumer goods sector for Scottish & Newcastle PLC.

He has two young daughters and, like them, is an avid reader of books. Colin has a degree in economics from the University of Manchester and an MBA from ESADE Business School. He is an invited member of the Global Agenda Council on Africa of the World Economic Forum.

Graham Brown-Martin: Colin, please tell me about Worldreader.

Colin McElwee: Worldreader is an organisation based on a very simple idea that I had in a conversation with my Co-founder, David Risher. In an increasingly connected world it was now possible to get a book to anyone who could get phone calls, which is really about 90 percent of the world as we know it. That's in response to a world where books ... only get to a small minority of people.

Graham: Can you give me a sense of scale in regards to numbers of books?

Colin: On our e-reader platform, we've distributed 800,000 books across nine countries. On our mobile platform, we have more than half a million people each month accessing our library of 2,000 books.

Graham: Your project led with the Amazon Kindle device. What were the specific reasons for choosing this platform and what about future platforms for Worldreader?

Colin: When we started, which was only three years ago – but three years in digital publishing is actually quite a long time – the Kindle device was pretty new, but it was clearly the leader in its category. We use two main platforms, e-reader and mobile phone.

On the e-reader platform, we work with the Kindle. On the mobile phone platform, we work right across many different types of phone using a technology that compresses data. This means that when we deliver books to mobile phones, the books get there fast, which means they get there very cheaply. This technology works right across Android phones and even Java feature phones, which cover about 90 percent of developing countries across the world.

Graham: What were the challenges and obstacles that you had introducing the Worldreader initiative into the countries you've worked with?

Colin: The governments used to say to us, 'Publishers are not going to like this. This is going to cut into their margins.' But when we went into a new country we got to see the publishers first before we talked to the government. For a publisher, going electronic makes absolute sense. They currently have their work electronically stored but only recently turned that into paper. What we explained and shared with publishers was that by taking that file and turning it into an ePub, an electronically published document, their market went from the local city or local country to a global market. For publishers, this was an enormous advantage.

Graham: By distributing Western content into another culture do you think this might be seen as sort of digital colonialism through content?

Colin: One of the things we realised early on was the vital importance of content in what we were doing. It wasn't about technology. It was about great content. Great content that resonates with the kids and the young people in our programmes really only comes from their local environment. That's why we've got over 60 African publishers signed up with Worldreader that are not only giving us their existing catalogue of content to distribute, they're actually bringing new authors and new writers to create new content for this programme and for the future. It's a very, very healthy and virtuous circle.

Graham: Back to the device; you're using a reader. Are you taking steps toward content creation?

Colin: We've been working very recently with some of the students that have been through our programme who volunteer for us. A number of these volunteers have written poems and short stories, which we've digitised and distributed. There's actually nothing so special for a child to see themselves number one as a reader, but not only as a reader, as a writer, to be recognised by their peers and the rest of the students. I have somebody who has actually created a book. It's certainly a pleasure that I never had as a child, but it is an enormously positive experience. That is something that actually drives greater interest in reading and writing.

Graham: What has been the response of parents in seeing this new device coming into the household?

Colin: When we start any project and go into any new community, we involve the school, we involve the administrators, but we also involve the community. We make a community launch. This is not so much to sell a new concept. It's really to share the possibilities that are behind this project. Parents have said to us, 'Previously, I would never have considered buying a book, because books are either too expensive or it was the job of the government. Now, I can see how exciting it is to see a book on an e-reader and a book on a mobile phone.'

It makes the parents feel that they can begin to think about purchasing a book, not at a price that's $5 to $10 a book, but purchasing a book at a dollar or less. That is super-important for the kids. They see the parents supporting this in a very real way.

Graham: Is one of the advantages of what you're doing, for example, in rural parts of

Ghana, providing access to books in the first place?

Colin: One of the fundamental aspects of Worldreader is that we're bringing books — and we're bringing access to many millions of books— to parts of the world where there was no access to paper books previously. This creates a very interesting and exciting dynamic because previously there was no access but there was an aspiration for access, meaning that you're going to have a latent demand.

For us to actually bring such great books — great African books, and some great international books — to places that never had access to books at all, and have such positive reception, not just from teachers and not just from kids, but from the community at large, is very exciting.

Graham: You're one of the few projects that has genuinely scaled up in this setting. What do you regard as the key to this success?

Colin: Scaling, for us, is one of the most fundamental challenges, as it is for any organisation, frankly. Scaling has been possible because what we have is a simple idea that dovetails into an existing need. People need books. Education systems need books. It's their lifeblood. Dovetailing into that need has meant that just by nature we're scaling. It will continue to scale and it will scale enormously. The costs of doing this three years ago were prohibitive, but what we saw was that within five to ten years, the cost would converge to a point where this could naturally scale. That's happened in three years. We're at that point now.

Graham: What do you think is the sweet spot for device cost that you believe could really have a transformative effect on the digital learning divide for countries like Ghana?

Colin: When we think about the cost of devices, we work on two platforms. We work on the mobile phone platform. That costs anything from $20 upwards. On e-readers, when we started this three years ago, e-readers were more than $300. You can get an e-reader now for less than $60.

We see that continuing to come down. When it comes to scale, the sweet spot is in the $20 to $50 range, depending on the segment of the population that you're addressing and the market that you're in.

Graham: From your experience, how do we stimulate innovation in education and what slows things down?

Colin: Innovating in the education sector, as we all know, is a big challenge. Education has certain characteristics that make it even more difficult. The first one is that there are so many stakeholders from ministries to teachers to parents to kids to parent-teacher associations and examination boards. If you want to innovate in an education sector, you generally have to have all of those stakeholders on side at the same time. That is a difficult task. If you really want to innovate in the education sector, you should be trying to work with the system.

One of the things that we found by working with books was the inherent unmet need for them in the existing system. Books are fully accepted and people don't see this as something that's disruptive in any way. It is actually something that is enhancing the current education system and making it work better. This has been our innovation.

Worldreader has achieved a lot in its first three years. I'd like to point out, principally, that what we're doing works and secondly, that what we're doing can scale. Really, it's: Where do we go from now?

There is a big, big job to do on this. Technology is changing quickly. It's changing in many shapes and forms. For us, it's actually keeping our eye on what is the best way to deliver books, deliver knowledge right into the hands of children and young people, right across the globe. You can expect Worldreader remaining on course ... toward books for all. It's knowledge for all. We'll use the best technology and we'll work with the best partners to make that happen.

'What we explained and shared with publishers was that by taking that file and turning it into an ePub, an electronically published document, their market went from the local city or local country to a global market.'

Ghana

'I arrive on a very busy day when a group of students from South Korea are working with a cohort of MWG's Ghanaian students.'

Mobile Web Ghana is one of a number of organisations based in Accra focused on lifelong learning, developing local talent, fostering entrepreneurship and incubating technology start-ups.

The significant investment being made in Ghana's digital infrastructure presents challenges and opportunities for the nation. The challenge is that much of the content on the web is not local; the opportunity is for Ghanaian businesses to leverage the digital world for the benefit of their own products and services. Thus Ghanaian citizens and local entrepreneurs require re-skilling in new digital and mobile platforms to take best advantage of the opportunities available.

Connected to the highest-capacity data cables that link the west coast of Africa to the Internet, Ghana offers one the fastest Internet speeds on the continent. Recent improvements in connections to the backbone of the Internet mean that the costs of reliable fixed-line connectivity will fall. However it is mobile broadband using the 3G and soon 4G LTE spectrum where Ghana is seeing the fastest growth. An International Telecommunication Union report[3] from 2013 shows that Ghana has the fastest-growing adoption of mobile broadband connectivity in Africa. Combined with the government's commitment to stimulating its own digital economy through privately funded projects such as the $10 billion Hope City technology hub, it is clear that Ghana is serious about its digital future. To be successful, this will require the nurturing of indigenous talent and investment in new high-tech start-ups.

Established as part of the World Wide Web Foundation's Mobile Entrepreneurship Programme, MWG is the first of a network of labs across Africa designed to stimulate an ecosystem of entrepreneurs to create mobile services that meet the social or business needs of the local market. The Web Foundation was founded by Sir Tim Berners-Lee, the inventor of the Web.

Formed in 2010, MWG is a non-profit incubator and training provider for a growing population of Ghanaians with a passion for information technology and an interest in creating local digital services. Through its training, MWG seeks to blend existing skills and passion with the knowledge required to start and grow businesses. MWG receives sponsorship from Vodafone.

The MWG training sessions last three weeks with local and international experts coming to teach and mentor 20 selected students in the creation of mobile applications as well as business skills. During the three weeks, with the help of the trainers, students develop their own service. Students, who are typically postgraduates, are asked to contribute a nominal $100 for the course.

The training is followed by a six-month period of mentorship and incubation where promising projects can be developed further towards becoming commercial services. The MWG mentorship programme links aspiring developer entrepreneurs emerging from the training with experienced entrepreneurs as mentors. With the goal of taking a project from prototype to release, the mentor collaborates with the developer to provide guidance, improve software skills, develop a business model, identify markets, manage intellectual property and find funding.

MWG provides inexpensive incubation and office spaces for early-stage start-ups that range from hot desks to complete office suites.

MWG's incubation and training lab is based in Accra in the district of Madina which, with its neighbouring district of Legon, is a positive hub of digital and technology activity where you will also find local video game developers and other incubators such as the Meltwater Entrepreneurial School of Technology. The district is also home to the University of Ghana, with multinational technology companies such as Google, Vodafone and MTN nearby.

I arrive on a very busy day, when a group of students from South Korea is working with a cohort of MWG's Ghanaian students. This is part of an exchange programme where culture is shared and the Korean students are coaching their Ghanaian hosts in Android software development and web creation tools. As I speak a rudimentary amount of Korean and Ga – one of the many Ghanaian languages but local to this district – I'm pleased that I can introduce myself to the group in both languages to the bewilderment of all. At least it caught their attention.

There's a real buzz in the atmosphere and it's clear that the Koreans are enjoying their experience as much as the Ghanaian students are learning new skills. One might wonder whether this isn't such a bad business move for the South Korean government, which funds this exchange. South Korea is home to Samsung, the world's leading supplier of smartphones based on Android software. With the rapid adoption of smartphones in Ghana as the expanding middle-income population migrate from feature phones, it may be the models with the most relevant apps are the ones that do best.

In the three years that MWG has been operating, it already has success stories that began their journey here. Farmerline[4] is a mobile data and SMS service that provides farmers with timely access to information that allows them to make more entrepreneurial decisions in their work. The organisation's vision is for an Africa where NGOs are not a functioning force in the market and where smallholder farmers are able to produce and sell more food. The training and mentoring that the founders received via MWG have affected not only their lives but those of the people they now employ and those who use their service.

www.mobilewebghana.org

Ghana

Florence Toffa

founding director, Mobile Web Ghana, Accra

Interview

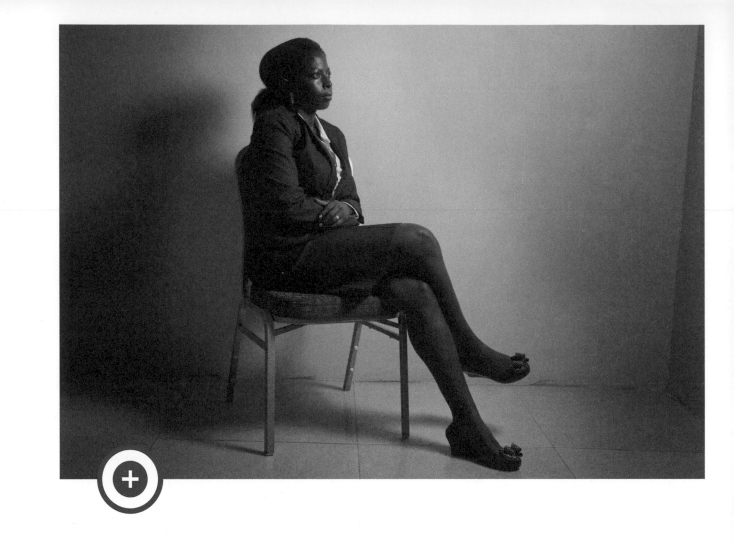

Florence Toffa is a perfect example of Ghanaian homegrown talent. She holds a postgraduate certificate in software entrepreneurship from the Meltwater Entrepreneurial School of Technology, based in Accra, and a degree in psychology and sociology from the University of Ghana. Florence has experience working with mobile entrepreneurs, content aggregators, developers, technology leaders and telco companies. She markets, recruits, trains, coordinates and manages a community of mobile technology entrepreneurs and has successfully implemented the mobile entrepreneurship project that is Mobile Web Ghana.

After graduating from MEST, Florence developed an online fashion portal to promote African fashion before being appointed by the World Wide Web Foundation as the regional community manager to set up an NGO to implement the mobile entrepreneurship project in 2010.

I met with Florence in the MWG Entrepreneur School in Legon.

Graham Brown-Martin: What is the background and mission of Mobile Web Ghana?

Florence Toffa: Mobile Web Ghana was conceived by the Web Foundation that was created by Tim Berners-Lee. It's an NGO to empower people to use the web. Unlike in the West, where the majority of people use the Internet on a computer, it's not like that in Africa. The only digital tool that we have that can change our lives, that can add meaning to what we do, is the mobile phone.

MWG is part of a Web Foundation project called Mobile Entrepreneurs in Africa. The idea is to create entrepreneurs to be able to develop value-added services on the mobile phone to improve the ordinary lives of Ghanaians.

Graham: With so much digital content being created outside of Ghana, why is it important that you create digital content here?

Florence: It's very, very important because even though people consume digital content, most of the content they consume is foreign. So if, for

instance, you are sick and you want to check your health status, I personally go to WebMD. I don't go to a locally created website. But there are some diseases in Africa that are not in the West. How then do you check the status and treatment of that disease using foreign content?

So we think that it's extremely important to tune the minds of people to start creating content that would be locally relevant to them. Because they live here. They know their culture. So we know the exact things to develop to be useful to us.

Graham: What are your challenges for nurturing local talent?

Florence: The challenge of nurturing and helping people to be independent or nurturing them to develop their intrinsic talent is sometimes that they have the skills but are unable to put them to use. In Africa, it can be very difficult for people to survive in terms of taking care of their baby's needs, let alone developing a business.

So there have been a series of challenges getting people to develop their apps after their training. They then seek jobs or go out looking for other things to do. That can be part of the success story if they get a job that utilises the skills that we helped develop. But our main goal is to develop entrepreneurs and very few people are great entrepreneurs.

It's very difficult in Ghana as a start-up. People don't get needed support in terms of loans from banks or seed capital to be able to bootstrap their business. So after their training, when they have the skills to make something and start a business, they still need something to go to market. Bringing an idea to market is a huge challenge here.

Graham: So do you think there are positive technology investments to be made in Ghana and what would you say to inward investors?

Florence: What I'd say to them is that we've got talent. There is a saying from a popular man

that talent is talent everywhere, irrespective of where it is located, whether in the West or in Africa. So we have the right people in Ghana to be trained. They are very deserving people who are ready to take up the challenge.

We have a stable political economy. It's easy to fly to Ghana from other parts of the world.

Graham: There are many examples of successful Ghanaians in the creative sectors. Do you think there's something unique and special about the Ghanaian people that would be a benefit in the digital economy?

Florence: I think that we're very creative people and we're friendly. There are a lot of people who have, for instance, succeeded in the fashion industry. We have a lot of graduate fashion designers here at MWG. They come with their content to learn how to use social media to market, to empower themselves, and to get exposed.

They have the talent to make stuff, but they don't know how to get exposure on the Internet. They learn how to put their stuff on basic applications like YouTube, to reach the market that they need. Even in the various industries in fashion, music and the arts, the opportunities are there. So if people got the right digital skills to expose themselves, to empower themselves, they would actually become very, very big.

Graham: Can you describe examples of successes, or ones that are moving towards success, that have come out of Mobile Web Ghana?

Florence: I think one successful example is Farmerline. They have an application that empowers farmers to get information on how to grow their crops. It's an SMS application and then an Interactive Voice Response application. So if you're a farmer, you just call a short code and you get information about how to plant your crops. Right now they've received a grant from Indigo Trust in the UK and they've got another contract from a multinational company. They won several awards from Canada and other places. They've travelled across Europe.

They spent 21 days with us. Those 21 days are transforming their lives right now. If you Google their name, they're in the top search engine right now. They have employed other people to join their company. So, they are not only changing their lives, they are changing the lives of people that work with them as well.

Graham: What about Ghana exporting digital content and competing in the global digital economy?

Florence: There is a company called Dropify. It's one of the companies that came out of the Meltwater Entrepreneurship School of Technology. They are now in Silicon Valley and have clients across the world. They started in Ghana and they're now making news. The last time, they were being interviewed by CNN and other international news agencies.

There is another called Retail Power. They provide online shops in [collaboration] with Amazon. They provide Ghanaians with the opportunity to create a shop on their platform. These are companies that came from Ghana and they're entering into the Western world.

Graham: How would you like to see Mobile Web Ghana develop?

Florence: I think we've just been known in the urban areas. We provided training in Kumasi. We did several trainings in the upper regions as well. We want to go to the rural areas, the grassroots people. We want to expose them to technology. We want them to know the power that they could derive from just listing themselves or their shops on a website. We want to reach out to people living in these areas and be known as the organisation that is specialised in teaching people how to develop mobile phone applications.

Over the past two years of Mobile Web Ghana, we've tried to give potential entrepreneurs the school that is needed. After the first year of setting up the organisation we realised that there was a need to bring people into a physical space. So we opened this incubation space for the start-ups and other people to come and work here.

So MWG is a central creation space. It's an incubation space. It's a mentoring place. It's a place to encourage people to innovate and to think creatively about solving local problems. It's not only about mobile applications at the centre, but it's creating a community that people can come to and work on their ideas.

'We think that it's extremely important to tune the minds of people to start creating content that would be locally relevant to them.'

Does technology really matter?
Thought piece

'There is one teacher for every 40 citizens in Cuba.'

When I was a child in the 1970s, I enjoyed *Logan's Run*, a science-fiction film set in the 23rd century where humans lived under surveillance in a perfect society enclosed in an environmentally controlled dome called Sanctuary. There were catches, of course: one of them was that citizens were forbidden to travel beyond the safety and controlled existence of their dome. Curiosity was not encouraged but inevitably some would wonder what lay beyond. Reflecting on my visit there, I wondered if the society beyond our dome might be Cuba.

My visit to Cuba during the *Learning {Re}imagined* project was partly a family vacation in between the official visits, so inevitably I viewed the country through the rose-tinted sunglasses of a tourist. But we did manage the occasional escape from the tourist features to explore some of the country's culture and meet some of its people. Being the summer break in Cuba, and without official permissions to visit schools, I was unable to dig as deep as I would have liked but I left inspired to return and discover more.

In response to my shout-out on Twitter to meet educators in Cuba, I received one response from a friend who suggested that I wouldn't find much to interest me and my project there, given that Cuba was the least 'connected' country in the region and that few people, if any, have access to the Internet at home and very few have access to it in public offices such as schools.

For me this was probably the most interesting aspect, given that without a hysterical rush to adopt 21st-century digital platforms and capitulating to PISA league tables, Cuba has achieved, according to the instruments and indicators applied by international organisations such as the Organisation for Economic Co-operation and Development and UNESCO, one of the world's best educational systems. An education system that is free to all students from primary to higher education and has achieved almost 100 percent literacy amongst its population. An education system that has led to a key export of Cuba being skilled healthcare and medical professionals as well as an effective literacy programme that has been exported across Latin America and as far as Australia and New Zealand.

A comparison between the educational systems of Cuba and Finland by prominent Ecuadorian educationalist and former Education Minister, Rosa María Torres, makes interesting reading.[5] Torres notes that Cuba and Finland have very different histories and cultures, and very different social, political and educational systems, yet they share high international recognition for educational and other social achievements. According to Save the Children's 2013 'State of the World's Mothers' report, both Cuba and Finland are amongst the best countries to be a mother and raise a child.

Both countries' education systems are public and free, covering all student-related costs, from initial education to the end of higher education. Cuba and Finland have been top performers in student achievement tests in school: Cuba in the Latin American Laboratory for Assessment of the Quality of Education (known by its Spanish acronym, LLECE) co-ordinated by the regional UNESCO office in Santiago, and Finland in the OECD's Programme for International Student Assessment. Cuba's performance in LLECE has been significantly ahead of all Latin American countries including Chile, long regarded as an educational model in the region, and the Latin American country that has so far achieved the best results in PISA. Torres concludes that whilst both countries demonstrate successful school systems, only Finland is internationally known and viewed as an inspiring model.

But for me what really stood out were the casual conversations with Cubans who I met along the way. One evening, it occurred to me that out of the 11 people I was chatting with, seven were educated to degree level, of which three held a Master's. No offence to my neighbours, but it's not like that in my local hostelry here in London.

Not everything is perfect in Cuba. It's a socialist state and since 1957 the economy has been regulated, meaning salary levels are nothing like you would find in Western nations. Some Cubans would complain about increasing unemployment, now running at a reported two percent but even if that was under-reported it would have some way to go to match 20+ percent across Europe, or Greece which has been effectively bankrupted. Occasionally I would find myself in 'grass is greener' type conversations but I couldn't help thinking that a university student in Cuba could complete a medical degree and not start their career already tens of thousands of dollars in debt.

After the revolution in Cuba, education and healthcare were given the highest priority under Fidel Castro and whatever other challenges are presented it has succeeded in this goal. There is one teacher for every 40 citizens in Cuba. How it will change in the coming years with embargoes lifted and the influx of Western brands remains to be seen, but something a taxi driver said to me on a journey resonated: 'Cuba is a safe country because of education.'

On that basis I say, 'Viva la Revolución Educativa!'

Dubai ○

Abu Dhabi ○

United Arab Emirates ◉

photo credit: Graham Brown-Martin

The United Arab Emirates is located on the Arabian Gulf, bordering Oman to the east and Saudi Arabia to the south. Qatar is across the Gulf to the west, and Iran to the north. It is a federation of seven emirates formed in 1971 after independence. Since that time, the UAE has grown into one of the Middle East's most important economic centres. Two of the emirates, Abu Dhabi, the capital, and Dubai, are the key locations of commercial and cultural activities. The discovery of oil in the late 1950s transformed an economy based on fishing and a declining pearl industry into what we see today. Abu Dhabi began exporting oil in the 1960s whereas Dubai, with much smaller oil reserves, has pursued economic diversification to a greater degree. Over 80 percent of the population of the UAE are expatriates.

Twenty-five years ago Dubai was a desert town with a population of 350,000 people. Today it numbers closer to two million. Six million people visit each year. During my visits to Abu Dhabi and Dubai over the past years, I've found it impossible not to be struck by the jaw-dropping scale of everything, where I oscillate between being super-impressed and feeling that I am in a parallel universe. From the tallest building in the world to the tallest hotels, to the world's first shopping resort replete with built-in skiing facility and snow park right in the middle of what should be a desert, it is just astonishing. You can find almost anything here, provided to the highest standard. It's absolutely no wonder that Dubai has become such a popular tourist destination.

There is a state education system in the UAE and a very large private sector. This is education in a free-market economy and, whilst the government carries out annual inspections of each school and the results are published, the real pressure comes from the market forces of parents who almost without exception are seeking an authentic 'Harry Potter' experience for their children that delivers high test scores and examination passes. With significant over-capacity and choice, the competition between schools is fierce. During my stay in Dubai I was speaking at an educational technology conference which was geared towards the adoption of 1:1 computing deployment in schools, principally around tablets. There were over 200 delegates representing a large number of schools in the region. All indicated that they were already achieving respectable results in examination scores so I was keen to understand why they felt the imperative to make an investment in digital platforms and whether it would change the way they taught. Whilst there was some dialogue around improving learning and teaching, I didn't gain a sense that the investments being made were intended to transform pedagogical practices. The focus, as a result of market forces, was firmly on the standardised test scores followed, of course, by pupil well-being, i.e. 'Do they enjoy being there?'

Beyond getting better scores in technology and computer science-related subjects, one might think that deploying iPads or other technology should rank pretty low against other factors, such as making sure the environment is one that children enjoy, or using teaching and learning styles that keep them engaged. This made the opportunity to meet and interview the recently appointed Chief Technology Officer of GEMS Education, Hervé Marchet, all the more interesting. Based in Dubai, GEMS is an international education company founded by a successful entrepreneur, Sunny Varkey, who owns a global network of schools providing education to more than 142,000 students from 150 countries. GEMS employs a high-profile executive team and numerous renowned consultant advisors to offer a broad range of curricula across various tuition-fee levels in order to expand market share. Before joining GEMS, Hervé held an executive sales and marketing position at Apple, focused on the education sector.

I visited GEMS Modern Academy whilst I was in Dubai. The school is affiliated to the Council for Indian School Certificate Examinations in New Delhi, India, and opens admissions from kindergarten level to 18 years of age. Day boarding is offered that provides academic tuition during the morning session and then activities for curriculum enrichment in the afternoon, consisting of study groups, clubs and sports. The environment is welcoming, the pupils of all ages are polite, interested, confident and, from those we met, extremely bright. The school is well-equipped, from fibre optic digital networks and AV systems through to fully equipped science labs.

I sat in on a chemistry class with a group of boys in the school's 3D Lab which features projection and a PC at every seat. The fact that the students were wearing 3D dark glasses, watching a video presentation floating off the screen in front, lent a future-retro effect to the scene. However, what really brought the lesson alive wasn't the classroom of students wearing 3D glasses, although it makes a great photo opportunity, but the energy and enthusiasm of the teacher who frankly loved the subject and enjoyed engaging in discussion with her students about what they'd seen.

So there we have it – Education 101: Engaged teacher plus engaged students equals learning. You could have taken this technology out of the classroom and the teacher would still have been able to teach that lesson. I'm not convinced that you could have put a less engaged teacher in the room with the technology and had such an effective lesson, however. This was a classic case where the teacher could have flipped the lesson and let the students review a video at home beforehand and then discussed it in class to make sure everybody got it. The real value in that room was the teacher.

Our next showcase was a primary class where eight-year-olds using iPads were learning about rocks and minerals. Once again the class was in the hands of a skilled teacher who encouraged her charges to use their devices in an *ad hoc* or collaborative manner to respond to the questions or directions that she offered. It didn't matter to her that some of the kids were faster at finding the answers than she was. If anything, it added to the buzz in the room. At the time I was there the class Wi-Fi network was malfunctioning but this didn't stop the lesson or faze the teacher who continued but changed tack, knowing that her students wouldn't be able to look things up immediately.

What I took away from my visits to classrooms was that the skill of the teacher would be at the heart of any transformation in learning to use use digital platforms, and that students would need to work in collaborative groups to share thinking and solve problems. It seems that the environment of the school or classroom influences the way in which technology is being used. It's as if someone thought that because kids are traditionally seated in rows with the teacher at the front, any digital intervention should work in that way also. Yet what I'm seeing is that the role of the teacher is shifting to one of encouragement rather than control, and that digital platforms used well can enable a hitherto unprecedented level of collaboration amongst so many people.

www.gemseducation.com

'You could have taken this technology out of the classroom and the teacher would still have been able to teach that lesson.'

Hervé Marchet joined GEMS Education after a long career at Apple where he held executive responsibility for the education sales and marketing strategy for Europe, the Middle East and Africa.

Based in Dubai, GEMS is an international education company that owns a global network of schools, providing education to more than 142,000 students from 150 countries.

Graham Brown-Martin: Hervé, can you describe your background and how you arrived as the Chief Technology Officer of GEMS Education?

Hervé Marchet: I'm a French citizen, even if I consider myself a worldwide citizen. I lived eight years in London and I was, for 12 years, the head of the education division of Apple for Europe, Middle East, India and Africa, where I discovered this mix between business and passion, meaning that I was, for a long time, a businessman, and I became even a more passionate person within the business, because bringing technology into the education world is a fantastic job. I was having a great time at Apple, and then one day I met Sunny Varkey.

He told me there is one thing that is very important – and I too believe this – which is that there is a human right to have education, so each kid should have access to education. This conversation changed a lot of things for me. My experience at Apple was great. It was a difficult choice to leave this company but, the day after, I decided I needed to move on. I called back Mr Varkey, the Chairman, and I told him, 'If you have something for me, I would be very happy to join your company.' He told me, 'I've got this global CTO post – Chief Technology Officer', and I said, 'I like it, but can I use the "T" as "Transformation" Officer? Can I come as a global Chief Transformation Officer?' And he told me, 'Yes, come. Join GEMS and let's do something great together.'

Graham: We hear a lot about transformation yet the promises made by digital pioneers over the last 30 years haven't arrived in the education sector. The needle has hardly moved, and when it has, it hasn't really scaled. What do you think the obstacles are for digital transformation in education today?

Hervé: We've heard a lot of discussion about substitution and transformation. A lot of people are saying that technology substitutes some ways of doing things, and a lot of people are looking for a real transformation. I believe that, for me, it's like politics: promises are only for the people that believe in promises. I think that you need to set up the right expectations, and very often people look at the ways it's going to transform education, piece by piece, but I'm more of a big-picture person, and I want to make sure that, when I talk about transformation, we don't forget any stakeholder in the education world. It's not only about teachers, it's not only about kids, it's not only about staff, it's not only about parents, it's the complete picture of what the technology can bring. That's element number one.

Then, a lot of people talk about transformation using technology but, for most of these kids, what we see as technology is not really technology. It's almost a commodity, it's what they use every day. That's this reality, to set up the right expectation, and see how can we come to a more blended learning way, rather than trying to totally transform or totally substitute but be, as always in life, balanced.

Graham: Our friends at Google talk about moon-shot thinking. A ten-times improvement or a 100-times improvement. As a vision from your own perspective, what would a ten-times-better education system look like to you, if you started again, with a blank sheet of paper?

Hervé: I'm always very careful to talk about percentage or time, in terms of how you multiply the learning. At the end of the day, it's to make sure that each kid finds his own potential, meaning that you want to make sure that technology did bring something totally different, that each kid could have access to what he needs at the time he needs it.

If we are back in history, there was tutoring, there was mentoring, so there was one-to-one. Then there was one-to-few, then school for everyone, and it was almost like a factory. I think that technology definitely changes this 'factory of education' mindset and brings the kids back into the centre of education.

It is not only about results, in terms of the achievement or assessment of a classroom. It is about each kid performing to his own potential, because we all know that the best university, or the best diploma, is not necessarily what makes a good life. Half of the companies in the world are managed by people with no degree. They didn't go to university, but maybe they are good in technology, or maybe they are good in the way they are living every day, and that makes a difference.

If I come back to your point about ten-times, I think that ten-times better will mean that ten times more kids have access to education. That's how I see the use of technology.

Graham: You present a case for technology putting young people, children, at the centre of learning. Is there another argument from policymakers that suggests technology as a way of automating the learning experience and getting kids through the tests – de-skilling rather than up-skilling teachers?

Hervé: I think that if you look worldwide, at any kind of system or any kind of culture, the magic recipe for a kid to achieve his potential and learn is a good teacher and parental involvement. Now, where technology could help is that some of the kids, half of the time, don't need the teacher, and the teacher can focus on the ones who need them. Instead of spending time with 20 or 30 kids all the time, he will spend time with one or two, five or six, and will allocate his time better. Definitely the teacher will have to skill differently, as with what needs to be delivered, and will have to involve more collaboration, but the technology will allow that, being multicultural, providing access to information, comparing information, challenging information. That's definitely different.

'Now, where technology could help is that some of the kids, half of the time, don't need the teacher, and the teacher can focus on the ones who need them.'

Then the teacher, certainly, also needs to interact with the parents, and that's another skill, because we know that if the parents are involved in the education of their kids, the kids will perform much better. We see that in the very old system, the teacher was like a *deus ex machina*, coming to the classroom, delivering a class with the kids. Now the teacher is also —and I see that very often at GEMS— involved with the parents' association, meeting with the staff, meeting with some other kids, meeting with other teachers, and definitely technology helps this communication and provides a total new skill for the teacher. Teachers are in the centre of the equation, the kids are in the middle —they are the heart of education, of course— but teachers are still very important, and will remain very important in a changing world, certainly.

Graham: We've seen great technology-influenced practice in pilot projects all over the world but there seem to be obstacles to scaling this practice across nations. What do you see as the challenge for scaling?

Hervé: If we talk about the scaling of technology —making sure that it's not only a few kids having the chance to have the good teacher, or to have the good content, or to have the good pilots— I believe that we need to look at a different aspect, from another angle. What's going on is that each education system does have its specificities, so I believe that policymakers need to look at their culture, what they want to achieve, and make sure that there is no digital divide, that each kid has access. Access is very important. The question of content is also very important. What very often did happen in technology that was not possible to scale, is that a lot of the things that we developed were based on the pilot. The pilot will always be very successful, because it's got all of the attention, it's got a lot of resources, so when you try and test something, it's going to work because it's on a smaller scale, and everybody will be concentrating on making it happen.

I'm more interested in the freedom of going large right away, making sure that what you try to achieve is going to be scalable. I have not totally answered your question, because I think it's case by case, curriculum by curriculum, culture by culture. The way I will answer your question is that if you look at pilots only, it will always be difficult to scale. If you go large scale right away to try something, and you evaluate after if it was working, at the end of the day it's new, it's bringing new advantages, it's bringing a lot of value and it's very often successful. So the scalability is right at the beginning and should not be thought of as a next step.

Graham: Do you see the way we assess as an obstacle to transformation? Shouldn't students be able to take their phones or tablets into examinations?

Hervé: One of the big things of technology is the fact that assessments can be ongoing assessments now, meaning that you don't need to test at the end of a semester, or a year, if the kid is good or not good, if he understood or not. If it's an ongoing assessment, it's real life, and in real life if you don't know something, you can take your phone, call someone, or you can go on your computer and find the information. So I believe that, yes, we should be able to use any kind of tool, any kind of device, to be assessed, because it's real life. Then there are different kinds of assessments which are the assessments that you need to determine whether you know particular information. It's not about knowledge any more. It's about context. Can I find information? Where can I find it? Can I see if this information is valuable? Can I confirm this information with another piece of information? And definitely, here, the only way to do it is to use devices, to use technology.

'It's not only about teachers, it's not only about kids, it's not only about staff, it's not only about parents, it's the complete picture of what the technology can bring.'

'This combined with our respective policy makers' inability to predict what kind of economy we would want to have in the future has led to a paralysis within our educational evaluation systems'

The rate and scale of transformational change within our educational systems must surely be governed by the way we test. We are not short of progressive thinkers and practitioners in the education sector, nor are we short of examples of outstanding practice to engage and excite learners in new ways. In many parts of the world we are not short of ubiquitous digital devices and access to the Internet. Yet where is the dramatic transformational shift in the education world that we've been expecting and that corresponds to other aspects of society that have been digitally transformed?

Today's assessment methods are usually based around standardised testing and intended to measure the level of success or proficiency a student has obtained at the end of an instructional period. The principle of this approach is to give the same test to all examinees in the same manner, thus providing consistency that permits reliable comparison of outcomes across those who took the test. This would be fine if, in fact, each of the test takers were the same and if the proficiency that's being tested is measurable.

This scientific approach to measurement has proven successful within industrialised and automated processes for manufacturing. The American management consultants W. Edwards Deming and Joseph M. Juran are widely credited for the quality manufacturing revolution that occurred in Japan after World War II. At the time, Japan had a widely held reputation for shoddy exports that were shunned by international markets. The strategies suggested by Deming and Juran represented a 'total quality' movement that, rather than relying purely on product inspection, focused on improving all organisational processes through the people who used them. The result was that Japan broadsided American manufacturing, with the most notable examples being the decline of US automotive and consumer electronic manufacturing.

Deming and Juran's manufacturing strategies originate from the demands of the Industrial Revolution as they evolved from the 1800s. Late in the 19th century the American engineer Frederick Taylor devised a series of theories that became known as 'scientific management' to transform craft production into mass production. This was achieved by management assessing and improving the production line by using scientific methods of evaluation: standardised tests to assess output and identify concerns.

Many have argued that these methods have migrated into our industrial-scale education systems that promote high-stakes testing. Concerns include the disempowering and de-skilling of teachers, teaching to the test, narrowing the curriculum, teacher-focused learning and the fragmentation of knowledge.

In order to improve the output of our schools and universities, numerous assessments in the form of standardised tests are conducted along the production line of learning. It would be wrong, however, to blame these American pioneers entirely for today's preoccupation with standardised testing in the education sector. Advocacy of British colonial administrators influenced by their economic occupation of China in the early 19th century encouraged a shift in Western pedagogy away from the Socratic method of debate and non-standardised testing that was common in Europe at the time to standardised testing. It was therefore from Britain that standardised testing spread not only throughout the British Commonwealth but throughout Europe and America, fuelled by the demands of the Industrial Revolution.

One might suggest that these industrial systems have served our society well, or at least a certain segment of society. The Industrial Revolution led to significant growth in human population, urbanisation, wealth, invention, healthcare and many other aspects of society. Indeed, the digital technology that we have today and which inspired this book is a result of this revolution.

But the revolution hasn't stopped and our society continues to evolve. The result is that the kinds of standardised tests that have been accepted since the 19th century are looking far from relevant for the individual or our society today. We shouldn't forget that the ballpoint pen, patented in 1888, was once regarded as technology. It wasn't until the first half of the 20th century that László Bíró perfected the pen that would democratise handwriting. This had a profound impact on education and literacy but not without controversy: in 1950 it was suggested that 'ballpoint pens will be the ruin of education in this country'.[6] Indeed ballpoint pens weren't allowed in school examinations until the late 1950s in the UK. Yet the ballpoint pen ushered in a world where writing became portable and could be conducted anytime, anywhere.

Historically our education systems have understandably been based around memorising details and facts. Relatively expensive printed books encoded information in a way that could be distributed and read, so it only seemed correct that to evaluate a student's understanding and retention they would be tested thus. Once the printed word became commonplace, the role of the teacher changed from being the person in charge of the information to being the person who told you where to find it. But today, in the digitally connected world, books point to other books and information so teachers are evolving into critical friends who question and encourage personal inquiry and problem solving by their students.

As a result of personal digital platforms, the potential is for society to return to the form of inquiry and discussion between individuals based on asking and answering questions that stimulates critical thinking and the illumination of ideas. This is, in effect, the Socratic method popular across Europe prior to the Industrial Revolution. One could argue that this is what we do on platforms like Facebook. It's not about skateboarding kittens.

The corner we have painted ourselves into is one where we are measuring skills that are no longer as relevant as they used to be. The skills that are now important, such as creativity, entrepreneurship, collaboration and critical thinking, have proven almost impossible to measure accurately under the standardised test regime. This combined with our respective policymakers' inability to predict what kind of economy we would want to have in the future has led to a paralysis within our educational evaluation systems that now rely on their standing in league tables like PISA from the OECD to direct their efforts.

Perhaps if we were to take a leaf from our Victorian ancestors' books and allowed modern technology to be used as part of today's standardised tests we might see a transformation taking place. At some point the technology of paper and pen was allowed in the examination theatre, resulting in a transformation in the way people learned and were taught. Yes, you can read and write anywhere!

Perhaps inevitably, given that we have retained the tradition of fact recall assessments written in ink, technology has also been used in the tradition of automating learning and de-skilling the craftspeople, i.e. the teachers. But imagine a world where it became compulsory and expected that students in a high-stakes exam would collaborate with their colleagues and use their connected devices.

Is that such a stretch of the imagination?

'Concerns include the disempowering and de-skilling of teachers, teaching to the test, narrowing the curriculum, teacher-focused learning and the fragmentation of knowledge.'

Singapore

Singapore

Singapore

Once a British colonial outpost, today Singapore is a high-tech, wealthy city-state in South-East Asia lying just south of Malaysia, to which it is linked by a one-mile bridge and causeway across the Straits of Johor. The OECD, in a 2011 report on strong performers and successful reformers in education, described Singapore as a poster child for education development. The OECD cited how Singapore 'aggressively pursued a policy of advancing in education and other arenas by system-atically benchmarking the world's best performance and creating a world-class education system based on what it had learned through their benchmarking'.[7] Consequently Singapore's test scores in the OECD's triennial PISA survey have consistently been among the global frontrunners.

Education has been one of the nation's highest priorities since it gained independence, but to understand why, it is worth considering Singapore's recent history.

Singapore was granted self-rule from the British in 1957 and, under the leadership of Lee Kuan Yew, the People's Action Party came to power in 1959. From 1963, lacking natural resources and employment opportunities for its growing population, Singapore briefly merged with Malaya and other regional states to form Malaysia but left the Federation in 1965 as a result of disagreements between the political parties of Malaya and Singapore that were exacerbated by racial tensions. In 1965, the Republic of Singapore became a sovereign, independent nation facing an uncertain future, challenged by conflict with its neighbours, unemployment, housing, education, sanitation, healthcare and a lack of natural resources and land. The nation felt a sense of political and economic vulnerability to larger countries and global changes whilst domestically it faced civil unrest.

As Singapore's first Prime Minister, Lee Kuan Yew set out two overarching goals as part of the country's recovery plan: to build a modern economy and to create a sense of Singaporean national identity. Lee recruited talented people into his early government who sought to promote economic growth and job creation. In the 1960s, the emphasis was on attracting labour-intensive foreign manufacturing to provide jobs for its low-skilled workforce. In the 1970s and 1980s, a shift to more skill-intensive manufacturing led to an emphasis on technical fields. From the mid-1990s on, Singapore has sought to become a player in the global knowledge economy, encouraging more research and innovation-intensive industry that seeks to attract scientists and companies from around the globe.

Lacking in other natural resources, human resources were and continue to be regarded as the nation's most precious asset. As a result, education and training were seen from the beginning as vital drivers of Singapore's successful economic development. The aims of education in Singapore are to deliver the human capital engine for economic growth and to create a sense of Singaporean identity. Education policy based upon clear economic goals means that education in Singapore is pragmatic with a strong focus on scientific and technical fields.

Ethnic and racial conflict in the early years of Singapore led to a deep commitment in creating a multi-racial and multi-ethnic society. At independence, Singapore had a population with multiple religious groups and no common language. There was no common schooling system or curriculum. Steps were then taken to realise Singapore's pledge of 'one united people regardless of race, language or religion'.[8] Four languages are recognised and taught – Chinese, English, Malay and Tamil – with English being the language of instruction and government. Compulsory national service and a government policy to mix ethnic groups within the government-built housing where most Singaporeans live have helped avoid ethnic and racial segregation. But it is the schools that play a major role in inculcating Singaporean values and character, where civic and moral education play a major part.

In less than half a century, Singapore made the transition from third-world malarial island to a first-world financial centre replete with a skyline of glittering skyscrapers and a thriving port. But this has come at a cost, most notably in Singapore's political system whereby the PAP have retained power since 1959. Though Lee stepped down in 1990, today Singapore's third Prime Minister is Lee Hsien Loong, his son. Some commentators have described Singapore as being governed by soft authoritarianism. With government exercising executive control over the judiciary and the legislature, Singapore is also noted for the conservatism of its leaders and its strict social controls.

A stable government under the same political party since 1959 has provided a basis for stable education policies. Teaching in Singapore is regarded as a highly honoured profession, in part because the standards for selection are high. Strong academic ability and nonacademic qualities are essential considerations during recruitment, so that only candidates who possess the character, aptitude and abilities to teach and develop students are recruited as teachers. Singapore has established a comprehensive system for selecting, training, developing and rewarding teachers to ensure the delivery of high-quality education that in turn would lead to high-quality student outcomes.

Teachers are trained at the National Institute of Education where they follow either a diploma, postgraduate diploma, or degree course, depending on their level of education at entry. They must commit to teaching for at least three years. The NIE maintains a close relationship with the schools whilst the Ministry of Education ensures that salaries are such that teaching remains an attractive occupation for new graduates. High-performing teachers can earn significant amounts through performance-related bonuses.

Once qualified, teachers are entitled to 100 hours of professional development per year, mostly at no cost to the teacher. They are appraised annually and their appraisal assesses their contribution to the academic and character development of their students, their collaboration with parents and the community and their contribution to colleagues and the school as a whole. This appraisal helps the teacher identify areas of growth that inform the basis of personal professional development plans. Teachers who don't perform are given help and are only invited to leave the service if they don't improve.

The results in terms of pupil attainment measured by standardised test scores, or global metrics such as PISA, speak for themselves. Singapore is a global leader. The government of Singapore has successfully designed and deployed a series of integrated systems, including education, that are part of an economic development plan. It is difficult to argue with the results, given the unprecedented speed at which the nation has metamorphosed from a post-colonial swamp to its standing today. However, one might suggest that this was only made possible by systems that ensured a culture of compliance held in check by robust social controls governing transgressions.

Critics cite the negative correlation between high scores in standardised tests and creativity or entrepreneurship, arguing that such tests kill students' creativity and desire to learn. They argue that an education system based around only the things we can measure means that creative disciplines will be undervalued. Pragmatic to a fault, Singapore might counter that its education provision has, through a series of rapid phases, converted a population with an education level similar to that of many developing countries to one of the best in the world that has led to its economic growth.

On the one hand, Singapore has benefited from having a one-party government able to plan its society and supporting systems, exert social control over its citizens and meet its economic plan. On the other, it is argued that the result is a compliant population devoid of creative self-determinism. It is the context that makes this discourse fascinating. Is it possible to simply take the genius of Lee Kwan Yew and transport that to another developing country and expect a similar rapid transformation? The answer is almost certainly, no. The context, scale, timing, location and history are just some aspects that are unique to Singapore and to industrialise Lee's approach across different cultures and context is likely to be a road to frustration and disappointment.

There are, however, lessons to be learned. In 1965, Singapore had a vision of what it wanted to be, supported by a plan of how to get there. As a state with a dominant political party, little opposition to deviate from this plan has been forthcoming. One might compare the iconic, quirky and visionary nature of Lee Kwan Yew to Steve Jobs. Both believed they could change the world.

As much of the developed world is now coming to terms with the digital economy and the impact of a connected society, one wonders how Singapore will next guide its systems and how that will affect its education provision. The Internet has often been seen as problematic for some regimes unable to curb this great engine of cultural change. More young people are questioning the trade-off between freedom and security, and even calling for freer politics and reduced social controls.

www.nie.edu.sgw

singapore

'The aims of education
in Singapore are to deliver
the human capital engine
for economic growth
and to create a sense
of Singaporean identity.'

Singapore

David Hung is currently Associate Dean of Education Research as well as a professor at the NIE, with teaching and research interests in learning, in particular social cultural orientations to cognition and communities of practice. Over the past seven years David has conducted research in learning and instructional technologies, constructivism and social constructivism, learning in communities of practice and other areas. In 2004, he initiated the set-up of the Learning Sciences Laboratory to focus research on Information and Communications Technology infusion in student-centred learning.

Graham Brown-Martin: David, please would you describe your background and role within the NIE.

David Hung: I've been a professor in this university, a full professor, for the last seven years. I've been here for a good 17 to 18 years in my career. I've been into technology and education because I've always been fascinated by it since my undergraduate days, dealing with computer science and technology. Because I had an interest in the learning sciences, cognitive science and, to some extent, neurosciences, I began to try to unravel how these theories could somehow find their way into education and schools –quite a difficult endeavour.

Graham: Technology has yet to make the big impact on education that we might have anticipated. Why do you think technology has had very little impact on improved outcomes so far?

David: This is my personal take. I just give my view as to why it's so difficult to change things in education vis-à-vis, perhaps, other practices. So I use the word 'practices' because technology in itself, as a tool, is just a small microcosm to a practice. So if we brought a doctor from 100 years ago back into the surgical theatre today, probably the doctor would be quite lost. But if you were to bring back a teacher from 100 years back and put him or her into a classroom today, any typical classroom, even if there were Internet sockets in the classroom, probably that teacher would still be able to perform.

So, there's something about educational practices that differs from practices, say, in the medical sciences. Now, my own view is that in the medical sciences, for example, the public would defer to doctors' specialisations for what they do, but in education, because everybody has been schooled somehow, the interplay between the school and the public becomes much more confusing, much more blurred, than in something like the medical sciences.

Let me try to articulate my own understanding of the history of ICT transformations in Singapore schools. We know that, back in 1997, the Singapore government felt that it was important that schools embark on this ICT journey. At the time, we had two terms, 'Information Technology' and 'Information and Communications Technology'. Now we know how important that particular 'C' is compared to those years, 15, 20 years back.

Putting technology into a classroom, into a school, does not necessarily change pedagogy or instructional practices. We did not all realise how daunting this transformational process could be. In 1997 when we started putting infrastructure into schools, we knew that, after a while, it would become out-of-date and then you would have to change infrastructure again. At that time, we thought that if we were to develop resources, if we were to give equipment to teachers, if we were to give some professional development for teachers, change and pedagogy would just come naturally, but they didn't.

Now, over the last ten years, we have done quite a lot of research in Singapore schools with respect to technology. I think, in Singapore, the contextual nuance of this setting is important because we are a system that performs exceedingly well in all international benchmarks. Also, I think many teachers believe that what they do with their kids can be achieved with or without technology.

There were many tried and tested approaches of didactic concept instruction, even through drill and practice, in which the stickiness of that knowledge actually reinforced a particular conceptual understanding. Very often we would feel that procedural knowledge would lead, as a complementary dialectic to conceptual understanding. So, one can be conceptually strong in certain ways, but not necessarily able to do procedural computations very well because of, perhaps, mistakes or otherwise.

In an exam-intensive context, you will find that students are required not just to know concepts well. They also need to know the procedures well. I think our top students in Singapore cohorts have no problem mastering either conceptual or procedural knowledge, but we know that we have a lower end of the cohort that may not do so well. We are trying to figure out how to help these particular lower-achieving students do better and what types of pedagogies we might put in place so that they can do better.

Technology has come in to help, particularly for the lower band of students, hopefully using different pedagogies that would be facilitated by technology. They might be able to do discovery and other forms of experimental learning that are more aligned with their dispositions and ways of picking up content knowledge.

Graham: Given that digital technology isn't allowed in the examination room, would you say that technology is used to reinforce teaching rather than transform learning?

David: This is a very difficult issue in Singapore because we do not want to give up the metric of students being assessed by typical examinations. We do not want to give it up because in Singapore's merit or credit system, we have not found a better alternative as of today.

'I think many teachers believe that what they do with their kids can be achieved with or without technology.'

So because we have not found an objective, publicly acceptable alternative to this metric, we have decided to keep those high-stakes exams as they are. Then, of course, the issue is how do we enable teachers to cultivate 21st-century dispositions including critical thinking, inventive thinking, collaboration, imagination and creativity? How do we do this and yet satisfy the demands of a publicly accepted rubric or metric for students to move in different trajectories in the educational system?

If you were to go to schools today in Singapore, compared to 1997 or even early 2000, quite a lot of innovations are happening. We have had many research efforts into these schools where we try to transform classroom pedagogies from a very didactic form into a much more student-participatory culture.

So our realisation is that the students are able to perform in these student-centred activities if given the understanding that this is not a traditional lesson but an opportunity to do more discovery forms of learning.

What really worked for these kids was when we started working with them in an out-of-classroom context. We created learning activities and designs that could marry the classroom learning with out-of-classroom learning.

We have two challenges. On the one hand, creating rubrics that would be acceptable in terms of assessing the 21st-century literacy, yet, on the other, these students are required to perform for examinations. So it's almost saying, 'Let's have the cake and eat it,' but it is possible. What happens is sometimes, at the crucial years such as Secondary Four, we don't normally do too much experimentation with kids because these are the years of high-stakes examinations. There is an exam practice at school that students need to be schooled in.

In these years, we make sure that the kids are able to perform for the examinations, but in the other years where there's more latitude for 21st-century forms of dispositional development, we do quite a bit of work with kids. What I'm saying is that we put on the right hat when we need to. So when we have to take examinations, we put on the examinations hat. We're trying to school a student who's able to take exams when he or she is required to take an exam, but when the exam criteria are taken off, he or she is able to exhibit the kinds of dispositions based on the practice which we are trying to inculcate.

Increasingly, we have been having success in doing this and we have characterised the teachers' performances using John Bransford's notion of adaptive expertise. We're developing teachers who are able to perform to the required goals. So if the goal is examination, perform to the examination. If the goal is 21st-century learning, create and design tasks that would be able to suit 21st-century learning. Not everybody can do that, but this transformational change takes a long time to develop.

'Technology has come in to help, particularly for the lower band of students, hopefully using different pedagogies that would be facilitated by technology.'

'We want to approach games as very open spaces for students to experience phenomena and develop a performance capacity with respect to their learning outcomes.'

Chee Yam San is an Associate Professor in the Learning Sciences & Technologies Academic Group and the Learning Sciences Lab at the National Institute of Education, Nanyang Technological University. He obtained his BSc (Econ) Hons from the London School of Economics and Political Science, University of London, and his PhD from the University of Queensland, Australia.

Chee's current research focuses on new media and new literacies in education, with a special emphasis on game-based learning in formal and informal learning environments, as well as identity construction through living online. Recent games developed include Space Station Leonis, Escape from Centauri 7 and Ideal Force. Current games being developed are Legends of Alkhimia and Statecraft X.

Graham Brown-Martin: The education system in Singapore is largely promoted, certainly overseas, as one of the global leaders in terms of the attainment of standardised test scores. Why do you think the education system in Singapore is so good?

Chee Yam San: I believe that our education system here is successful because of the well-trained teachers who are part of the system, and the very rigorous standards by which they adhere to the requirements of the curriculum that basically prepares students very well for these forms of standardised assessments. So while they do very well on PISA and TIMSS, and this is envied worldwide, there are certain costs at which this achievement is actually attained.

Graham: Tell me about those costs. What is the consequence of attaining these high standards?

Chee: My personal sense is that while there's a spoken importance concerning all-round holistic education, the importance of students being seen to do well in school assessments tends to make these assessments very narrow. And students tend to focus just on accomplishing their best within these very narrowly defined sets of requirements. And so the kinds of thinking that

the 21st-century world requires tend not to be something that is being given due attention.

Graham: Policymakers tend to refer to creative subjects, the ones that are hard to measure, as soft subjects. Do you think there's a blind spot on creativity and the arts in Singaporean schooling?

Chee: My personal sense is that there is attention being given, at least officially, to developing 21st-century competencies, but it rarely extends beyond a need for so-called sub-skills. So there's much emphasis being put on collaboration skills, for example, but really where I think we see the serious weakness is in thinking skills, especially the capacity of students to think independently on their own. They tend to be brought up on a diet of content, and sort of knowing stuff, but they then lack personal opinions and deep convictions about the knowledge that they learned.

Graham: You've recently led an investigation into the creation and use of video games within Singaporean schools. What were the origins of that project?

Chee: We entered the video game space with respect to education because of a unique funding opportunity that came our way courtesy of the National Research Foundation in Singapore. It supported a fund to do research that involved the use of interactive visual media related to education. So games were like a perfect example of the kind of work being invited.

So we were successful in two funding grants, and therefore we developed two very different games as part of this work. One was for chemistry, for 13- to 14-year-olds. This is a four-person

'Games are engaging because they place the learner in the role of first person.'

multiplayer PC-based game using a LAN. The other is a game for social studies. It deals with the topic of governance in relation to citizenship. And this is a game that we developed for the Apple iPhone as a highly multiplayer game involving 20 concurrent players in a single session.

The games have been used in schools. They've been trialled, they've been tested, they've been the subject of research. And the findings that have emanated from that fieldwork have been published.

Graham: How were these games designed and created?

Chee: Our video games were designed and developed entirely within the NIE. And this was a very important principle, because my past experience of trying to develop technologies in education indicated that if you were to outsource the development of the technology, especially something that's very closely coupled to content areas, you would tend to get back something that's not quite what you wanted or what you need. So by being able to bring the design development in-house, we were able to constantly apply a pedagogical lens to how the design and development was evolving. I think this has been vital in terms of providing that coherence and integration between the final developed artefact and the pedagogy that we embedded in, when you take it and offer it to schoolteachers to make use of in the classroom.

Graham: And what did you discover?

Chee: We could take the Statecraft X iPhone game for social studies as a concrete example. One of the issues concerning social studies' assessments is that students are required to look at passages critically and then write an essay that involves making comparisons, identifying gaps, information, etc., with respect to claims. This is a very structured kind of exercise that students can master with sufficient practice.

In our Statecraft X game we were very concerned about tapping into students' own views concerning governance. Governance is an important topic within social studies because there are no necessarily absolute right or wrong answers concerning what constitutes a good government. So we were interested in giving them a space wherein they could actually articulate their views, and then through a dialogic kind of pedagogy, be able to participate in an expansive form of learning.

There's obviously a textbook that is used, and that tends to be a very authoritative source of information. Students often refer to that source as definitive and use it as a basis for their essays. So the space for thinking on one's own, for relating to the events, etc., that are current, because the textbook was written some time ago, is fairly limited.

In our essay that we got them to write after they completed the Statecraft X curriculum, we posed a problem situation concerning the situation in our nation, Singapore. We asked them to suggest solutions, and we were assessing them for multiple perspectives on the solutions, to what extent they reflected a sense of ownership, of vested interest in the answers that they gave, and also to what extent they showed personal voice and commitment to what they were writing about. So these are very different criteria from what I use as part of the standard assessments. And this in turn created some challenges in terms of doing our classroom work.

Graham: Picking up on that point, there are different schools of thought about using video games in education. One school of thought is that video games are the almost perfect, ultimate rote-learning technology that allows their use to support a 19th-century teaching practice. Another school of thought says the games can reinvent and transform the learning experience in ways that haven't been measured. How are you influenced?

Chee: We want to approach games as very open spaces for students to experience phenomena and develop a performance capacity with respect to their learning outcomes. So in relation to citizenship, the crux of the issue is: Do you want students to learn about citizenship or do you want them to learn to be good citizens? The two are vastly different goals. So I go into the

'So by being able to bring the design development in-house, we were able to constantly apply a pedagogical lens to how the design and development was evolving.'

classroom with this curriculum and I ask the 15-year-olds: 'Would you prefer to learn to swim, or learn about swimming?' They very quickly say they would like to learn to swim. So it's this personal value that's associated with learning that is important for us. It's about learning to be good citizens, not learning about citizenship.

This assimilation underlies the Statecraft experience. It's a very open simulation in which students have the liberty to enact the kind of government that they want by virtue of being placed in the role of governors of towns in this medieval fantasy world that we call Velar. There are various indicators to show them how well they're doing. We play upon the tension between citizen happiness and the economic wealth manifested in their towns. Because when you work the citizens harder to drive the wealth up, you pay a price in terms of their happiness.

Students are forced to confront the values that they bring to the role of governing, making them ask: 'What do I value as a citizen?' It creates a dialectic tension in the conversation between government and what they do, and citizens and what we are. It allows them to even get a feel for what it's like to be in the shoes of the government.

Graham: There's a cultural context to this as well. Do you think that having a safe, open digital environment where you are encouraged to question and test numerous things that you might not do, or be able to do, or feel comfortable doing in the less safe real world, can have an influence on the physical world?

Chee: Sure. I think our curriculum provides a safe space within the classroom context for teachers to facilitate this kind of learning where kids are helped to understand the assumptions under which governance actually takes place. Kids tend to be on the receiving end of things and they tend to just be forced to accept doctrine. But this game, designed as a game to learn rather than a game to teach content, allows teachers to use it as an instrument, a tool, because it instates a very rich learning experience. But the content, the take-aways, are not really messages proposed directly within the game.

It's a mobile game. Kids do not play the game during social studies class time. They play in their own time, wherever they are. In the class, teachers … invite students to share what happened, what difficulties they experienced, and then make connections to the principles of governing a nation.

This kind of open space for dialogue is really the safe space where students can articulate their *bona fide* thinking without any fear. And then, within the safe space of a classroom, the teachers can help them to understand more deeply the assumptions that underlie governance, as well as the values that they bring to the enterprise. Governance is a very value-based kind of process, and so whether one prefers more control or one is comfortable with a more libertarian mode of governance, there will be repercussions. There will be side-effects in terms of more liberty.

So we play on this tension between the happiness of the citizens and economic development. This mirrors the whole Singapore tension very nicely because there is a constant rhetoric from the government, especially in the past, that economic survival is the key challenge and that we need to prioritise this goal. But then that takes a toll upon citizens' time for other kinds of pursuits, the work-life balance issues, etc. And then the question is: What do you value?

Graham: Looking at the wider society issues in Singapore, what do you sense is the public debate happening around education?

Chee: In Singapore it is a slightly unusual dialogue now in the sense that education focuses upon the stress that students face going through the system, especially at the primary school level. So at the age of 12 they take a primary school leaving examination, and the score that they get from that examination then determines their eligibility for the secondary school that they get into. And Singapore being such a small pressure-cooker place, parents are very competitive in trying to get students into what are perceived as the best schools. And this has been the issue that has framed national conversations around education of late.

But ultimately the issue is one about the administration of schools and the criteria by which students progress from one level of education to another. Unfortunately it hasn't touched on the deeper issues of what actually takes place under the label of education in the classrooms. I think this is a deeper issue that parents need to be concerned about.

Graham: What do you think it is about video games that children find so engaging? I think most teachers would almost give their left arm for children to be as engaged in their lessons as they are with some video games. What can we learn from video-game design?

Chee: Games are engaging because they place the learner in the role of first person. And this represents an epistemological shift compared with the way that they traditionally learn in the classroom, where information is presented to them and they are basically in the third person. So you learn about 'them' and 'it' and 'they', etc. But in a video game, it's 'I'. That's the great difference. So engagement is something that you cannot not have when you play a game, because it's 'I'. I am doing things. I am governing. I am working as a chemist. And so the engagement comes very naturally.

But having said that, different genres of games also get associated with different degrees of engagement. Our game for chemistry, Legends of Alkhimia, is a first-person action game, so the level of engagement is very intense. The students encounter strange monsters and we use this device to instantiate the workings of chemistry for them to engage in scientific inquiry. So when they encounter these monsters, they use a certain weapon whose ammunition ... interacts with the kind of substance that the monster is comprised of – a chemical reaction. So that kind of game is extremely engaging. The classroom goes wild with screaming when these creatures appear.

Our Statecraft game is a strategy game, a much slower-paced game. We found that that the demands for thoughtfulness in the gameplay were much greater, and not all students necessarily took to this slower-paced game. So we have to be mindful of the different types of genres as well as some potential issues related to gender. Boys tend to like action games that move at a very fast pace. Girls tend to prefer something a little slower. So in Statecraft, it's a slow-paced game, but then there is a battle that looms because the neighbouring kingdom ... begins to assemble its forces along the border ... and this gets the boys excited. So the different aspects of the gameplay are also something that we have to attend to in order to bring in the participation of both boys and girls.

Graham: How do you see the future use of this kind of platform, the technology and ideas being developed in Singaporean education?

Chee: The potential for widespread use of games with the associated technology is first and foremost dependent on teacher capacity to enact the kind of game-based learning pedagogy that is vital. Teachers as gatekeepers of the classroom are important agents, and they need to both understand and fully buy into what games offer with respect to education. And this is where, with regard to empirical work, we have found deep tensions that arise as teachers wrestle with whether or not, and to what extent, they will accept the use of games as knowledge within the curriculum.

'Is it a coincidence that so many of our recognised entrepreneurs didn't complete their formal education?'

I was recently invited to take afternoon tea at a rather swanky establishment in London to meet with the chairman of a university sector college. The college has a long and respected history in the arts but is in the process of reinventing itself as a centre of excellence for digital design and entrepreneurship with the aim of attracting and establishing long-term financial relationships with key design industry players. Recognising that higher education is undergoing a radical transformation in itself, the recent retirement of their CEO has presented the college with the opportunity to identify new blood that will challenge the status quo. It turns out that one of my [it has to be said] quite influential colleagues had tipped me as a possible candidate. Having recently been appointed to the advisory board of the renowned EMLYON Business School in France, the idea of helping to transform higher education appealed to me.

My background before writing this book was as a serial entrepreneur who had created, built and sold a number of successful enterprises since I was 21 years of age in the creative, digital and education sectors. One of these enterprises employed nearly 200 people, plus a similar number of contractors. Without trying to inflate my own ego, I had built these organisations from the germ of an idea – sometimes gambling my own home to raise finance and sometimes negotiating multi-million-pound investments – into businesses that had value. After working overseas for a number of years I returned to the UK in 2005 to devote more than ten years to establishing global dialogues about the transformation of our education systems and finding the smartest people in the world to mentor me. This book marks a particular point in this lifelong learning journey.

Now there is almost certainly somebody out there who will be the safe pair of hands to become the CEO of that college, but it won't be me. Somewhere after the second cup of tea, I mentioned that I had left school at 15 and then taught myself all that I know aided and abetted by far too many people than I could ever mention here. I should say, though, that if these people were the faculty of a university it would be the best faculty in the world, and I'm very lucky. But the catch in all this – and it has happened to me on a number of occasions – is that I don't have the stamp in my metaphorical passport that allows me into the club of academia. How could somebody without a degree possibly know how to transform higher education, whose principal business model was monetised by awarding them?

I'm not experiencing a narcissistic breakdown here. The point I am wanting to make is that our education systems and other public-sector organisations don't take into account or recognise the actual experience that people have gained. I can't turn my experiences or my knowledge in design, invention or other works into anything that would be accepted as a substitute for the university degree that would allow access to the magic kingdom. At this point in my life, as much as I would enjoy the opportunity to research and participate within the academic world, it is closed to me. Perhaps I'm just not smart enough.

So it's interesting that so many conversations with policymakers and educators arrive at a destination that wonders why there aren't more Mark Zuckerbergs, Steve Jobses, Richard Bransons, Larry Pages and Sergey Brins, et al. All of those high flyers who, you know, dropped out of college. Is it a coincidence that so many of our recognised entrepreneurs didn't complete their formal education? Did Zuckerberg et al become Zuckerberg et al because of, or despite, their schools? Is it possible to design schools to nurture creative and entrepreneurial talents like Zuckerberg? If so, what do they look like?

The global education reform movement recites from the college and career readiness songbook that is crafted from uniform curriculum, common standards and assessments, data-driven instruction, high-stakes testing and globally benchmarked practices. PISA, TIMSS and other international benchmarks are measured as the gold standard of education quality and linked to future national prosperity. Yet student loan debt in the US stands at $1 trillion with nearly five million graduates unemployed. For the first time in US history the number of jobless workers aged 25 and up who have attended some college now exceeds the ranks of those who settled for a high-school diploma or less. If college degrees do not guarantee gainful employment or a meaningful life, what is the point of preparing someone to be ready for college?

I'm indebted to the work of Dr Yong Zhao,[9] Director of the Institute of Global and Online Education, College of Education, University of Oregon. Zhao took the scores from the Global Entrepreneurship Monitor, an annual assessment of entrepreneurial activities, aspirations and attitudes of individuals in over 50 countries, and cross-referenced them against scores from the OECD's PISA. What he discovered was that countries with higher PISA scores have fewer people who are confident in their entrepreneurial capabilities. Zhao noted that, 'Out of the innovation-driven economies, Singapore, Korea, Taiwan, and Japan are among the best PISA performers, but their scores on the measure of perceived capabilities or confidence in their ability to start a new business are the lowest.'

What we need to ask ourselves then is what does this mean?

We know that it is possible to engineer and design our education systems so that learners perform well in standardised tests. We can even deploy digital technology to reinforce the skills required to attain high test scores. The excessive investment made in private coaching outside of school hours by parents of children in South-East Asian economies to achieve better test scores demonstrates this unhealthy obsession with standardised tests. But is this what we want when we understand that it is at the expense of curiosity, creativity and entrepreneurship?

Zaatari

Amman

Jordan

Jordan

We arrived in Jordan from Singapore, via Abu Dhabi, in the middle of the night at a deserted airport in Amman.

This was my first time in Jordan but I'm certain it won't be my last. It is a country that slowly seduces you with its charm and feels comfortable, like a surrogate home. There was something in the culture that felt familiar. Conversations with people were both interesting and easy to start.

Jordan, officially the Hashemite Kingdom of Jordan, is an Arab kingdom on the East Bank of the River Jordan. It is currently host to the world's largest refugee camp at Zaatari, now home to over 150,000 Syrian refugees, making it the fifth highest population centre in the country. An additional camp for 130,000 refugees is being opened at Azraq. The country is also host to more than 300,000 refugees and asylum seekers from Palestine and Iraq. The vast majority of refugees live outside the camps, representing a significant challenge to, and demand upon the resources of Jordan, a country of six million people with a displaced population of more than one million.

Jordan is not blessed with abundant natural resources like some of its neighbours. More than ten percent of the nation's GDP is derived from tourism, as the country is home to the world-class historical and cultural sites of Petra and Jerash, the seaside recreation of Aqaba and the Dead Sea, as well as the site of the first baptism and Mount Nebo. It is hardly surprising, then, that education is regarded as a priority by the Jordanian government, and the country has developed a highly advanced national curriculum. But there are challenges.

A 2009 USAID report suggests that, faced with a growing youth population, the Jordanian government must ensure that the quality of education and skills imparted can help new generations to compete effectively both at home and abroad. Presently a mismatch between the skills taught and the skills required by employers is leading to high unemployment. Teaching methodologies that have become outdated, a lack of relevant teacher training and limited use of technology are just some of the challenges the Ministry of Education is facing.

I was in Jordan to meet the principals of the Jordan Education Initiative, who have been tackling the challenges of education reform and technology in Jordanian schools with some remarkable results. I also had the opportunity to travel to the Syrian border and visit the Zaatari refugee camp to see at first hand the challenges of providing schooling to a displaced population.

'...education is regarded as a
priority by the Jordanian government,
and the country has developed
a highly advanced national
curriculum.'

Jordan Education Initiative

Amman

Case study

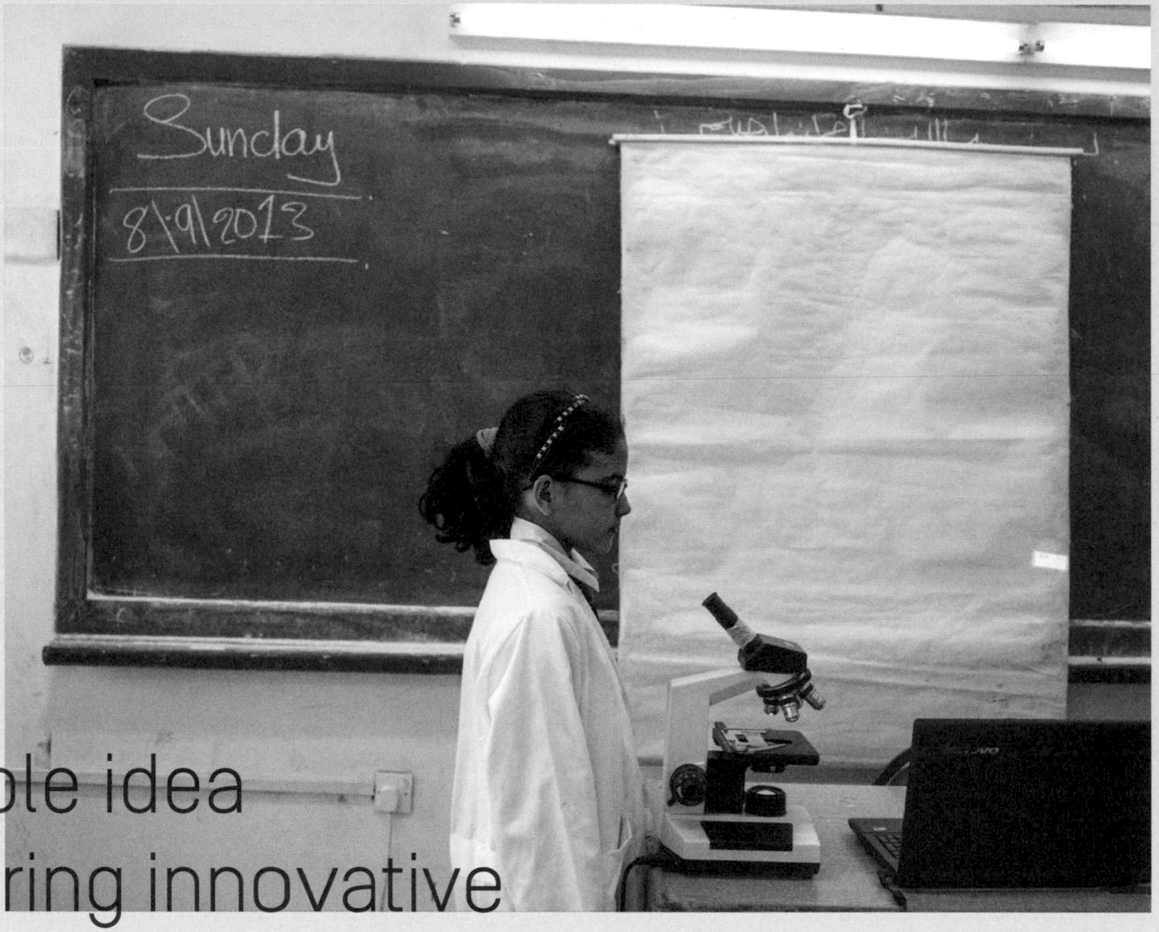

‘The whole idea
was to bring innovative
ideas to change
the education system
in Jordan...’

I had an inkling that I was going to enjoy meeting Rana Madani, the Deputy CEO of the Jordan Education Initiative, when we initially spoke on Skype whilst I was in London scoping out the visit to Jordan. She wanted to make clear that I wasn't coming to Jordan to make comparisons with Westernised implementations of technology in schools and make sure that I understood the context in which the JEI were working.

As it turned out, Rana had nothing to worry about. Our visit was one of the most enlightening, with genuinely forward-thinking and well-implemented digital strategies that were entirely relevant to the cultural context of the nation. The passion for positive change and improvement of the Jordanian education system was palpable with Rana and the JEI team as well as with the teaching staff, principals and learners we met.

The JEI was established as a public-private partnership involving both local and international partners aiming to improve education in Jordan through effective use of ICT and to create a model of education reform for other countries, particularly in the Arab world. The initiative was launched at the World Economic Forum's annual meeting in 2003 at the Dead Sea, attracting 17 global corporations, 17 Jordanian businesses and 11 governmental organisations and NGOs working together with the Jordanian government and with the support of their Majesties King Abdullah and Queen Rania.

Rana explained that the whole idea was to bring innovative ideas to change the education system in Jordan that ran in parallel with two other simultaneous programmes, the Education Reform for Knowledge Economy programme and the ICT Ministry's roll-out of national broadband. Involving local businesses in the JEI was an intrinsic aspect of the initiative to ensure local knowledge as well as enterprise creation.

The work from 2003 to 2007 produced three main pillars. The first was the infrastructure to enable a number of schools to pilot working practices that embedded digital platforms. One hundred of the Discovery Schools chosen were in Amman, the capital, to discover what worked and what didn't. The concept was to learn important lessons about implementation so that successful practices could be scaled up to all the country's schools. Rana emphasised that it was not the mandate of JEI to roll out to every school in Jordan; that would be the function of the Ministry of Education. The role of JEI has been to act as an innovation lab or think tank to explore, test and evidence new ideas for learning for the Ministry to inform their education reform process.

The Discovery Schools in Amman (55 boys' schools, 45 girls' schools, across primary and secondary) were chosen based on their location in relation to the data centre and current broadband provision. There are two distinct areas of Amman: the more affluent districts to the west and the more densely populated and socially diverse districts to the east, somewhat similar to the split between West and East London in the UK. This was an important aspect of the initiative to judge impact within different social conditions. Most of the schools were in the east, and more in need of change. These 100 schools were a good representation of what was happening in Jordan as a whole.

Wireless and broadband connectivity was a core aspect of the JEI programme. Whilst prior to JEI there were computer labs in schools, it was JEI that was pioneering the use of digital platforms across the curriculum, within each classroom and for each student. The focus was to explore how digital and connected technologies could be integrated within the curricula and not limited to a computer lab where ICT was a subject in itself. Thus 1:1 access for each student and the ability to access wireless networks wherever they were within the school were key.

The second pillar was the creation of digital content. Rana explained that simply introducing infrastructure and devices into the classroom would not mean that teachers would be ready to create their own content. The lack of resources in Arabic adds to the challenge. There is plenty of teaching material on all subjects, and lesson plans, on the Internet but these are not in Arabic. So an important part of JEI's work has been to create digital content rather than simply translating and customising existing content. The idea has been to bootstrap a local industry of digital learning materials and content that can be used in the region. International corporate partners, for example Cisco, would support digital content development by working with a local partner in Jordan such as Rubicon Studios.

The six areas of digital development were around maths, Arabic, science, ICT, English as Foreign Language and civics (citizenship), deployed via the EduWave learning management system, in which every teacher, student and parent is provided with a login.

The third pillar of activity was the professional development training of teachers that was initially provided by the project's commercial partners and content developers before a 'train the trainer' approach was adopted to ensure local expertise that would provide ongoing continuing professional development.

In 2007, USAID funded a comprehensive impact assessment to measure the impact of JEI. The study found that JEI was an effective catalyst in growing the work and activities under the partnership and was able to facilitate the sharing of global expertise in innovation with the local expertise of Jordanian schools, culture, values and needs. It also identified areas for improvement that led to the next phase of JEI that would lead to an expanded team (between 2003 and 2007 there were just seven people) and methods of monitoring and evaluation that would provide diagnostics to identify where improvements were occurring or where additional focus was required.

Jordan

Capacity building and change management have become important activities within JEI. Ongoing continuing professional development for teachers has become vital, especially programmes and workshops that they have developed themselves rather than brought in. Relevance was everything, Rana said. 'If teachers can't see the benefit of using technology they won't use it,' she explained.

Rana invited me to visit three schools in Amman: the Princess Rahma School in West Amman, a relatively wealthy and attractive residential neighbourhood that is home to the National Gallery and most of the upmarket hotels, cafés and quirky retail outlets; the Shefaa Bint Awf School, also to the west of the city and described as a mentor school; and Balqees School, situated in East Amman, the historic centre of the city that today is densely populated with failing infrastructure, and that featured a one-laptop-per-child approach.

Princess Rahma School, described as a leading innovation school, is an elementary school that was buzzing with activity and full of enthusiastic learners in every class we visited. In one second-grade class I witnessed one of the most energetic and enthusiastic teachers that I have encountered. She was animated around the room, engaging her young pupils in a geography lesson about the Arab countries using a blended combination of her own physical theatre and a physical globe, a poster map, and driving an interactive whiteboard in a way that wasn't exclusive to herself – young pupils were frequently encouraged to join in and use the board.

A fourth-grade science class about atomic structure in which each child had their own Classmate laptop featured an acted-out play by some of the students in costume, explaining by showing the different characteristics of atomic particles. It was quite obvious that the children here were enjoying their lesson and learning by participation and doing. In another class a group of grade-six children were debating (in English) the relative merits of using technology for learning, no doubt for our benefit but nevertheless very impressive, with well-reasoned arguments, although the motion for the use of technology was upheld!

Our visit to Sheefa Bint Awf School was equally inspiring. An interactive whiteboard was used in one science class as a multi-touch collaborative surface by the students. I have often had my doubts about the benefits of interactive whiteboards in classrooms but here the device was used skilfully by the teacher as a means for the students to use it rather than to simply project Powerpoint slides in a preset lesson plan. In all cases there was an abundance of locally created Arabic content as had been described by Rana *(see interview on page 98)*. Once again students were involved in a theatrical performance as part of a maths class, discussing the concept of volume via play-acting involving a popcorn seller filling cones. This struck me as an engaging way to learn whilst at the same time students were creating their own digital content about the subject, digital animations using Oracle's Alice, to share on the maths group's Facebook page.

Yes, that's right: every teacher and student was encouraged to use Facebook as a place to share learning. Indeed, the principal was very keen to show me the YouTube channel that she had created and maintains for the school. Coming from a Western perspective where social media and even YouTube are all but banned from the classroom, this was quite a revelation. I asked one of the students, a 13-year-old, how she learned to create such interesting digital content. She gave me the same look as my own 13-year-old daughter does when I ask a dumb question – a look which says that I'm an idiot which, of course, I am.

It was at this school where we also met the annual intake of interns that join JEI to spend an entire year mentoring and assisting schools participating in the JEI programme. Most of these interns are from an IT background and join the programme to gain working experience whilst at the same time provide vital support and encouragement to the teaching faculty in the schools.

Our last visit was to Balqees School, located in the district of Jabal Al-Kalaa on the eastern side of Amman. The school is nestled between the dense conurbation of buildings perched on the side of a large hill. The school building is, in fact, a converted house, providing education for children from less affluent homes. Despite its size and very small classrooms, the school is bright and positive. This isn't one of JEI's Discovery Schools but a *madrasati* (meaning 'my school') which is an initiative to repair and rebuild schools with community support.

The students at this school and others like it lack access to the kind of digital platforms for learning made possible by broadband Internet and so JEI, in collaboration with Qualcomm, are supporting a pilot that provides every child in the school with a 3G-connected laptop computer that they use in the school and take home to their families.

Despite a reduction of space and resources, there was nothing to suggest that the children in this school were receiving less of an education. The atmosphere was positive, the children clearing enjoying the freedom and access they have via their laptops supported by a hardworking, committed team of teachers. I asked a pupil what she planned to do when she was older and she told me that she was going to be a heart surgeon. There was a sense that anything is possible for these children, regardless of background.

JEI has nurtured an environment that encourages innovation, a place where teachers can explore new ideas and new approaches without fear, and that is something I think we can all learn from. I came away from my two days with JEI genuinely impressed by the determination, ambition and ongoing learning that is happening within the team and participating schools. They have truly grasped the understanding that innovation is messy, that it is risky, that mistakes will be made and that you must have courage.

'JEI has nurtured an environment that encourages innovation, a place where teachers can explore new ideas and new approaches without fear...'

Jordan

'Every teacher and student
is encouraged to use Facebook
as a place to share learning.'

'At the end of the day, with these students we're not just talking about their school grades any more.'

The Jordan Education Initiative was established as a public-private partnership aiming to improve the provision of education in Jordan through effective use of ICT and to establish a model of reform that could be used across the Arab world and beyond. The initiative was launched at the World Economic Forum's annual meeting in 2003 at the Dead Sea and attracted the support of many global and domestic corporations, with governmental and non-governmental organisations working together with the Jordanian government, with the support of their Majesties King Abdullah and Queen Rania.

Rana Madani, their energetic and enthusiastic deputy CEO, has worked with the project since 2005. This is what she had to say.

Graham Brown-Martin: Rana, what are the aims of the JEI?

Rana Madani: The aim of the initiative is to change education and to add innovation by using technology.

Since 2003, one of the biggest education reforms happening in Jordan is the Education Reform for the Knowledge Economy programme. Also at that time, we had the National Broadband Network plan, and we thought maybe we could put all these efforts together by having another initiative to bring innovation, to bring new solutions to the education system, so we can make a change in the delivery of information to the students, and of course in the whole environment of teaching and learning.

Graham: What challenges did you encounter introducing new technologies into an existing education system and how did you solve them?

Rana: Actually, in any intervention, the first thing that you're going to face is the ability of people to change. Because first of all people are really happy with what they're doing. They have their own personal zone that they're just comfortable in. When you come up with a new idea or with any intervention where they need to do

something new, where they need to change, there will always be resistance to that change.

The main player in the whole game is the teacher at the beginning. You need to work with the teachers on changing their mindset towards the change or towards the new intervention. That's why from the beginning we work with the teacher and the whole school as a unit.

But when people start believing in what you're giving them, and if they believe that this will actually make their life easier and they can do their job better, they will start believing in that intervention and they actually adopt it and they start using it easily.

We do a lot of capacity building and training for the administrators, for the teachers themselves. We work on a change management component, training them on the new technology that we introduced into the school, in addition to our own training material which tackles the 21st-century skills for students such as project-based learning, collaborative work, critical thinking, and the important role of the social media in learning and teaching.

We also work with the community. We do a lot of orientation sessions with the community and the parents, because in order for you to ensure that the technology is used in schools, you need all the players to be part of the game. They have to be introduced and they have to be part of it, taking part and making decisions towards what they want to have or what they want to see in their school.

Graham: It's interesting that the JEI is actively promoting the use of social media within learning whereas many other parts of the world are actively banning it. Please tell me more.

Rana: The social media are widely used in different schools in Jordan but, again, this is controlled, it is monitored. I mean by that, for instance, in certain cases for a teacher it's easier to create a group on Facebook where the students are working on a certain project together,

and the teacher can be part of the same group, so the teacher can really supervise and monitor what is happening and give feedback and comments.

Many of the students do a lot of projects and they really want to market and promote them, so they use Facebook to create a page in order just to talk to people about their work and to spread the word about what they're doing. Many of the schools also have their own Twitter account. They tweet about their achievements, they tweet about their projects, they learn about what is happening in other schools by following certain educators in different parts of the world. We believe that the social media, if well-used in order to serve an educational purpose, can actually be very beneficial.

Graham: How does the JEI work with the government in Jordan?

Rana: We look at the JEI as a think tank that talks to international partners and the private sector, local and international. We try to look into the latest trends in education and then we talk to the government and we work hand in hand with them in order to bring these innovations into the schools.

At the end of the day, the schools that we're working with are the schools that belong to the Ministry of Education in Jordan. We really talk to them at the beginning or at the inception of any project, we share our ideas with them, and also we try to be on different committees where we can give advice to the Ministry whenever it is needed.

Graham: As a public-private partnership with international technology companies, what impact does the JEI have on domestic capacity building and the economy?

Rana: The public-private partnership in this initiative is a bit different because we think about it as a win-win situation for everybody. The schools and the private sector are gaining out of this experience, and we are exposing the Ministry of Education in Jordan to the new and the latest innovations or solutions that are taking place in the world, and we bring them into Jordan. There has been a big investment from the private sector in the state schools in Jordan.

Another objective of the JEI is to help the ICT industry in Jordan. That's why we opted to create our own digital content, which is mapped with the learning objectives and outcomes of the education system in Jordan and certain curricula.

The international partners, with their experience, funded development of the content, working with local companies helped by the Ministry of Education, who were the ones who actually wrote the script because they know exactly what type of content they would like to have in the schools.

Our local technology companies added multimedia and simulations in order to make it more engaging, rather than a scanned copy of the book. It's full of life. It's full of simulations that can really stimulate critical thinking and problem-solving skills for students.

Graham: To what extent do you think that improvements in education will be linked to improvements in the economy and productivity?

Rana: Productivity is really important. Also being good citizens, because at the end of the day this is about what they're going to do for their country. Now, if you have more educated citizens, this means that the economy of the whole country is going to move forward. This is what we need specifically in Jordan.

We don't have too many resources, which is why education is the main thing here in our country. The human brain is our treasure, it's our jewel, you may say. That's why we need to work on it very hard to make it suitable for the job market in the whole region. The job market in Jordan cannot support all Jordanians and that's why we are competing with everybody. It could be in the States, it could be in India, it could be anywhere. That's why the competition is really, really high, and we need to have really well-prepared students in order to be able to compete and find good jobs for themselves.

'Many of the schools also have their own Twitter account.'

At the end of the day, with these students we're not just talking about their school grades any more. We're talking about well-rounded students who can really communicate well. They need to have good skills in terms of presenting themselves, talking about their country, talking about what they learned in a very innovative way, and in order to be able to find good jobs in the future.

Graham: Is it possible for the JEI, working as a regional think tank, to become a digital learning hub for the Middle East?

Rana: The beauty of the JEI model is its flexibility. It can fit into any environment according to the needs of that environment. That's why when we started our project in Palestine – and we are currently using the JEI model in 20 schools in Jerusalem – we really were able to use this model and have it fit into the environment in those schools. Whatever we can do, we can do it anywhere.

Being in Jordan and in the region allows us to be more accepted by our neighbouring countries, because we understand the culture, we understand the language, and we have the know-how, the experience and the expertise. We've been doing this for the past ten years. We've been dealing with technology and we believe that technology is there to modernise education.

Graham: Thinking about the last ten years of this initiative, what would you say are the lessons that you'd like to share?

Rana: The beauty of this journey is the challenges we faced at the beginning and the lessons learned. This is what we'd always like to share with anybody who wants to use ICT in education – our experience in designing the strategy or vision or policy for any country wishing to use ICT in education.

There are challenges regarding the infrastructure itself, and connectivity issues. These are challenges that any country needs to look at when they start working with technology.

The second thing is professional development. What kind of professional development do we really need to offer or give our teachers, how do we do it, are we going to force it on teachers, or are these teachers part of the whole journey? What kind of policies need to be in the country? Is there a strategy that is really clear for the country to use technology in education?

The other thing is the availability of resources. What kind of resources do we have in schools in order for the teachers to be innovative and to use technologies? What decisions need to be made regarding the technologies we need to have?

These are things that you always need to think about. You need to see how you're going to do it, and sometimes you opt to use something and then it turns out that it's not what you need, and it's not achieving your goals or your objectives. That's why you have to stop, think, reflect, and see what you're going to do next.

Again, remember that we're talking about education, we're talking about human beings, we're talking about generations of people and students who are going to shape the future of their countries. That's why you need to be really careful with what you're doing. You have to be really patient because change does not happen in a second.

'We believe that
the social media, if
well-used in order
to serve an educational
purpose, can actually
be very beneficial.'

Jordan

The Zaatari refugee camp, Jordan
Thought piece

> 'Education is, quite simply, peace-building by another name. It is the most effective form of defence spending there is.'
>
> Kofi Annan

While we were in Jordan we decided to make an unofficial visit to the Zaatari refugee camp on the border with Syria. Tensions in the region were heightened by the possibility of US intervention in Syria in the wake of allegations of the regime's use of chemical weapons. We felt a responsibility to provide a window into the lives being affected: the mothers, fathers and children whose lives have forever been changed and displaced.

Of the two million Syrian refugees who have escaped conflict in their home nation, one million are children. According to the United Nations High Commissioner for Refugees, refugees in 'protracted situations' can expect an average camp residency of 17 years. What is certain is that many of the families and children currently residing in camp will be there for years. Nearly five million others have been displaced within Syria itself. These numbers are expected to increase with the escalation or spreading of conflict to neighbouring countries. And this is the tip of the iceberg. There are many other refugee camps around the world with a population of some 10.5 million people of concern to the UNHCR. On average, 850 children are born every day in the world's refugee camps; too many children spend a large part of their lives growing up in the camps.

I've been interested in what happens to the education of child refugees since a chance meeting with my friend Alek Wek at the

2012 WISE Summit where she helped launch the Educate A Child initiative. Alek is a British supermodel, former refugee from South Sudan and goodwill ambassador for UNHCR.

Education through schooling within refugee camps is not just an ongoing investment in children's future wellbeing; it also provides a sense of normalcy in challenging conditions. Statistically, children who attend school in camps are less likely to be taken into military service and are at lower risk of sexual abuse, violence and disease. Few people would deny that basic schooling is a humanitarian right, yet education programmes for child refugees have longer-term political significance as well as immediate humanitarian consequences. Education pushes humanitarian action beyond saving lives to a project that also shapes futures. Therein lies a tension between the kind of education provided, what is taught and its purpose.

When we visited in September 2013, Zaatari had become the second largest refugee camp in the world with a population approaching 150,000. It had opened just over a year earlier with 100 families. With many thousands more expected to arrive in Jordan, a new camp of similar capacity is being prepared nearby in Azraq.

After receiving our official permissions, we travelled 90 minutes from Amman towards the Syrian border. At the camp we were

left & right photo credit: Graham Brown-Martin

ushered through several checkpoints where our paperwork and passports were examined before arriving at the administrative and police compound for an interview with the site commander who had the final say on our access to the camp. Explaining our mission, we were granted approval and were provided with a guide to take us to points of interest and to meet families in the camp.

It was clear from the buildings that organisations such as UNICEF, with supporting nations, had made considerable effort to provide a good schooling infrastructure. However, given the rapid expansion of Zaatari it has been reported that two-thirds of the 30,000 children eligible for school do not have a place. We learned during our visits to schools in Amman that some Jordanian schools are operating double shifts to accommodate child refugees. As one might imagine, having a rapid influx of people whose numbers are similar to the populations of the UK city of Norwich or the US city of Knoxville presents an enormous challenge on resources.

Considering the challenges presented, the camp was well-organised and we were welcomed by the majority of those we met who were often willing to tell us their stories. Children were especially happy to see us and stop us to ask questions, play or have us take their photograph. There are 'high streets' where entrepreneurial refugees have set up shops and trading posts for those who have money, so an economy of sorts operates within the camp. The main street has been jokingly called the 'Champs Elysées'.

The festival-like feel to the camp quickly fades when one considers the reasons why people are here in the first place and the uncertainty of what they might return to. For many this will become a permanent settlement rather than a temporary safe haven. We arrived on a hot summer's day, but winter can be cold – it snows in Jordan. Life can be harsh, with the biggest challenge being security. Gangs operate in the camp and attacks are becoming more frequent, particularly against women. It's a staggering challenge for the Jordanian government and the UNHCR that one can only respect them for taking on. I have no doubt that they will be successful but it will take time, resources and, inevitably, things won't always go to plan.

I was unprepared for the size and scale of the camp. It is absolutely enormous and leaves you in disbelief and then in shock at the consequences of human conflict. I have the utmost respect for the spirit and welcoming kindness that many of the people living at the camp showed me.

My visit to Zaatari was truly life-changing. It has made me question a lot of things about the human condition, our society, the media, our global leadership and myself. It has given me a much-needed shove to consider what I should do next with my life. In the meantime my hopes and wishes are with those who have been displaced.

United Kingdom

Newcastle

Bolton

Cambridge

Bristol   London

If there are problems with global education, then you can probably trace them back to the United Kingdom of Great Britain and Northern Ireland. The British Empire, with vast power and influence, shaped societies in all manner of ways, and, for better or worse, had a massive impact on the history of the world. Impressive for an island nation with a landmass smaller than the US state of Oregon.

Quite what combination of circumstances allowed Britain to expand itself across the world is a subject for debate, but there can be no question that the industrialisation of the schooling process owes much to the invention of the steam engine and the birth of the Industrial Revolution in 18th-century Britain. Industrialisation, albeit as a slow process, was already well under way by the time the steam engine appeared, with textile factories, for example, being constructed across Europe, Asia, the Middle East and Africa since the 15th century. Harnessing the power of steam, however, changed almost everything it touched. Horse-pulley systems used in coal mining were incredibly slow and inefficient, unable to keep up with the demands of the nascent glass-blowing industry of the 17th century. The power of steam transformed manufacturing and mining. Factories could now be built anywhere, untethered from the necessity of being near a fast-running stream or the wind of a mill.

The story of the Industrial Revolution as the engine of the expansion of the British Empire is well-documented. It was a time of dramatic social, economic and techno-logical change. It was a period defined by a major, rapid transition from an agricultural and commercial society (an economy based on manual labour) to a modern industrial society dominated by new technology (an economy based on complex machinery). It drove phenomenal growth in population as a result of improve-ments in standards of living, sanitation and healthcare.

On the eve of the Industrial Revolution in 1750, humans numbered around 750 million; just after 1800, world population reached one billion. Today there are over seven billion of us.

In 19th-century Britain, relative world peace, the availability of money, coal and iron ore, and the invention of the steam engine, all combined to facilitate the construction of factories for the mass production of goods. The factory system increased the division and speciali-sation of labour and resulted in large numbers of people moving to the new industrial cities, especially in the Midlands and the north. It also resulted in low wages, slum housing and the use of child labour.

The Industrial Revolution exacerbated the division between those who had land, capital or a profession and those who had none. The Peel Factory Act of 1802 was perhaps the first indication that the state acknowledged some responsibility for the conditions in which the poor, and particularly poor children, lived. The Act required employers to provide instruction in reading, writing and arithmetic during the first four years of the seven years of apprenticeship. Instruction was to be part of the 12 hours of daily work.

The Reform Act of 1832 gave a million people the right to vote and this dramatic social, political and economic transformation served to reveal the inadequacy of Britain's educational provision, with reports highlighting the deficiencies and calling for more and better schools. To provide for the nation's newly industrialised and partly enfranchised society, various types of school began to be established to offer some basic education to the masses. Yet at the same time there was hostil-ity from influential taxpayers and industrialists towards educating the poor on the basis that, as a Justice of the Peace in 1807 put it, 'knowledge would produce in them a disrelish for the laborious occupations of life'.[11]

Despite hostility towards universal education, new schools were built and attendance increased so that by 1835 the majority of Britain's school children attended some kind of school for a period. The average duration of attendance in 1835 would have been one year. The industrialisation of Britain led to the urbanisation of the growing population as workers migrated from the country to cities to find employment. It was the demands of employers who favoured literate and numerate citizens able to work in their factories that drove a requirement for education, yet it wasn't until what is regarded as the second phase of the Industrial Revolution that human capital was placed at the heart of economic development.

This second phase, also known as the Technological Revolution, started in the latter half of the 19th century with the advent of electrification and the mass production line. The first half of the Industrial Revolution was based around textile, iron and steam-based technologies; the second half was founded on electricity, communications, chemicals and transportation. The demand for skilled labour in the growing industrial sector markedly increased. Human capital formation was designed primarily to satisfy the increasing skill requirements, and industrialists became involved in shaping the education system. The significant increase in schooling during the 19th century lowered the costs of education, thus generating a significant increase in the number of educated workers.

Britain transformed itself from a feudal economy with the lord and his windmill to an industrial one with the industrial capitalist and his factory. This transformation swept across Europe, America and, as a result of the British Empire, a great deal of the world. The demands of economic development combined with the advent of new technology platforms to change society almost beyond recognition. We are now on the precipice of what some call the third phase of the Industrial Revolution.

The demands for economic development are ever more present and transformation revolves around the new technology platforms of digital data and surveillance, placing new and uncertain demands on human capital formation. If we are to learn anything from the past, we can be certain that the future will bring forth a new world order. The question is: Who will be the new masters of this epoch, who will be the workers and who will be the poor?

In light of this history of transformation, it is perhaps appropriate that our case study for the United Kingdom is a school in Bolton, a northern town in England that witnessed the complete story of the Industrial Revolution. Bolton was a production centre for textiles in the 15th century, and during the 19th, it had become the third largest engineering centre in the region with Oldham and Manchester. Essa Academy in Bolton is one of the first state schools in England that has fully embraced a 1:1 computing strategy in which every student has their own iPad.

In Cambridge we met the creators of Raspberry Pi, an inexpensive computer to stimulate an interest in technology amongst children. We met Professor Sugata Mitra in Newcastle who is developing what he calls a School in the Cloud. We looked at 3D printing and making in London's Shoreditch, and then travelled across to Bristol to learn about the future of universities.

'We are now on the precipice of what some call the third phase of the Industrial Revolution. The demands for economic development are ever more present and transformation revolves around the new technology platforms of digital, data and surveillance, placing new and uncertain demands on human capital formation.'

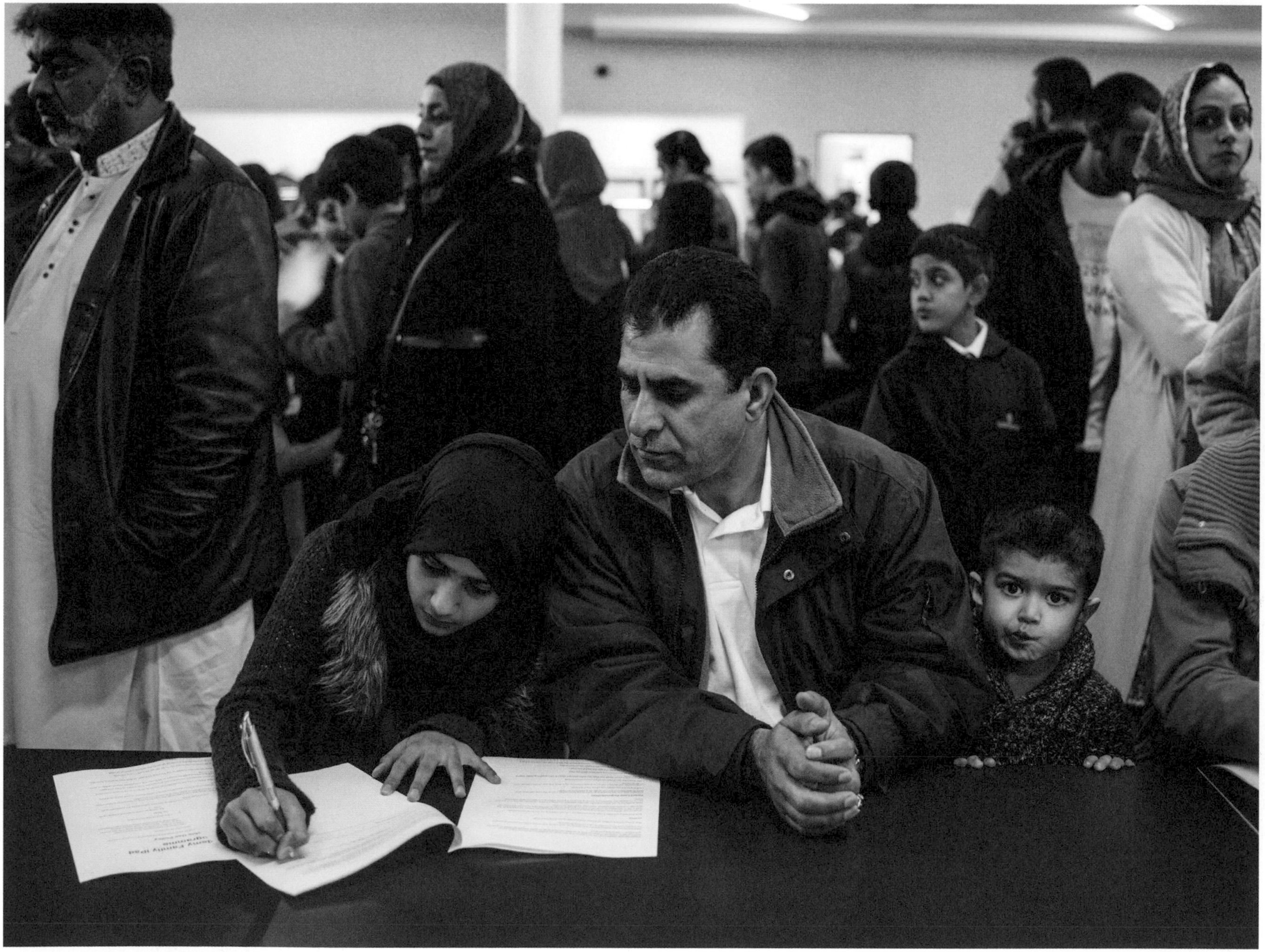

United Kingdom

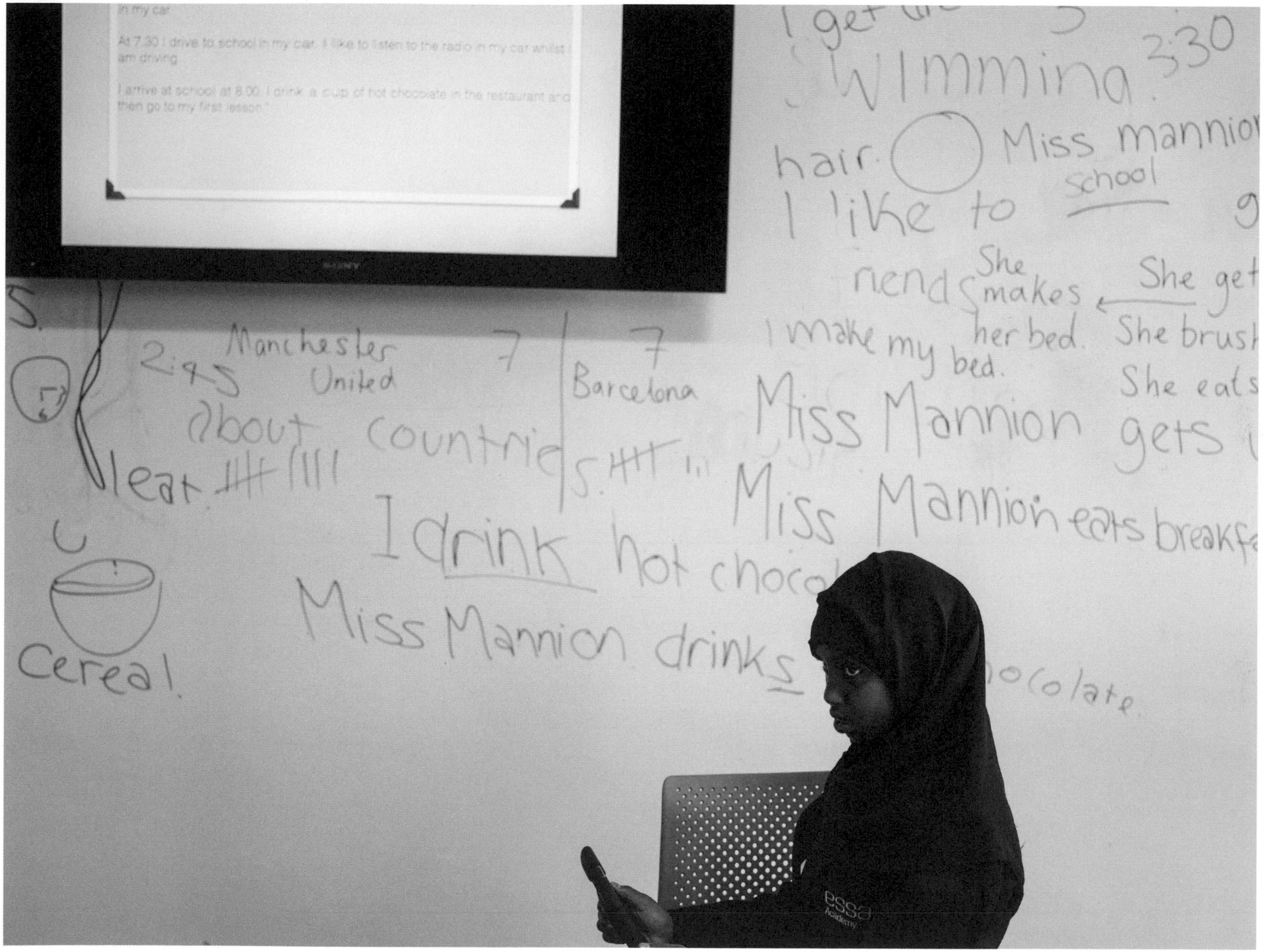

United Kingdom

'How do we create meaningful ways of earning a living that combine multiple ways of being?'

I've known Keri Facer for many years as a colleague, intellectual sparring partner and friend. She is gifted with a fierce intellect, unconcerned with popular opinion and suspicious of the kind of evangelism that stifles the discourse around digital technologies and learning.

I first met Keri when she was the Research Director of Futurelab, a UK think tank, where she conducted horizon scans beyond the year 2030. She has led large-scale design programmes for curriculum change and today works on rethinking the relationship between formal educational institutions and wider society. Keri is particularly concerned with the sorts of knowledge that may be needed to address contemporary environmental, economic, social and technological changes.

With the world and their accountants talking about MOOCs and the changing role of universities, I met Keri to learn where her thinking had brought her and this is what we talked about.

Graham Brown-Martin: In the discourse about digital technology for learning, do you see technology as a force for transformation or automation?

Keri Facer: That's a really tricky question. I think, fundamentally, it depends what sorts of social context it finds itself in. That's it. The technology doesn't make the change. The issue is: What's the culture, what's the society, what's the context it drops itself into? If you drop any technology —whether it's cognitive enhancement or whiteboards or laptops— into a culture that says education is about individual competition and drilling kids in the most efficient manner, then that's how you'll get the technology used.

If you drop those technologies into a culture that says education is about the development of the person and the creation of a good society, then you get a completely different approach to technology. The technology doesn't drive it. It creates conditions of possibilities, but in terms of what education then looks like, it's the social and cultural context that matters.

Graham: It seems that many digital deployments in schools and universities have been layering technology over education. Are we not thinking hard enough?

Keri: I think the issue with these massive investments in technology is that some of them are going to be beneficial. There's no doubt that technology changes what is possible to do, but at the same time, unless people have had the fundamental conversation about what they think education is for, this stuff is essentially pointless.

We're not going to get a sudden change in education. We've spent the last 15 years, if not longer, expecting that a revolution will come, and we're still waiting. We have to find a way of engaging parents and kids and communities and educators and everybody else in the conversation around the question: What do we think our education system is for?

The problem is that we take parents seriously when we hear them say, 'Oh, I just want my kid to get these qualifications,' or, 'I just want my kid to get into this university.'

What we hear is that they therefore want an education system that is about exams and results. I genuinely think that what the parents mean in those situations is: I want to get security for my kids. I want to get wellbeing for my kids. I want them to be able to live well in the world. I want them to be OK when they're in old age. I think

'The problem, at the moment, is all that creative energy that invents stuff is about taking us further and further away from nature, embodiment, materiality.'

the mistake that we've made is we keep having the conversations about the proxies, the exam results, the certification and not about the more fundamental questions, which are: What does it take to live well in the world? What is it that we're going to need? That's why we need to have the conversation.

Graham: What do you think are the challenges that future generations will face to live well?

Keri: There are a whole set of things that look like they are challenges at the moment. But the future doesn't exist. We need to remember that. It's not a real place, so we can't predict it. The challenge actually is to figure out how we live well with not knowing the future, not with predicting it. There are things that are happening at the moment that we need to address. We're looking at radical and increasing global inequalities, and that's inequalities within countries and inequalities between countries, to the point that we're ending it with Green Zones.

We have small groups of people who are sequestering themselves from the rest of world and large numbers of people who are, frankly, being left on the heap to sort themselves out. That's a massive problem. We have a massive problem in terms of how we're using our resources. This is not sustainable.

We can't continue to live in the way we are at the moment. We have really interesting questions about how we live with an ageing and globally diverse population that sees a much greater degree of movement. How are we going to live in those sorts of settings? Those are just some of the challenges that I think we're facing, not to mention the slightly more edgy end of the technology development, which I think raises huge questions for us as to whether that's the way we want to go or not.

Graham: Isn't there a conflict between the physical economy of the present and the digital economy that is being presented to us as the future, that these problems are just a click away from solving?

Keri: The question is the challenge that we have to face. How do we square the creative tendencies that allow us to invent things which are beautiful and amazing and good —and that's what we're trying to do— with the conditions in which we find ourselves?

The problem, at the moment, is all that creative energy that invents stuff is about taking us further and further away from nature, embodiment, the material. We need to shift that creativity back to some of these more fundamental questions about how we live with our material environment.

What does the economy look like? How are we going to work over the next few years, really? The material is going to continue to be important. For example, we don't take seriously the fact that there's a huge demand for horticultural workers at the moment, and this is completely overlooked in most of the accounts of the labour market and where we're going. We actually really need people who know how to work in agriculture, who know how to grow things. This is all stuff that's important.

The question we need to ask ourselves is: How do we create meaningful ways of earning a living that combine multiple ways of being? None of us wants to be just one sort of person, and that was the mistake that we made with the industrial shift, the shift towards one way of being.

There are sides to me that would happily go and spend my time gardening. There are sides to me that would happily spend my time running around the country, having conversations with people or sitting at a desk. The question is: How do we create an economy that allows us to express what it means to be fully human in all of its complexity? That's not a question about how we make the economy work. It's a question of how we create a world where the point of life is life.

Graham: Human consciousness shifted after the Industrial Revolution when we took identities from our function or work. How might the Digital Revolution impact our psyche?

Keri: We are being pushed down roads towards both fundamentally unviable economies and fundamentally destructive ways of living. The road that we're being pushed down is one of continued growth supported by technological change with little respect for the people that are involved in that sort of machine mentality and way of living. It's a road that increasingly accrues rewards for a very small number of people... That road is not inevitable... Actually, there are really interesting things happening amongst those other people, a large majority of people on the planet who are experimenting with and creating new ways of living. The challenge is to figure out where the cracks are in this inevitable trajectory, to see the light coming through and to figure out how to open them up.

Graham: You've coined the term 'anticipatory research'. What is this about?

Keri: The problem that we have in terms of how we think about the future in education is that we tend to either operate with one dominant vision of the future, and we figure out how to get there, or we throw that out the window and say, 'Ha-ha! We need to figure out how to cope with uncertainty.' Neither of those positions is particularly helpful. What we're seeing emerging is a new science of anticipation, which allows us to recognise the way in which our ideas and our assumptions about the future operate on us in the present.

It starts from the premise that the challenge isn't to figure out how to predict the future. The challenge is to figure out how to live well, how to uncover the creative possibilities of the present because we don't know the future.

It's profoundly exciting because I think it's opening up the possibility for us, as humans, to realise that we are deeply anticipatory animals. We work with our ideas of the future all the time and yet we're very bad at reflecting on, and thinking about, all of that. I think it's a new science, and I actually think that it will change the way education works.

'It's a question of how we create a world where the point of life is life.'

'The technology doesn't make the change. The issue is: What's the culture, what's the society, what's the context it drops itself into?'

'People seem
to miss the tangible
a lot, people who
maybe spent
their life working
in digital.'

I first met Alice Taylor when she was a commissioning editor at Channel 4, a respected UK television station, where her focus was on educational output. These were the most exciting and innovative years for Channel 4 from an educational programming perspective because, realising it had to reach its audience where they resided, the station devoted its entire programming budget to interactive digital programming across the web, gaming platforms and social media rather than traditional broadcasting.

Alice was and continues to be an avid gamer, both a player and designer of video games. She left Channel 4 during 2011 to start MakieLab, a toy and game company based in Shoreditch, London's hub of digital start-ups. MakieLab has developed a system of creating objects using game technologies and then 'transmogrifying' them into 3D-printable toys. Their first product, Makies, allows children to design their own doll via the web and then have MakieLab produce it for them using their fast 3D printers.

I caught up with Alice to see how the new venture was going.

Graham Brown-Martin: What was your inspiration for MakieLab?

Alice Taylor: The inspiration for Makielab came from a combination of all of the stuff that I'd seen as an educator: How kids play, what they want to play with, mainly video games, that kind of stuff, and amazing technologies. The advent of 3D printing, laser cutting, all this kind of stuff that is now way more affordable. Really the inspiration came from being at the toy fair at the same time as the digital stuff and thinking: Why can't you turn avatars into dolls using 3D printing, or toy cars into remote-controlled cars? Just realising that now the digital and the physical can come a lot closer together.

Graham: There's a shift in thinking about consuming versus creating and the emergence of the 'maker' movement. What is happening here?

Alice: It's an explosion. Maker Faire started in the States and is the big annual fair where everyone shows off their stuff. It started six years ago, and the 2012 Maker Faire on the west coast alone involved 120,000 people. So it's gone from nought to that in six years flat. It's reflective of, I think, a long history of passive consumption of media, and now the sudden ability to be an active, collaborative creator of media across all forms, whether that's making your own videos to building your own drone. Making, collaborating and creating is obviously a lot more interesting to kids and parents alike than just consuming. I think that passive consumption has its place. You can watch a TV show that will educate you for a little bit, but we all know that if a parent is sitting with a child while they're watching that show, and they're actively doing something, talking about it —'Did you notice that? Did you see that?'— they'll learn a lot more and remember a lot more than if they're just not doing anything. Doing is the key thing. The maker movement is spreading across the world rapidly. There are many Maker Faires all over the place. You can set one up yourself if you want to.

Graham: Do you think the emergence of the maker movement demonstrates that the world isn't ready to say goodbye to the physical economy?

Alice: Physical versus digital, or the other way around. My background has always been in digital until recently. I'm also noticing it across the Maker Faire stuff. People seem to miss the tangible a lot, people who maybe spent their life working in digital. All my work, for instance, from 1994 to about 2002, is gone, it's archived or just gone, just overwritten. I helped build the first ever Channel 4 dot-com, but now it's on version two thousand or whatever, and the original one is long gone. But a physical object can sit on the shelf forever. There's something real —I hate to use the word, but people do use the word 'real' versus 'virtual'— even though digital is as real as anything else these days. There's something about the physical object in your hand.

The way I see it, 3D printing is one of a number of technologies that finally reached a price point that means many people can take part. And in the next couple of years we'll reach a price point that means everybody can take part. We're at the last bit of a long journey of something that 20 years ago cost hundreds of thousands of pounds is now going to be 50 quid, which is amazing. That means that anybody will be able to teach themselves how to make a physical thing if they want to.

Making physical things is really hard. With digital, if you make a mistake you just change it. With physical, you can't just change it; 3D printing makes it easier because you can. It's still a digital file that produces a physical object, so you change the digital file and the next physical object is changed. The fact that you don't need to have a PhD in mechanical engineering to go out and make a toy is awesome.

Graham: Do you see this new kind of making becoming popular in schools?

Alice: If teachers want to incorporate this kind of stuff into the classroom, the machines are now at a price where it's pretty affordable, so you can pick up a 3D printer, a very simple one, for

around £500. If you don't know how it works it doesn't matter, just set the kids on it and say, 'Figure this out, use Google, read the manual.' And they will figure it out. There are plenty of resources out there, resources like thingiverse.com, which is an enormous repository of free, printable models. Because they're Creative Commons you can take a model that somebody else has made, download it, send it to the 3D printer and it gets going, starts making something right in front of your eyes.

Kids absolutely love it. My kid's five and a half and she's learning Microsoft Word in her ICT class, and I'm thinking maybe you could move on from Word. Fundamentally it's a case of pick up, have a go, learn as a group, because everyone's learning this stuff. Teachers should not be expected to know how to do it because it's so new, so do it together.

Graham: 3D design used to be a steep learning curve. Do you think it's easier for children today?

Alice: I think there's a huge convergence in video games and learning about 3D stuff, because most games are 3D. With games like Minecraft, they're creative and collaborative, and now with third-party things like Mineways you can just send your Minecraft village through Mineways to the 3D printer and you get back a little model of what you've made, which is fantastic. That's landscape gardeners at work right there.

There's a lot of free software out there. Autodesk, for instance, give away their modelling software for free to educators and individuals. If you're turning over less than $250,000 a year, you get their $30,000 worth of software for free. It's being actively encouraged, so just pick it up and have a go.

www.makieworld.com

The Raspberry Pi is a low-cost computer designed to stimulate an interest in digital creativity. Launched in February 2012, the first 10,000 units were sold within hours, demonstrating that the non-profit Raspberry Pi Foundation had significantly underestimated demand. Within two years of release over two million units had been shipped.

The Raspberry Pi was inspired by the BBC Micro computer that spearheaded a UK government campaign in the 1980s to foster computer literacy amongst the nation's schoolchildren. The BBC Micro was fabulously successful at the time and, for a while, the UK was a world leader in computer-enhanced learning and software engineering, spawning a generation of technology entrepreneurs and video-game designers. It's fair to say that my own personal career was shaped during these years by events in the UK.

Despite originally being conceived for use by children and schools, most of the Raspberry Pi sales have been to adult computer enthusiasts who already have knowledge of computer programming. A dramatic shift by the UK's Department for Education in 2013 —demanding a school curriculum change to support computer science rather than simply ICT— left many teachers without the knowledge or skills to respond. Simultaneously, a concerted media campaign to build awareness around a requirement for children to code, largely promoted by enthusiasts and the private sector, has stimulated a further demand from parents.

I met with Clive Beale, Director of Educational Development, at the Raspberry Pi Foundation in Cambridge, UK, to find out how he planned to meet this surge of demand from the education sector.

> **Graham Brown-Martin:** Clive, what's happened in UK schools' computing since the BBC Micro?

Clive Beale: The background of computing in the UK is that we really haven't taught it for 15 years, although that's changing massively as we now have changes in the curriculum and a lot of grassroots pushing to get computing back in.

This subject called 'ICT'[12] wasn't always as creative and inspiring as it could have been. In the late 1990s, there was a government report that decided what the 'C' in ICT should be and created this new subject. So it was decided that the best thing to learn would be office skills and those sorts of things. That was one thing with the curriculum change, but also gadgets started to get more and more refined and more and more consumer-orientated. We've become consumers, I think, and really the creative element was taken out of the classrooms, the ability to get your hands dirty and mess about. Systems became locked down, you can't install software, you can't put things into it, and this is what we've tried to reverse.

> **Graham:** Do you think there is a capacity problem with the number of teachers who can teach computer programming?

Clive: There are issues and it would be wrong to say there aren't. Research suggests that only one in 20 teachers of ICT in this country actually has a computer science qualification. So there are obviously issues of training but they're not issues that can't be overcome. But there has to be a structure in place to make this happen and we can't just hope that overnight teachers are going to suddenly have all these skills because they aren't.

Things are changing but there are issues with teacher skills and knowledge because we haven't taught it in 15 years so it's as if an English teacher never had to teach *Romeo and Juliet* or Shakespeare and suddenly it's kind of 'Bam! You've got this whole new canon of work that you've got to deliver.' So there are challenges to overcome.

> **Graham:** Do you think that coding and this kind of work actually belongs in the school rather than after-school clubs where you have enthusiasts?

Clive: It's like learning a musical instrument. It's the three hours you put in every night learning that instrument that count, not your 40-minute lesson at school, and definitely that's where the hard-core talent can come from. But unless you expose people to computing at an early age they're never going to have a chance to understand if they enjoy it or if they're very good at it.

We don't teach music in schools to turn out generations of concert pianists and hope everyone is going to join an orchestra when they're in school. We teach it because it's useful, it helps your thinking skills and some kids love it and some don't. Just the same with art —you don't teach art to turn everyone into a Picasso. You've got to give kids the opportunity to say, 'You know what, I'm really good at that and I love doing that and I'm going to pursue it.'

But the other thing is that people confuse coding with the whole computer science thing, and I'm not a fan of the media saying that coding's the new Latin because it's almost like saying everyone should learn poetry and then ignore the English eco-system that surrounds it.

When we talk about computational thinking and understanding problems, breaking them down, problem solving, those skills are central, those skills are vital and we're teaching them to 16- and 17-year-olds at A level with this thing called critical thinking. We should be teaching them that at age five. Say, 'Here's a problem, how do you break it down? How do you solve it?' That's where computing comes in. It's not the coding; it's the abstract skills that filter into everything you do if you can think well.

Graham: Why is Raspberry Pi different from buying a laptop or a tablet computer?

Clive: Raspberry Pi is a general-purpose computer. It runs Linux on an SD card, you plug into a phone charger and you plug it into a telly and so the whole idea was to go back to the BBC Micro vibe. I've got my own little personal computer that just belongs to me. As a kid it was, 'Hands off to anybody else! This is my computer. I can plug it into my TV in my room and I can start to program.'

Two things on this are non-negotiable. First, the price is $35 and that is what it gets sold for. Wherever you buy it in the world it's $35.

'It's not the coding;
it's the abstract
skills that filter into
everything you do
if you can think well.'

The shipping and taxes we can't control, but this is what we sell it for. Second, the size; we wanted to make it really small and personal. It's quite a cool form factor. You can stick it in weird Lego cases, you can put it into robots and you can send it 40,000 metres up in the air. So it's a tool for experimentation. It takes us out of that locked place with tablets, a locked place with aluminium and glass and away from the fear of breaking something and ruining all the data. But with Raspberry Pi I can just re-boot and re-install in a few minutes. It's a tool for thinking, messing and experimenting. We want you to try and break it in a sense and find out how things work.

Graham: What sort of things have come out of the education sector that have impressed you?

Clive: Again this is the first term that the Raspberry Pi has been in schools so we're two weeks into the new term and I'll be visiting a few schools in the next two weeks to collect stories.

What we've been really impressed with at the moment, until the whole schools come on board, is what individual teachers are doing. It's their initiative. They're spending their own time and their own resources. Some are even buying Pis for their classroom because budgets are limited and they've actually been using that to turn the ICT thing on its head. Instead of just making something move on-screen in Scratch for example, which is a programming environment for younger people, they've been connecting that up to the outside world and making things happen.

What we want to see is for this to spread to schools, realising that this is a tool that they don't have to ask the technicians to come in and install. From my experience as a teacher for ten years, that's really tricky.

This isn't instead of a PC suite or a Mac suite or a bunch of tablets. It's in addition. It's this little extra tool where I don't have to be too careful about what I do with it —in fact, quite the opposite really. Individual teachers are doing fantastic things and we'd like to make that broader and expand it.

Graham: How much interest in the Raspberry Pi have you seen outside of the UK?

Clive: There's obviously a big chunk in the UK because it's a UK-made product, it's UK designed and we've got a real history in the UK of being quite innovative, with the whole BBC Micro thing and everything that came out of that. Then there's the States and other developed countries, but what we're seeing at the moment —which is just fantastic— is a movement into developing countries and elsewhere in the world where you don't see technology and computers because they're expensive or inaccessible. Take the power requirement of the Pi, for example. It uses about a watt, so I can leave that running in my house for one or two pounds a year but you can also run it off batteries, you can run it off solar cells.

You're actually seeing it being put in places you wouldn't expect— in schools as whole computer labs set up in Cameroon and Ghana and Burma and places like that, so the penetration is really starting to excite us.

They're being used to set up little networks with Khan Academy and you can use one as the server. It can actually serve lots of other Pis in the classroom wirelessly, so you don't have to have an Internet connection. There's a system called Rachel which takes that further. It's got Khan Academy, things like Wikipedia —all offline— and it will serve this out to whoever is on that network. You can be effective in a lot of rural communities even in this country and certainly in developing countries without access to the Internet. Certainly not with bandwidth, anyway.

'It's like learning a musical instrument. It's the three hours you put in every night learning that instrument that count, not your 40-minute lesson at school'

'I'm actually inspired by children because I find that they are amongst the most imaginative people we have.'

Alan O'Donohoe, it has to be said, is a force of nature whose natural enthusiasm for teaching and learning could fill a room of any size. By day, he is the principal teacher of computing at Our Lady's High School in Preston. His alter ego is the Founder of both Hack To The Future and Raspberry Jam, the global community of clubs inspired by the Raspberry Pi, a $35 computer designed to inspire an interest in computing amongst children.

I managed to get Alan to sit down just long enough for this interview.

Graham Brown-Martin: Alan, tell me about the inspiration that drives your passion.

Alan O'Donohoe: I've been teaching for 20 years. About four or five years ago, I realised that I felt there was something wrong with what I was teaching. Children weren't enjoying or getting excited about what I was doing and I changed what I was doing and suddenly, now, they get excited and interested.

I'm actually inspired by children because I find that they are amongst the most imaginative people we have. They come up with these great ideas about things, and they ask the most fascinating questions that make us stop and think and question what we're doing. School is quite an ineffective thing because it seems like the purpose of school is to take that away from children, and turn them into homogenised units so that they will conform and follow rules and think in straight lines.

By the time the average child in the UK is 14 or 15, they've become constricted by the machine, and they think the way that the machine wants them to think. Earlier than that, much younger than that, children seem to get really excited and enthusiastic about their learning and they want to take control and possession of what they're doing. I really want to tap into that.

Graham: There's been a recent shift in thinking about what is taught about digital technology in schools, to balance the learning of tools with the creation of new works. What is driving this change?

Alan: In the last four or five years, there's been this obsession that's been helped and made stronger by the likes of Apple devices, like the iPad. Now they're becoming commonplace. It's a piece of glass. You don't have to know how it works, you just magically do this, do that, and it does everything for you. It just becomes an extension of your brain. What we really feel we're missing is: How do these things work? All those kinds of questions that children would ask when they were younger like, 'Why is it this size?' 'How does it do that?' We're almost saying to children, 'Oh, you don't need to worry about it. It just works.'

I don't really buy into that kind of mode of thinking because, with devices like the Raspberry Pi, you've got a platform, a very slimmed-down, scaled-down platform that you can customise to do whatever it is that you want it to do. We've had children working on projects where they attached a Raspberry Pi to a webcam, set it up with a time-lapse sequence of photography, and situated it in a few different places over a

period of days. Basically, they were collecting data about what was happening in their garden, and sure enough, a squirrel was all over the bird box, all over the bird feeder. The birds were going to go nowhere near it.

Graham: What is it about the Raspberry Pi platform that you like so much and what are you doing to build a community around that?

Alan: In a lot of the projects that I used to teach in school, there was a lot of emphasis on interactive media, or just media. We might set a project where children have to record a podcast or a radio advert, or they might have to make a video. If you've got a tool that's got a camera on, it's got editing tools, then something like a tablet device really fits into that kind of mould.

If you're actually trying to teach children how to build a piece of hardware that's going to solve a problem, a problem that the children have identified — and they see that as being really important because it's their problem— a tablet device is not necessarily going to be the best device. We really needed a low-cost, versatile computing platform like the Raspberry Pi.

On the day that the Raspberry Pi was launched they could have sold two million but they only made 10,000. My neighbour came to me and said, 'Alan, you'll be really pleased, I've got a Raspberry Pi.' I said, 'Why don't we have a party, we'll bring some kids along, we'll show them what we can do with the Raspberry Pi.' My wife said, 'Oh, like a jam!' I said, 'Yeah, let's call it a Raspberry Jam. We can have people who have Raspberry Pis, and know what to do with them. They can come along... They can get ideas and then we can have this bigger group. We all jam together, we do things, we create, we share ideas.'

So I used a site to list an event on-line so that people could see what it was... We have a space in our school that we can open on a Monday night. I thought, 'We can get 30 people in.' In half an hour of me listing, all 30 tickets were gone. I thought maybe I'd made a mistake, maybe it was being spammed. These were all genuine people who lived in Liverpool or Manchester and wanted to come to Preston.

I rang up a friend at the university in Preston and said, 'Can we get a space for maybe 100 people?' He agreed and 100 people came. I thought, 'This is incredible.' Now, at the same time, a gentleman in Australia said, 'This was a fantastic idea. Can we have one? How much do we have to pay you?' I said, 'No, no, just have a Raspberry Jam.' Within a week, Singapore and Silicon Valley and Mexico, and places all over the world were suddenly saying, 'Hey, I'll have a Raspberry Jam.' Then, everyone was looking to me, like, 'So, what happens at a Raspberry Jam?' It was very much trying to respond to demand, and then it just got crazy. I was getting 100 emails a day. People saying, 'Right, we've listed our event. How do we promote it? How do we do this?' It just took over my life.

Graham: Do you think it's important that every child should learn how to code?

Alan: I wonder how that question, or the answer to that would be different if we put a different word instead of code. Should everybody learn how to play a musical instrument? Should everybody learn how to read? Should everybody learn how to write? If we can read, do we really have to have writers?

I really feel if we're not giving children an opportunity just to discover what coding is, to see what it is, to unlock the potential of it, we're as good as denying them access to music, or to art, or to drama, or to a foreign language.

www.raspberryjam.org.uk

'The presence
of technology alone,
no matter how
advanced, does not
equal transformation.'

Essa Academy lies in the northwest of England in Bolton, a former mill town that has been a production centre for textiles since the 15th century when Flemish weavers arrived, developing a wool and cotton-weaving tradition. By 1929, it was home to some 216 cotton mills and 27 bleaching and dyeing works, making it one of the largest and most productive centres of cotton spinning in the world. The British cotton industry began to decline in the early 20th century with an upturn just after World War II that led to the arrival of predominantly Hindu and Muslim settlers from as far away as India, Pakistan and Mauritius. After a period of heavy industry in the region, during the latter part of the century the town entered a period of decline and unemployment. Some engineering jobs were replaced by service industries including retail, call-centres and leisure.

Today Bolton looks to the future with the challenge of developing new skills and competences that will provide employment opportunities for school leavers and the economic development of the region.

Essa Academy opened its doors in January 2009, the first of a new type of specialist, state-funded independent academy replacing the former Hayward School. Taught in mixed-year classes, Essa has 900 pupils aged from 11 to 16. The Academy specialises in modern foreign languages and sciences with a strong business and enterprise ethos. Its new purpose-built premises opened in 2011.

Located within a large community of immigrant and refugee populations, ranked among the most economically disadvantaged in the country, the old Hayward School suffered from lack of investment in staff and resources resulting in years of under-achievement. Technology was often regarded as irrelevant to the learning process in the old school and was undervalued and underused. The school was split across three sites and yet there was no network in place. Education was failing as a result of low expectations and morale amongst pupils and teachers alike.

The principal of Essa Academy, Showk Badat, grew up in Bolton but wasn't allowed to attend Haywood School. 'Parents like mine believed that if you went there, you were never going to succeed,' he tells me. This remained the prevailing belief in the community when Badat returned there to turn the struggling school around. The school's dingy, neglected environment and sometimes dangerously under-maintained buildings were reflected in the low test scores of its students. With a failure rate over 70 percent, the school risked being closed.

Applying for academy status and renaming the school Essa Academy gave Badat and his administrators more autonomy to make decisions about curriculum and staffing, allowing them to pursue new investments to supplement state funds. This included financial support from the Essa Foundation, an educational charity set up by local business people to 'encourage research, development and introduction of best practice across the schools and curriculum, for use by head teachers, staff, governing bodies and students in schools in the UK and worldwide.'[10]

From past experience leading another school, Badat had witnessed the potential for technology to engage students. Believing that reinventing Essa as a hub of technology-assisted learning would reflect the new leadership's commitment to the community and, more importantly, remove barriers to academic achievement, Badat engaged Abdul Chohan, a Director of the school, to research platforms that would lead to a more dynamic learning environment. Chohan, a former chemistry teacher from the failing predecessor school, had experience working as a researcher for Glaxo Pharmaceuticals before becoming a teacher and recognised the need for his pupils to have 21st-century skills when they set out to find work. He also believes that too much attention is focused on exams rather than developing life skills. Chohan is scathing about the way technology is often used in schools as a way of reinforcing outdated teaching practices. He describes the interactive whiteboard as a good example of technology reinforcing the 19th-century position of the teacher at the front of the class.

Essa's first move was to provide all of its students with iPod Touch devices from Apple. 'We needed to give them direct access to information,' says Chohan. Teachers were provided with iPads. It was the first school in the UK to adopt such a bold move and had a positive impact on student engagement and morale that was quickly noticed by the school's administrative team. Using online learning materials and apps, student test scores improved and this early success helped Essa secure funds to build a new school.

Every aspect of the new school was designed to support interactive learning. Interactive whiteboards were abandoned in favour of integrated Apple TV devices connected to large HD screens that populate classrooms and collaborative learning spaces, allowing students to display and share material wirelessly from their iPods and iPads with teachers and their peers. Essa installed a state-of-the-art 3D imaging theatre; a range of data, video and VoIP applications and services further enhance this technology-rich learning environment. Teachers were encouraged to find creative ways to integrate the iPad into their teaching, directing small groups to record conversations in French and practise their pronunciation, or filming PE sessions and playing back the video to help students improve their game.

With the ongoing success of the programme, it was decided that every student would move up to an iPad which would be the hub of their anytime, anywhere learning in the classroom and at home, letting them learn in a more hands-on way. Students create Keynote presentations to share in class and use the built-in camera to snap photographs for reports. Non English-speaking students, who were originally pulled from lessons for 1:1 language tutoring, are more able to stay in class and use translation apps to improve their comprehension. Cloud-based solutions have been deployed for student and teacher convenience. For example, teachers can save information on their Dropbox rather than school servers. All printers have cloud-printing options enabled, meaning that students can print to an email address and use the Academy's Follow-Me managed print solution to collect their print jobs. All of this is supported by the installation of a robust, secure wireless academic network but with an open guest network to which personal devices can connect. Access points are located around the school to ensure pupils never lose connectivity.

Essa Academy is one of the first schools in the UK to make all its courses available through Apple's iTunes U which the school uses as its free learning management software or VLE. Students use the iTunes U app to access all their learning materials in one place, keep track of assignments and receive notifications any time a teacher updates information. Teachers use the iTunes U collection to discover podcasts, videos and other resources to enrich their lessons. They use iBooks Author to create and distribute interactive textbooks to the students' iPads as a simple way to refresh their textbooks to reflect current events and to weave together traditional reading materials with multimedia content. As a personal device that students own, the iPad helps them to do their homework and gives them the opportunity to email their teachers with questions whenever they like. While some tutors set aside a specific time slot to answer pupils' queries, others will fire an answer back within ten or 15 minutes. Chohan believes that being continually in touch with their teachers gives the approach a crucial advantage for the students. 'If there's something they want to know, why should they have to wait until the school gates open at nine in the morning?' he asks.

The environment of Essa Academy is indeed breathtaking in both its modernity as well as its calm. I spent a whole day there from morning until the evening, when I had the opportunity to welcome a new intake of students who were joining the school and attended an evening gathering with their parents to collect their iPads. There was excitement and interest amongst all the faces who had come to learn about this new way of schooling. I spoke to many parents, all of whom were enthusiastic about what is happening and who have made a commitment to their child's education at Essa.

With all this talk and excitement about iPads, one might be forgiven for believing, as many newspaper and media headlines have described it, that Essa Academy was 'the iPad school' and that this was somehow the transformation. But the presence of technology alone, no matter how advanced, does not equal transformation. In fact, it can mean quite the opposite. This was demonstrated by the world's infatuation with interactive whiteboards, something that schools and education authorities rushing headlong into providing every student with a tablet

computer or other technology would do well to consider. It doesn't matter how much technology you throw at a school. It won't transform anything unless you have a very clear idea of what you think transformation looks like and a strategy to make it happen.

I do believe that Essa Academy has transformed the learning and teaching experience to a remarkable degree, innovating within the limitations set by an out-dated assessment system and curriculum. This means that, after learning in an environment of rich collaboration with information at their fingertips, students must return to the 19th century to take a high-stakes handwritten test that will determine their future.

The transformation that has occurred isn't so much that students and teachers are continuously connected via their digital devices and software platforms but the massive efficiencies that this brings, allowing more time for learning and teaching in a really focused way. Rather than shredding the school day into six or seven one-hour study periods of different subjects, students have just two three-hour study periods per day either side of lunch. This doesn't mean that teachers must prepare lesson plans that cover a three-hour period but it does mean that students have the opportunity to explore and reflect upon what they're learning. Essa Academy was flipping the classroom long before it became fashionable, with teachers being active users of iTunes U, committing the repetitive or research aspects of their teaching to digital so that they can get on with dealing with their students' individual understanding. Creating more efficiencies in the administrative tasks of teaching means that teachers are now able to participate in active face-to-face continuing professional development with each other all the time rather than on some obscure day that happens once a term and then is quickly forgotten.

The results from Essa Academy speak for themselves and are very encouraging. Within two years of the pilot iPod programme, the pass rate at the school jumped from 28 percent to 100 percent. Test scores have increased significantly for all students. Whilst Chohan believes that an overemphasis on exams is wrong, there is no denying that the new method of learning has acted as a catalyst in improving results. Last year, every pupil achieved five A* to C-grade passes at GCSE, compared with 40 percent previously. This was achieved whilst operating costs for the school decreased as hefty budget items like tech support, 1:1 tutoring, textbooks and even photocopying have all been slashed.

Today educators from all across the UK and beyond visit Essa Academy to learn from its successes and best practice, including staff from Eton College, Britain's leading private school and educator of the country's future king.

www.essaacademy.org

'...the massive efficiencies that this brings, allowing more time for learning and teaching in a really focused way.'

'Students will have the option
of picking the courses that they're
doing and they have access to
those courses and their content
through their iPads.'

Essa Academy is a secondary school in Bolton for students aged 11 to 16 years. It has been regarded as a leader in the UK for the adoption of 1:1 computing where every student and teacher is provided with their own iPad.

I met with Abdul Chohan, a Director of the Academy and the person responsible for driving the digital transformation of the school, with the support of the Principal, Showk Badat.

Graham Brown-Martin: Abdul, please tell me about your background.

Abdul Chohan: My background really is predominantly in teaching. I've been a chemistry teacher for about ten years, and then for the last four years, I've been part of the senior leadership team here at the Academy.

Graham: What is the local community like?

Abdul: Predominantly, there are a lot of Indians and Pakistanis that actually came over in the late '50s, early '60s. A lot certainly from my grandparents' generation came via Mauritius because that's where they worked on the ports and the docks and so on. Then, because of the cotton industry and so on, many of them came and settled to work in the meadows in Bolton.

The community still stands. Many people, even though they may go away for education and so on, come back and then still reside here. Beyond that, much of the community is still operating in quite a deprived setting. We find that certainly for the students that come to Essa Academy, we're looking at almost 80 percent of the student population coming from 20 percent of the most deprived communities in the region.

In the last few years, we've also seen quite an influx of Somalis. We've found Eastern European communities growing within the area as well. Generally speaking, pretty much people live quite well side by side, although the migrant community that's here occupies pockets of areas, rather than being completely spread out throughout Bolton.

'What would you do if you weren't afraid?'

Graham: What was the transition from the predecessor school to this one like?

Abdul: The predecessor school had been here since the '50s. It was a school that my parents came to as well, but as time went on, it became the school that was not the school of choice. There were issues around the physical nature of the building which had suffered, so you could see cracks and roofs falling off when the winds were strong, and so on.

But there were also questions raised by various inspecting bodies and local councillors at that time about the quality of the provision. It was at that point that the government introduced the academy programme that many schools and governing bodies were taking up around the country. The Essa Foundation got involved with the sponsorship of Essa Academy.

The Essa Foundation is a charitable non-profit organisation. Its founders include two brothers. One is an accountant, the other a pharmacist. They've been quite successful with their businesses. They are from the local community as well and understand the needs of the minority population and other communities who have settled here.

They decided to set up a new leadership team that completely reorganised the school itself, including getting a new building as part of the academy change. It was at that point that our principal was appointed — Showk Badat, who was from Nottingham, but originally from Bolton as well. It was under his leadership that we began to see some of the changes that we're seeing today. That's been the key to a lot of the change that has happened.

Sometimes, it's just this idea that in education, we are very good at doing the wrong things really well. The question that can be asked is: What would you do if you weren't afraid?

Graham: What would you do if you weren't afraid?

Abdul: Let me give you an example. Traditionally, we were buying laptop trolleys, laptop computers. We asked: What would we do if we weren't afraid? When you ask that question, you wonder about spending £22,000 on 30 laptops and a laptop trolley that people will fight over, that not everybody can use at the same time, that is locked down, that may not work, that doesn't connect to the network regularly, that actually is a hindrance to learning quite often. If you were to take that money, what would you spend it on if you weren't afraid?

We looked at it and answered that question. It was quite simple. There would be a device for every student. We explored that possibility. We looked at a whole variety of different things, and at that time it was the iPod Touch. We did it. We took the last step further. Rather than piloting things, testing things out, we had a belief that we could do this. We put our feet into it. Then we made it happen.

We didn't just run it as a pilot project for months, and then create studies and write plans and reports and wait for somebody to tell us whether we can do it or we can't. We did this. Of course, this is a leadership decision but the leadership was thinking that it's not just about planning things and talking about things, it's actually making things happen. Very quickly, we found ourselves in a position where every student had a device. It was simple. It was reliable. It was operational. It was personalised. All these [are] things that we in education have been asking for, for a long, long time.

Graham: How have efficiencies brought about by the use of these technologies led to a transformation?

Abdul: There are certain obvious operational efficiencies. People use technology to make life easier. There was a time when if I wanted to transfer funds from one bank account to another, I would actually have to go out at lunchtime, get to the bank, fill out forms, and all that sort of stuff. That was the only way that I could have transferred funds. With technology, I can now take a device, log in, and just do that within minutes. It's transformed the way that this process happens. Organisations, businesses, ministries are doing this all the time. Why should it be any different in education?

What we've done is we've taken technology and allowed it to pay back in terms of efficiencies. In the past, teachers may have printed worksheets of paper and on a Monday morning are waiting at the photocopier because they've all got lessons on and they've prepared things. With digital, you don't necessarily have to go through that experience. We use iTunes U here which is a free resource, where a teacher planning a lesson makes that Word document available as part of the lesson plan. All the students receive that on their iPads.

What that means is it frees the teacher up to actually start the lesson, welcome the students, invite them in, and make sure the lesson starts on time. It's not about physically walking around, giving out papers, and those sorts of things. That's just one example. If you multiply that into other types of resources that teachers have to set up and make available and so on, technology allows you to save on so many of those things.

For example, interactive whiteboards. Schools across the UK, across the globe you could say, had this idea that the interactive whiteboard was suddenly going to transform things, and you found schools spending serious amounts of money installing them into every classroom. You had to provide teachers with training for this technology to be used. Once the technology was installed, they then started to create resources that were only usable on that piece of technology.

Then there was the whole difficult thing around plugging your device, laptop, into the right port and making sure the speakers were working, making sure the sound was working, and all those sorts of things. What we've done here is we've simplified and made the technology very, very

reliable. We've taken away the need for plugging things in and for uploading things to a virtual learning environment and so on.

What we've done here is just made things very, very simple. Teachers are the administrators on their machines. They can download content whenever they want. What it means is that they can now concentrate on the real job which is to provide a level of cognitive development and help students with their ability to think and understand processes.

> **Graham:** Essa Academy has been described as 'the iPad school' but it seems that there is more than just iPads here. You have changed the timetable and teaching practice. Tell me more about that.

Abdul: To present it very simply, take the idea of teaching and learning. Teaching is when a teacher stands up and is imparting information and is trying to ensure that the students will learn. The learning is a completely separate process. It's how well the students have actually understood the concept and ideas. There is a big gap between those two things. A teacher can feel, I've taught, and they will have jumped out of the classroom, and screamed, and shouted, and all sorts of amazing things, but when you measure the learning that's happened, it may be that not much learning has actually happened. On the other hand, you may get a teacher that doesn't do all of the singing and dancing, but has put key processes in place. At the end, when you ask the students about their learning, you find the students have actually learned quite a lot.

In order to get a workforce and in order to get teachers to the point where they actually understand this and are able to deliver it requires face time. It requires time to sit down and actually convey the ideas and make sure people understand this. In order for that to happen, we've had to change the school week.

Typically speaking, in a school you would have an in-service training day at the beginning of the term. Teachers come in, they talk about what they've done, and maybe clear the rooms

out, maybe some vision statement from the head teacher. That's it for the rest of the term. There will be great ideas there. There will be lots of amazing things that will happen. But they actually just fall by the wayside because there's nothing to capture them.

What we've done is on a weekly basis. We've changed our school timetable and it gives us time to be able to have this dialogue and have this conversation. There is this idea of cognitive surplus where people have lots of ideas and thoughts and different things that they think about, but it falls by the wayside. If you could find a way of collecting these thoughts and applying them to solving problems, you would get perspectives. You would get ideas about the same thing from different angles, and it would be easier to solve problems and issues, and you would be able to innovate and have new ideas.

If you take a school environment, and you look at the issues, and you look at ideas, and you look at the idea of cognition, and you look at cognitive functioning, demand mapping, and so on, and you apply different perspectives to it from all of the different teachers, and you have a time and a space that's made available for that to happen, you're going to get new thoughts and ideas. You're going to be able to solve problems. You're going to be able to have a more intelligent debate about what needs to happen in terms of change.

> **Graham:** The school day consists of just two, three-hour sessions for the students. How does that work?

Abdul: It means that if you are going to embed this idea of cognitive development, you need the time to be able to create that level of change. It means that you need time for reflection. It means that you need time for students to be able to create their own learning, for them to be able to work through problems then solve problems, and so on.

That's not possible in a 50-minute lesson or a one-hour lesson where kids take five minutes to get settled in the room and five minutes to leave. You've got 40 minutes or 50 minutes left. Within

'We use iTunes U here which is a free resource, where a teacher planning a lesson makes that Word document available as part of the lesson plan. All the students receive that on their iPads.'

that, you're still dealing with everything else and you've got 30 students in the class. It's not the right level of time for the sorts of change that we want to happen. This isn't just about preparing students for exams. It's about getting students to change the way they think, to be able to apply their learning to real problems.

It is one thing sitting in an exam and being able to regurgitate something but different when you can actually go to France, walk into a coffee shop, and order in French. It's that sort of gap that needs to be bridged and we don't feel that that's possible within a 50-minute session or a one-hour session. What we have are longer sessions, morning sessions and afternoon sessions, where the learning is much deeper and much broader, where questions can be asked, where investigations can happen, where if need be, and if the class needs to, we can go outside the school. It's possible to make use of local amenities, local facilities, to be able to make the learning happen. It's not necessarily constrained to just within that space or just within that classroom.

It also lends itself to the way in which those lessons are planned because as soon as you say 'three-hour session' to a teacher, it causes a pain because you begin to think I'm going to stand there for three hours, just talking. But a lot of this activity is investigation, a lot of this is creativity in the way in which the students are learning and bridging that gap.

Graham: You also stream by stage rather than the age of the students?

Abdul: That's basically just around the readiness. If you explore the idea of readiness, what we mean by that is when the student is ready to take their exam, we will put them in for that exam. In order for that to happen, students need to be in the right places to learn the right things. It's not necessary for us to group the children just according to their ages. You're 12 years old, you're amazing at maths but cannot take the maths exam until you're 15.

Of course, there are a lot of measurements they're going to put in place that allow us to monitor the students quite realistically in terms of how well they're doing. If there's a strong need, or the head of department feels that actually this child is ready for the exam, and can get a grade B or a grade A, we're going to put them in.

It is about making sure the child achieves their full potential and the full benefits of being here at Essa Academy. We've had students that have left with more than 12 General Certificate of Secondary Education passes. Why? Because, actually, in year nine, the student was very, very good in maths. Maths was completed. They then picked a different option, a different module to study, and did an additional GCSE as well. It's those sorts of things.

We have 48 different languages spoken here. If a child that comes in and is fluent in French, why do they have to wait until they're 15 to be able to take their French exam? They can come in and sit the French exam in the first year because they're fluent and they get the GCSE. We have students who are like that.

We're trying to do the best we can for every student. This idea of personalisation is very, very important. Students will have the option of picking the courses that they're doing and they have access to those courses and their content through their iPads. As soon as the teacher plans a lesson, it's made available to the student. It's very transparent. They can see what's happening. Parents can see what's happening. It's a far more efficient way in which learning happens.

Jake Davis

digital activist, London

Interview

photo credit: Graham Brown-Martin

This is a story about an alternative learner, the kind that we rarely consider when we use the term 'Learner Voice' in the discourse about education, particularly when we discuss digital.

On 27 July 2011, Jake Davis was arrested at his home in the Shetland Islands, a remote archipelago of Scotland that lies northeast of mainland Britain, by six police officers from London. Jake, 18, was accused and subsequently charged with a number of offences including unauthorised computer access and conspiracy to carry out a distributed denial of service attack on the UK's Serious Organised Crime Agency's website.

Jake had been playing in the digital playground with online activist groups including Anonymous and LulzSec, the latter being more akin to a team of digital pranksters making practical jokes and creating stunts in cyberspace than to the kind of cyber-terrorists some of the media would have you believe.

Under his online pseudonym, Topiary (@atopiary on Twitter[11]), Jake came to prominence in the hacker community after participating in a live radio phone-in discussion[12] with a member of the Westboro Baptist Church whilst their site was hacked and replaced with a message from Anonymous. The Westboro Baptist Church is widely recognised as a hate group for its extreme ideologies. Whilst illegal in terms of the law, the live hack of the website could be regarded as an act of protest within the digital world against the proliferation of online hate speech.

According to Jake, LulzSec was formed during a moment of boredom inside an online chat room with fellow users, none of whom had met in the physical world or knew each other's real identity. The group's objective was initially to rail against what they saw as the absurdity of online marketing by using the digital world against itself. They launched a number of notable campaigns which he tells us about.

The LulzSec group gained notoriety across global mass media and, as if to prove the point about digital marketing, their @LulzSec[13] Twitter account managed by Jake Davis accumulated more than 400,000 followers. Legality aside, one can only admire the *chutzpah* of a group of teenagers using their laptops to create mischief within a digital world barely understood by their parents' generation.

LulzSec lasted a matter of months before Jake's arrest, but already there was disagreement within the amorphous group with the suggestion that government-hired hackers had infiltrated the group to encourage less whimsical campaigns and more carnage.

After his arrest, Jake was banned from using the Internet for two years, wore a location tagging device that enforced a curfew and was sentenced to 37 days in Feltham Young Offenders Institute, a prison in southwest London more commonly used to accommodate young people with a history of committing violent crime or involvement with narcotics distribution. Whilst serving his sentence Jake became an informal teacher helping fellow inmates write letters home or enrol for education provision within the prison.

So often the young people of Jake's generation are described as apathetic and disengaged from the society around them. Whilst Western nations describe the transformative effect of digital platforms within emerging democracies and, for example, throughout the Arab Spring, the flipside is that they are not prepared for protest or even pranks within the emergent digital economy. The brightest minds of Jake's generation are now actively nurtured and recruited by our respective intelligence agencies to commit acts of espionage and civil surveillance on behalf of their nations. I wanted to understand more about the world in which current and future generations are expected to grow, learn and, where necessary, demonstrate dissent.

Graham Brown-Martin: Jake, please tell me about what it was like for you growing up and your experiences in school.

Jake Davis: I grew up on this remote set of islands called the Shetlands. The island I lived on had a population of 900 people, all of whom knew each other. I went to a small school with about 100 kids. I got a tiny bus from my house across this large river to the school, from about the age of six. After a few years, I started getting incredibly bored with it. I then moved up to secondary school which was the first time you got to pick your subjects. I thought it would be fascinating, until I realised I was bored with all of them.

At about the age of 13, after nothing was particularly stimulating, I decided to stop going, mainly to see what would happen. I was sort of rebelling but also just as an experiment.

Graham: What had inspired this rebellion?

Jake: It was boredom. I just wasn't excited. It's that kind of forced structure of learning I didn't enjoy or appreciate. I felt like all this knowledge was being thrown at me and not sticking. I wanted to learn in my own way and they didn't like that. Modern schools aren't like that, but in the Shetland Islands, they're rooted in it and they don't like change... They like nice, traditional, linear kinds of upbringings.

The kids who I went to school with, their parents and grandparents, had literally not once been outside of the Shetland Islands. They had no concept of the outside world. It was a lack of wanting to. They didn't like to think of themselves as part of the UK, or any other country... They were Shetlanders.

I wanted to think outside of that. I asked questions about what's going on in the rest of the world at the time. We didn't get taught that. I found that when I went home and used the Internet, I could speak to people through it. I had a friend in Delhi who I would speak to every day. I thought, 'He's not from here. He's from somewhere else.' He would tell me stories about his day. I just found that fascinating. Despite having beautiful Shetland scenery outside one window, through the window of my computer I could see the rest of the world, and what it was up to, at a far more granular level than I would have had otherwise.

None of my classmates were interested in that. They were interested in who won the football between Rangers and Celtic, or the local gossip from the town, or sheep herding. One day, it was a combination of things: I just left, and I stayed in my room, at 13. I decided: I'm not going to school, because it's boring. It's a waste of my time.

I had teachers who were quite bewildered by it. I guess in England you would have more of a system set in place to deal with that, because it could happen far more frequently than in the Shetlands. This didn't happen a lot up there. Six months went by of people just going, 'No, you have to go to school.' I would ask why, and there was never really an answer that convinced me to go, so I didn't.

For the next three or four years, I stayed in and just learned what I wanted to learn, when I wanted to learn it.

Graham: What things were you into? What sort of things were you teaching yourself?

Jake: I was just reading whatever I could online. I played a lot of online games at a young age, which I found to be far more fascinating than anything at the time. It just opened up different worlds. You have control, you have the immediate gratification, that sort of community we're all so used to now through social media.

So for about three or four years I did that before I became so immersed in it that I started trying to tinker with the system itself, the online system, which had ironically become almost like a system I was bored with, just like school. I started getting involved with this hacker group, Anonymous, a collective of online hacktivists, whatever you want to call it.

When WikiLeaks released 500,000 US diplomatic cables in December 2010, I joined this chat room full of these Anons, these hacktivists. It was about 8,000 people. I joined under the nickname I'd made up at the time: Topiary.

Graham: How old were you?

'After his arrest, Jake was banned from using the Internet for two years.'

Jake: I was 17 or 18. I just thought that that was fascinating, how there was no need to divulge anything. At this point, I didn't want to talk about myself. Myself was very dull. I think that was what a lot of others on there thought as well. We like to kind of forget that the other person behind the screen is probably just some nerd as well, with a pack of Doritos and Mountain Dew or whatever, and just get sucked into their alias or their persona. I stayed there. I got so sucked into it that it became part of my life. I started getting involved in what they were up to.

Graham: At what point did you get involved with the hacktivist community?

Jake: I think in February 2011. There was this organisation called the Westboro Baptist Church. They describe themselves as a church. I would describe them more as a cult that pickets the funerals of dead soldiers. They come out with signs saying *God hates homosexuals*. They think everybody apart from them is doomed and is going to Hell for their positions.

They're led by this kind of older generation, and the people I was around online decided to attack them. I thought that was interesting, both because it was a new way of protest but also ironic that these people genuinely think that the Internet was invented for them. We did a live radio interview on the David Pakman Show with Shirley Phelps-Roper, one of the leaders of the church, where we broke into their website live. I sort of acted as the spokesperson for that, and it went quite viral. She gave some very clever answer about it being God's intent for that to happen, so that I would be sent to prison.

For me, at the time, being a young person, it was very, very exciting to be able to have that kind of collaboration. It was a case of wanting to shut the laptop and then realising: What else do

I have apart from that? It was all I really had. It just kept building up and building up until we decided to create this hacker group, Lulz Security, which was basically a Twitter account with a very amusing avatar which I picked at random of a small stick man in a white suit with a top hat and a monocle, drinking a glass of wine.

Graham: What was the significance of that aesthetic?

Jake: It was random. I had folders of thousands of images, and I just picked it at random, for being a Twitter header. It was just kind of amusing, for people to wonder, 'What's going on here? This doesn't belong on the Internet.' It was something that went against the grain of the Internet. That could evolve. It wasn't about breaking into websites. It could have involved anything. It was just something that was supposed to go online. At this point, things started to get centralised. Facebook started really taking over. Everyone was talking about social media.

Television adverts started using hashtags at that time to promote ridiculous products, and have preposterous conversations around it, and put together statistics about how popular they were, based on the number of people that used the thing that they're promoting, which is absurd. So we did the same thing.

They have these large teams behind that, driving that. We decided to just go on Twitter, without any sort of funding, no money, which was unprecedented.

Graham: No social media consultants?

Jake: We didn't have Clive from marketing or anything come and look at our page. We just started posting what we thought and it got very popular very fast due to websites being hacked. The X Factor database was hacked and it went up on Pirate Bay with a very smug picture of Simon Cowell's face with one of his red buzzers there, and it had a description below that. It was fun and amusing. We had this little personality, the top-hat man who interacted with people on a regular basis. It grew in Twitter followers. We had about 400,000.

Because of its popularity, once a couple of people realised we had this following, we had eyes on us. People thought we could do whatever we wanted and it would hit the news in some fashion. We got these people on board who were really attempting to use that for their own sort of anti-police regime.

But then the phone hacking scandal hit, with News International [now rebranded as News UK], and we became active again for one final adventure, which was replacing *The Sun* newspaper's home page. We decided to create an account for an administrative journalist with a fake name to post a breaking news story article, like a genuine article, reporting that Rupert Murdoch had killed himself in his garden by ingesting poison out of shame for the phone hacking scandal.

It was this little parody of what Murdoch said at the time – that he knew nothing about the scandal and couldn't remember a thing. I played on that for his getting dementia and losing his mind.

When Sky News started reporting, it had the live page open. Because our group had full access to the website, we could therefore make it so that anyone that visited TheSun.co.uk would be redirected to any page we wanted. Malevolent hackers might point them to a virus or something. We just pointed them to our Twitter page. You would go to TheSun.co.uk and you'd be redirected to the @LulzSec Twitter page, which would speak to you as if you meant to go to *The Sun*. 'Hello, *Sun* readers, we're sorry for the inconvenience.'

Graham: It was after this that you were arrested. Do you think that tampering with the mainstream media is what finally landed you in trouble?

Jake: When you go after something that breaks down the fabric of society, the media, the people that are reporting, you take them, and it becomes part of the real world. The real world is suddenly aware of it.

I was arrested ten days after that. I think at that point the officers in charge obviously had an inkling of who we all were and thought,

'They're really breaking the Fourth Wall with their activity. Let's take them out now.'

I was just sitting around in the Shetlands, living on my own at the time. I was speaking to my friend from Delhi, actually, that I'd met online at 13. He was the last person I spoke to online, completely innocently. I got a knock on my door. The only knocks on my door were the neighbours complaining about loud music or a mental health team coming to have a chat with me about my not eating or not leaving the house or something.

But it wasn't. It was about six serious-looking individuals. At that point, I knew who it was but I said, 'What is it?' kind of thing. 'Are you Jake?' I said, 'Yes, that's who I am.' They showed a warrant, and wanted to come in, said they were from the Metropolitan Police. They said I was arrested on suspicion of conspiracy to commit a denial of service attack, which I'm sure sounded ridiculous out of their mouths as well. They must have understood that they'd been flown to the Shetlands to say that.

They went through all of my stuff – CDs, under my couch, in my toaster, actually, in my fridge, opening up packets of food, looking for micro-SD cards, or USB sticks or something. I guess they were just looking for proof that I was the alias that they knew was involved in criminal activity. They were just looking for devices. They knew they wouldn't get into my house again, in the Shetlands. They had to go back to London. They were going to get one chance, they'd just gather up everything they could. Most of what they took was useless stuff.

They drove me to the airport … loaded me onto this small plane with all of these bags of evidence taking up the back storage area, and [we] flew straight to London.

It was my first time ever in England, my first time off the Shetlands, since I was very young. They kept me for the maximum 96 hours, at which point I was released outside of a magistrate's court on bail, after they tried to deny me bail based on their conclusion I was a threat to national security which they convinced a police sergeant

was the case, and he didn't let me go. I had to go to a court to apply for bail the next morning. I couldn't have legally been held any longer at that point.

The judge kind of looked at me and looked at them and thought, 'This is just some kid. Just let him go on bail. Give him a tag.' I had this large electronic device on my right ankle. They put me under house arrest, and made sure that between the hours of 10 PM and 7 AM I had to be in a specific house. If not, it would beep, it would go off, and vans would come to my house.

I was released to my mother's house. She had moved to England. With that electronic curfew and an Internet ban, I couldn't access the Internet, or ask anyone to access the Internet on my behalf. If I asked someone to look up a video on YouTube for me, or look up some ticket prices online, that was illegal. I guess they thought I would tamper with evidence, or tamper with witnesses, or send hidden messages or something like that.

For two straight years, while I was awaiting trial, I was banned from the Internet. I couldn't access it once in two years, which posed difficulties in getting work. For most work now you're required to have an email address or some access to technology.

I had a really old phone and a sort of computer with all of the Internet stuff ripped out of it that I could use for writing and preparing my case. The trial against me was so set in computer evidence, but I couldn't access it in computer format. I had to have chat logs printed out on paper, computer viruses printed out on paper, nullifying them. I had thousands of these pieces of paper.

The prosecution had an electronic presentation of the evidence, and we had paper. I have an entire cupboard filled with stacks of paper, thousands of pages. There was this evidence of what we said online, which is recorded by the FBI or something, but it wasn't printed properly, it was tiny on the page. They wouldn't give it to us in disk format, because they thought it was too dangerous.

I was defending myself against one of the most modern cases in the country, using the most old-style court methods, and they couldn't keep up with that.

I got sentenced to two years. It was originally three years, though I pleaded guilty at the earliest opportunity, which was to get a third off.

Graham: What was that like?

Jake: I got in and I was nervous at first. You're put into sort of a section area and given this tray of food. They have BBC News playing constantly, and my face was on the news, while I was eating. I had these large, stereotypical prison inmates around me. I thought: This is not going to end well. They started going, 'That guy, he's on the news. This is a bad-ass guy. He goes against the man.' I was completely praised by these hard-core London gangsters.

Graham: So you got respect there?

Jake: I got a strange level of rep from the fellow inmates. They're a bunch of 18- to 21-year-old guys. We all kind of think in the same way. Everyone had been there because they'd gone against the system. They all hated the idea of authority. This, to them, was amazing.

Halfway through my sentence, the Edward Snowden story broke. I had questions from the guards who kept asking me about Snowden. My cellmates were asking me. They were writing stuff down about computer hacking. It was brilliant. We were talking about spying, and stuff like that.

In my time in Feltham, I tried to help people read and write. I was with three separate cellmates at that time: one who smashed his dad's car with a pickaxe, another who ran quite a large drug business, and someone else who allegedly —he's pleading not guilty— robbed a very rich couple's house.

Graham: Your case really set a precedent. Do you think this will help young people in your situation in the future?

Jake: The first time this came to mind was when I got a standard letter from my lawyer about sentencing guidelines, comparing my case to another case... This is kind of the high bar of what you may receive as a prison sentence... What my lawyer wrote in that entire section was just a couple of sentences that said there's no case like this in history. I can't advise you on this...

The judge in our case had to really think about this. What that means for the future is that this case will be used as a precedent. If any computer hacking case comes up with any sort of pranking, any sort of ideology that doesn't involve just damage to a computer system, this will be used.

In the future I think we're going to have cases where we understand a little bit more, so the judge is going to look at a bunch of 16-year-olds that are committing pranks online, and go, 'Look, just get a job somewhere' —which is what happened in Ireland recently, with two Irish hackers who were my co-conspirators, who hacked into the Fine Gael website, and translated it into Gaelic, and just left it like that. They got a £1,000 fine, and were told to just go off and get jobs. They didn't get a sentence.

I would question sending a hacker to Feltham. I don't know. The two-year Internet ban was far tougher than 37 days in Feltham. It was far tougher than being in a cell with a drug empire leader. Really, being banned from Google was far worse than that.

'It's that kind of forced structure of learning I didn't enjoy or appreciate. I felt like all this knowledge was being thrown at me and not sticking.'

United Kingdom

'...environments that don't feel oppressive, that don't present like institutions, that encourage collaborations and multi-disciplinary learning, will lead to a different output than ones that present like a workhouse, gilded or otherwise.'

Early in 2011 the UK government's Department for Education under the Secretary of State for Education, Michael Gove, published a report that would form part of a policy 'to make the construction and maintenance of school buildings more cost-effective'.[14] The James Report was led by Sebastien James, the Group Operations Director of Dixons plc, a popular chain of electrical retail outlets in the UK. The team supporting James in the creation of the report included senior representatives from a UK supermarket chain, a clothing retail chain and a car manufacturer. Gove welcomed the report and said, at the time, 'The system we inherited had profound problems. We must have a system for school building which is much simpler, less bureaucratic, and which targets priority projects.'

This happened just after Gove's party took office and promptly scrapped a £45-billion programme initiated by the prior administration called Building Schools for the Future. BSF was an investment programme by government to reinvent and rebuild secondary schools in England with the objective of making them fit for the 21st century. The programme was extremely ambitious in terms of costs, time-scales and objectives. It also placed more emphasis on the building rather than the learning or, for that matter, the future. A school of the future would, according to the construction companies winning the projects, be like a school of yesterday but made from glass and steel like a trendy office for a financial services company.

It doesn't really matter what side of the political spectrum you're on. It's easy to spot the foolishness on both sides in the lack of ambition of the respective governments for the country's youth. On the one hand, we have a report commissioned from a group of shopkeepers and retail specialists, and on the other, architects and builders fitting shiny body kits on Victorian carriages. Given these scenarios, England is either aiming to be a nation of shop-keepers, as predicted by Napoleon, or a nation of office workers.

The 2011 report was followed up by a set of guidelines published by the DfE in 2014 that, in a bid to standardise school design and cut costs, indicated templates that placed restrictions on room sizes, storey heights and building shapes for 261 replacement school buildings planned across the country. The notes call for 'simple, orthogonal forms' with 'no curves or "faceted" curves' and having 'minimal indents, "dog legs" and notches in the plan shapes'. They also state that buildings should have 'no glazed curtain walling or ETFE roofs'. Gove was reported as saying, 'We won't be getting Richard Rogers to design your school, we won't be getting any award-winning architects to design it, because no one in this room is here to make architects richer.'[15] Thus, with a sweep of the pen, the notion of design as well as architectural enhancements for learning were abolished.

So does the environment, the physical space, in which we learn matter? Is a well-designed environment simply an irrelevance provided you have good teachers? Can school buildings be stand-ardised in the same way that we roll out fast-food restaurants and retail stores?

The reality probably lies somewhere in between all these points. Given that the alma mater of the majority of the senior UK govern-ment members is Eton College, then one might assume that the environment has, at least, some part to play. But this is a complex issue and in the design of a school or learning environment there are many things at play including the building itself.

The British Design Council defines design as what links creativity and innovation. It shapes ideas to become practical propositions for users and customers. Design, the Council says, can be described as creativity deployed to a specific end. Thus, if we were designing a school, who do we imagine are the users and customers, and what is the specific end that we have in mind?

This straightforward definition of design seems less straightforward when we apply it to the design of an environment in which people are supposed to learn and even more difficult if we apply it to the design of education itself. And education as a system can be designed, as has been shown by Singapore which designed its education system to match its economic development programme. So it really begs the question of our policy leaders and the people who make decisions over learning environments: Who and what are they designing these environments for when they offer up variations on pop-up retail outlets or office complexes?

The schools I visited as part of this project that had an answer were the ones that felt more transformational in their approach. Whether it was Noyaa Association Community School situated on a beach in the fishing port of Jamestown, Ghana or High Tech High in San Diego, California, there was a clear intent and ambition in the form and function of the learning environment combined with the curriculum and approach of the teaching practice. It's fair to assume, and demonstrated in practice, that environments that don't feel oppressive, that don't present like institutions, that encourage collaborations and multi-disciplinary learning, will lead to a different output than ones that present like a workhouse, gilded or otherwise.

Learning (Re)imagined # Qatar

Qatar

Qatar

O Doha

For the past five years I have been travelling to Qatar, and more specifically to Doha, its capital, principally to attend the World Innovation Summit for Education which commissioned this book and project. Each time I return, the vista across the city has changed as vast infrastructure projects reshape the skyline. At first glance one might imagine that Qatar is similar to other young countries that are thrusting into modernity, but my experience suggests that there are subtle and not so subtle differences.

Qatar is a peninsula in the Arabian Gulf, attached to the larger Arabian Peninsula. It shares a land border with Saudi Arabia, while the United Arab Emirates and the island kingdom of Bahrain are close neighbours. Evidence of human settlement on the Qatar peninsula goes back many thousands of years. Archaeological studies show that Stone Age inhabitants fished, built encampments and worked sites for flint. Despite an inhospitable environment and a scarcity of fertile soil and drinking water, people have been consistently settling its shores for more than 7,000 years. The adjacent waters were a reliable source of fine natural pearls which offered a livelihood until the introduction of cultured pearls in the 20th century.

Oil and gas were discovered in 1938 and rapidly replaced pearling as the country's main form of wealth. Production was suspended during World War II and resumed in 1949. The State of Qatar became independent in 1971, and in recent years has become the world's largest exporter of Liquefied Natural Gas. It is conscious of its dependence on this commodity and is energetically pursuing economic diversification and sustainability.

His Highness the Emir Sheikh Tamim bin Hamad Al-Thani, who assumed power in 2013, has continued the policies of His Highness Sheikh Hamad bin Khalifa Al-Thani, the Father Emir, who placed education at the forefront of national development. Qatar is now the highest ranked country in the Arab world for a number of human development indicators.

The country is investing in education at all levels, from literacy to research-based higher education, and Her Highness Sheikha Moza bint Nasser, Chairperson of Qatar Foundation, is a driving force behind the development of education in Qatar and internationally. She has guided the establishment of Education City which is home to branch campuses of universities based in the US, UK and France, as well as a wide range of other educational, research and community development initiatives.

His Excellency Sheikh Abdulla bin Ali Al-Thani, PhD, serves as President of Hamad bin Khalifa University, an emerging research university at Education City, and he is Chairman of the World Innovation Summit for Education. A key initiative of Qatar Foundation, WISE brings together foremost thought leaders, policymakers and practitioners from all sectors to serve a changing and connected world in which education is a prerequisite for inclusion and social progress. The WISE Awards initiative has supported innovative projects all around the world that are making a real difference to the lives of individuals and communities.

'The country is investing in education at all levels, from literacy to research-based higher education...'

Qatar

Qatar

Awsaj is a desert plant that despite a challenging environment bursts into a beautiful flower. Awsaj Academy is a specialised school that has served Qatari children since 1996 who are at risk of school failure because of the learning challenges they face. The school is unique in Qatar and is among a handful worldwide that dedicates itself to working with bilingual Arabic-English speaking students who have demonstrated aptitude in certain areas while facing academic challenges in others.

Awsaj Academy began as a small programme serving 20 students from Qatar Academy and the community. Today, the K–12 school serves 365 students within its modern, purpose-built facilities situated in the sprawling Education City development. Supported by an impressive cohort of teachers, psychologists, speech and hearing specialists, and researchers, the school tackles a broad range of learning challenges that children present including Down syndrome, autism, ADHD and cerebral palsy.

One approach used throughout Awsaj Academy is digital technology that includes a 1:1 laptop programme for grades five to 12. Students use Google Apps to create blog sites for every grade level that allow teachers, students and parents to communicate and collaborate regarding assignments, schedules and other announcements. Additionally, assistive technology is used to increase the opportunities for physically challenged students to learn and participate in all class activities. I met two young boys, aged nine and ten, both of whom had severe motor coordination difficulties. One of the boys had cerebral palsy with a speech impairment; the other a degenerative condition. Under the guidance of an occupational therapist, each boy was working with specially adapted assistive keyboards, while the rest of the class used touchscreen tablet devices.

The most important objective of the school is for all students to graduate from secondary school, prepared either for advanced education or a career in Qatar or overseas. I met two recent Awsaj graduates during my visit, one who now works as an administrative assistant at Awsaj and another who will soon be attending a business school in Oxford, UK. Awsaj Academy is providing vital opportunities to these young people who might not have succeeded with a conventional approach. Most importantly, parents who might have had the mindset that their children with Down syndrome were 'ill', now have a more advanced understanding of their children's needs and capacity to learn.

Awsaj Academy operates as a not-for-profit private school. The Academy is comprised of a K-12 school with students separated by ages into the elementary, middle and high school. The centre also includes units that conduct applied research and provide outreach services. Qatar Foundation supports Awsaj organisationally and financially because it is seen as a centre of excellence in the region

Qatar

'Awsaj Academy's success has also opened a more informed dialogue in the region about special needs children.'

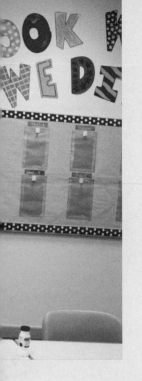

that meets the needs of children who might otherwise not be served. The school aims to ensure that each graduate can demonstrate proficiency in reading, writing, listening and speaking in both English and Arabic, has the knowledge and skills to begin post-secondary education or a career, takes pride in their own culture while respecting the culture of others, has an understanding and respect for Islamic values, and has a commitment to lifelong learning.

Dr Ralph Pruitt, Director of Awsaj Academy, describes Awsaj as a 'university lab school' where the teaching and support staff only implement evidence-based practices that are constantly being studied in order to determine whether the practices are effective within the Qatari context and culture. He explains that the school has adapted a mastery-based, explicit direct instruction approach, encouraging high student engagement. Each classroom has ten children and one or two teachers. The class is fast paced. Students must answer correctly on cue in order to advance to the next level. The research and development centre works with the school to evaluate and guide the instruction while giving technical assistance to other schools interested in adopting the 'Awsaj Way' of instruction.

Awsaj staff members use the AIMSweb assessment system as a reading and math screener, progress monitor, and a benchmark tool for all students school-wide. Reading and math growth is measured three times a year using the Measures of Academic Progress (MAP)[16] system, a computer-based, formative testing regime created by the US-based Northwest Evaluation Association. In 2013, Awsaj Academy began using Ballard & Tighe's oral IDEA Proficiency Test (IPT)[17] in all grades to establish a baseline of its students' English listening and speaking skills. The IPT test is administered annually to measure growth because English is not the first language of 95 percent of Awsaj students. According to the school's 2014 annual report, 38 percent of the students increased their MAP scores from the autumn to the winter. More impressively, 64 percent increased their MAP scores in mathematical computation. Finally, students demonstrated on average a 71 percent increase in words-per-minute scores from one test to the next for oral reading fluency on the IPT.

The reliance on continuous testing wasn't especially appealing when I first learned about the school. What I realised, when discussing the process of continual evaluation with Dr Pruitt, was that these tests were being used as diagnostic tools to provide vital data and evidence upon which the teachers and the specialist teams were able to constantly improve each student's instructional program. The outcomes of what Dr Pruitt and his team are achieving at Awsaj Academy, with a student body that would have been a missed generation, are testimonials to the approach. Students have graduated to go on to universities in the region, and as far as New Zealand, the UK and the US.

Awsaj Academy's success has also opened a more informed dialogue in the region about special needs children. Demands for its services have increased among families within Qatar as have consultation requests from schools locally and regionally. Awsaj is responding with outreach and continuous professional development programmes for schools in Qatar. An estimated 20,000 children in Doha alone would benefit from having specialised support for their learning. Awsaj's influence appears to have sown the seeds for a field of blooms in Qatar.

'The outcomes of what Dr Pruitt and his team are achieving at Awsaj Academy, with a student body that would have been a missed generation, are testimonials to the approach.'

Qatar

Dr Ralph Pruitt is a US educator with a Doctorate in education leadership and international education leadership from Lehigh University. His Masters was in the area of leadership and special education.

Graham Brown-Martin: Public awareness and open discussion about 'at risk' children who had learning challenges have been inhibited in the past. Have you found that this is now changing?

Dr Ralph Pruitt: Absolutely it is changing. I think in the last four years we've been able to openly communicate and visit about these challenges. Even at the last graduation, I pleaded with those who may have influence to start more schools like Awsaj and to provide more training to local schools so that they can incorporate all children. Not just kids who are capable of learning, also kids who are at risk of failure or have already shown failure at school, and so that they can have the services available in every neighbourhood school for all kids.

Graham: What about affordability, for the children who are at risk but whose parents are unable to afford an environment like this?

Dr Pruitt: That's the key question because we only have capacity for 500 children; but based on numbers in typical countries, there would be 20,000 children who need this attention. We can't provide all of the help for them. That help has to happen through every school's taking on the mission to educate any child who walks through their door, not just a lead group or those who are easy to teach but all children. Every child has potential. It's our job as educators to pull that potential out of them. There are many examples of great people in history who have had learning challenges –presidents, inventors, entrepreneurs– who have had these challenges, but because of educators, caring teachers and parents who believed in them, it made a difference in their lives. They become quite an influence to the community.

Graham: Do you imagine that schools here might follow the European or US model where

'A child that has low motor skills or strength because of a truly physical disability now has the opportunity to compete against the norm.'

state schools are obliged to provide support for children with learning challenges?

Dr Pruitt: I think this country could learn from other countries. In many other countries, the reason why they have the special education services and labeled children in that is because of the bureaucracy that's in place to receive funding. You label a child because that gets you a certain amount of funding so that you can provide these services. What is unique here, is that you don't have to label because of funding. There's good funding here. You're doing it for the right reason. You want to educate all children. You want the entire population to succeed.

To answer your question, though, I think that there will be more inclusive practices in local schools here as they learn how to do that. It's not easy work, as the USA and UK have found out. There's not always one way to teach a child, you've got to figure out how to do it. There are certainly best practices and some common steps that you go through, but each child needs to be worked with. A whole team needs to really work with them.

Graham: Do you think labelling children with specific challenges has become a trend now?

Dr Pruitt: Absolutely. There was a cartoon the other day that showed a picture of a child, probably in a 1950s classroom, looking out the window and daydreaming. They labeled that child a daydreamer or bored. Today, you have another child that's looking out the window in a modern classroom and you label him ADHD.

There's very little purpose to labelling. There may be in medical conditions, you need to label a child who's diabetic because there are certain medical procedures... But why can't we work with every child who comes through our door and have the skills and the ability to do that?

Graham: That's almost a general observation about education –one size doesn't fit all. Do you think some of your approaches here could be adopted at a more general level?

Dr Pruitt: Yes, whether in an exclusive setting

where it's all kids without risk needs or it's in an inclusive setting. There are tiered systems of support based on a child's performance [in which] you can help that child succeed and ratchet up the intensity of interventions and support based on their performance and needs.

Graham: How would you describe the teaching practice within the school?

Dr Pruitt: One area that we are seeing some good progress in our children is via direct explicit instruction where you model something. You model how to read a word. You practice it, you make sure they're successful on it, you reinforce it. You test it and make sure that they've understood it. [Then] you go on to the next level. If they don't, you have to re-teach.

We do behaviour the exact same way. We teach behaviour just like we teach a math lesson. If a child is not respectful to others, then he needs to be taught how to be respectful to others. They can go through lessons about how to be respectful. If he is still not respectful, he may need additional intervention, like private tutoring, the social skills class in order to develop skills in respecting others. Rather than thinking the problem is all in the child, we've got to think as educators, what can we control and do? We can control the quality of instruction.

What we believe is that after children get a strong foundation using a direct explicit instruction, then they can go to more inquiry-based instruction where they get to experiment where the answers aren't all there. You've got a higher-level problem solving. Until they're at a basic level, you have got to get them to read and write, and to be able to speak, and to access the text that they're reading. If they can't do that, you don't start with more [thinking that] maybe they'll learn because I'm teaching this way.

Graham: How do you see the use of digital technology enhancing students' learning here?

Dr Pruitt: I think it's to access good education. It's to support a child who, because of physical limitations, may need something in

order to access that instruction. So it's another tool to access education. A child who has low motor skills or strength because of a physical disability now has the opportunity to compete against the norm.

Graham: What does the future look like for the Academy? How would you like to see things developing in Qatar and the region?

Dr Pruitt: A lot more dialogue about how to support children who are at risk. A lot more dialogue around prevention and more advocacy. There is a lot of advocacy going on and some grassroot efforts among international schools to promote more inclusive practices.

To really study the effect of practices that are contextualised here, oftentimes consultants or trainers will go to schools and they'll say, 'I can't implement that here because this is a unique setting...' What we say and what we're really proving is that our kids are different, and that's why we've got to research effective practices because nobody has done that yet. All of our kids are at risk. All of our kids are second-language learners. All of our kids are from this country, primarily. There's no norm group to compare them to.

The future is that we can actually write about that, have dialogue about it and create models and systems that can be replicated and sustained in the future. That's what's going to happen here. I think it's going to happen here faster than in many countries because of the interest, the resources in a knowledge-based economy, the nature of how innovation is so fast-paced here. The challenge is keeping leadership, keeping the focus. Anytime you implement these kinds of strategies, and we have that here now, the top leadership must be highly supportive.

Learning {Re}imagined # Lebanon

Beirut

Lebanon

Lebanon

I had wanted to visit Beirut for many reasons, not least of which was the recommendation and invitation of numerous Lebanese friends I've made over the years in London and Paris. The school I was visiting had seen its fair share of challenges since the 1970s and the war in Lebanon, and I was aware there would be teachers helping children make sense of what was happening.

The city of Beirut relies on tourism and it seemed everybody was really pleased to see us there. We arrived at the start of the Beirut Art Fair, featuring a week of exhibits and gatherings for the national and international community. On arrival at the airport we were greeted by our hosts from Eastwood College, and separated from our luggage which went to our hotels. We were then taken for an incredible feast of Lebanese cuisine at a quayside restaurant overlooking the harbour. We continued to an opening party of the Art Fair on the top floor of a very trendy hotel with an incredible view across the city.

At the time of writing, Lebanon is receiving a significant population of Syrian refugees from across its border. Lebanon has a population of over four million of which more than 1.25 million are refugees from Syria and Palestine. The government of Lebanon provides access to education and healthcare for refugees but their presence also imposes a burden upon political, economic and social stability, as well as upon the labour market and infrastructure. Arabic, French and English are commonly spoken in a land that has a diverse mix of cultures and religions. The dominant cultural background is Ancient Syrian, Phoenician and Byzantine as a result of numerous occupations and settlements over the millennia.

Despite the scars of a violent past, Beirut feels very much like a Mediterranean melting pot. It's a beautiful place, sweeping down from the mountains and hills to meet the sea. It's a lively and welcoming city that is struggling with many complex issues to achieve a peaceful future for its children and future generations.

I was only there for a few days but I'll certainly return. There definitely is an edginess to the place, but also a good spirit. I'm looking forward to going back.

'It is a beautiful place, sweeping down from the mountains and hills to meet the sea.'

Lebanon

'Lebanon has a population of over four million of which more than 1.25 million are refugees from Syria and Palestine.'

Lebanon

'Beirut feels very much like a Mediterranean melting pot.'

'Every teacher and
student has an iPad
and inexpensive Apple
TV devices in each room
allow material from
any iPad to be shared...'

Eastwood College is a K-12 private international school founded in 1973 by Amine Khoury, who remains president of the school today, and Hazel St John MBE. Before founding Eastwood, St John, who was British, was a teacher and the headmistress of the British Syrian Training College for Girls in Beirut from 1950. The college provided girls, who had limited choices for education in the region, with classes through the eighth grade, in addition to college preparation and teacher training. She was awarded an MBE for her services to education for children in the Middle East by Queen Elizabeth II in 1971 and passed away in 2003. Khoury was just 19 years of age when his passion for educating children formed a vision of founding a school of excellence.

The school operates from two campus locations on the outskirts of Beirut. The first campus opened in 1973 and is located at Kfarshima and the second, which I visited, is in Mansourieh. Since opening, the original school in its various incarnations has been bombed and reconstructed three times, collateral damage in various domestic and non-domestic conflicts. It ultimately relocated to its current location some distance from the 'demarcation line' of past sectarian disputes. Originally founded on Christian principles, today Eastwood College is effectively multi-faith, supporting a cohort of students from more than 40 nations as well as local children. The school also has an intake of students recently joined from Syria as a result of the diaspora.

The campus I visited has a population of around 300 students from kindergarten up. Students are in learning groups of no more than 15 to a teacher in small classrooms that benefit from a light and airy aspect overlooking Beirut from the school's hillside location. The school works to an American-based international curriculum within the context of the Lebanese Baccalaureate.

Eastwood College already has an enviable reputation in the region that is by no small measure due to the efforts of its founder and driving force, Amine. However, the recent return to this family education legacy of his grown children, son Michel and daughter Joelle, seeks to maintain the school's ongoing success and relevance well into this century. Both had been living in the US following their own paths in higher education and high-profile careers before returning to Eastwood. In addition to an MBA and an MA in economics from Columbia University in New York, Michel Khoury was one of the candidates selected by Apple to join their Distinguished Educator programme from which he graduated in 2013.

Armed with new skills and vision, Michel and Joelle, a graduate from the American University of Beirut with an MA in curriculum and teaching, also from Columbia University, have embarked on a programme of transformation for the school. I started to see how the seemingly disparate locations and contexts of my various visits on this project begin to connect. I discovered strong links, regard and sharing of knowledge with Essa Academy, the school that we visited during our UK tour, and it's clear to see some similarities of approach with the Khourys' work to transform the learning and teaching in the school.

Like at Essa, there are no interactive whiteboards. Instead, each classroom is fitted with flat-screen HD televisions and walls that invite being written on. Every teacher and student has an iPad and inexpensive Apple TV devices in each room allow material from any iPad to be shared with the class on the HD screens. Extensive use is made of the free iTunes U software where the school has already created a wealth of material, some of which we had seen being shared in the UK just a week earlier. The software allows teachers to present materials, set tasks and provide students with almost 24-seven access as well as out-of-school-hours email response.

I sat in on numerous classes and discussed what was happening in the school with different members of staff. The Khoury family were eager to know what I thought, despite my reassurances that I wasn't there to judge, review or compare with other schools. My reason for being there was to understand how they were approaching transformation within their own context. Where, for example, at Essa Academy broadband was in plentiful supply, here in Beirut bandwidth is tightly restricted, immediately creating challenges for any school in the nation wishing their students to benefit via connected learning. The restrictions on bandwidth in Beirut aren't as much for ideological reasons but because paralysis within government means policy decisions are either protracted or just never taken. Digital access doesn't seem to have been made a priority within Lebanon as an enabler for economic growth, let alone education, which seems at odds with other aspects of its forward-thinking population.

I really enjoyed being at the school and had a genuine sense that the student cohort were enjoying their experience there, making sufficient academic progress for many to go on to be accepted at Ivy League universities in the US or similar in Europe or in the region. As for the bold digital transformation programme initiated by the Khourys, I believe that they will be successful, but what I saw was what I'd regard as a moment in time, the first steps in the right direction rather than what might be regarded as an end result. It should be said that the end results based on the metrics of standardised testing with which we are familiar are very good, so what is being attempted here is to keep the school ahead of the curve.

If I had to be critical I would say that what was happening at Eastwood College today was a transition that has yet to impact pedagogy in so far as the initial benefit is that the large number of print books that weighed down a student's shoulders has now been reduced to an iPad. Like the example in Ghana, this transition does not require a significant change in teaching practice and so is a low-skills threshold approach to introducing digital platforms, but nevertheless is a Trojan Horse for change.

Lebanon

Classes that I saw seemed somewhat reminiscent of classrooms-plus-technology rather than environments where the technology was embedded within the learning. This is what usually happens when tablets and so on are introduced within a classroom. The teacher inevitably teaches to the platform. But my feeling was that at Eastwood this was a transition to a change in pedagogy, curriculum and timetable perhaps in a similar way to Essa Academy, which had taken the benefits of technology's time-saving and efficiencies to allow students and teachers the oxygen of time and space to transform.

I also felt that the small class sizes and 1:1 approach of Eastwood would lend itself well to the work that Sugata Mitra has been conducting in the field of self-organising learning environments in which students collaborate together to solve big problems and the teacher switches from the 'guide on the side' to the critical yet encouraging friend.

But all this was the unintended, unexpected outcome of my travels so far. I was beginning to see the jigsaw puzzle where different people have different pieces and, if we manage to bring them together, there's a chance that we will see the whole picture and change together.

Since 1973 the school motto of Eastwood College has been 'Children, Our Purpose, And Our Future'. I think this pretty much nails it within the school that I saw and the leadership, staff and students whom I met.

The founder and directors of the school mentioned the word 'love' many times before and during my visit. Surprisingly, this wasn't mentioned in the context of love of teaching, in what has become a modern cliché used by almost anyone who talks about the teaching profession. Does anyone ever publicly admit to hating teaching or hating children? Although I'm pretty confident there are a lot of teachers and policymakers who secretly do. No, the context in which the Khourys meant it was the creation of a loving, family environment within the school itself and I can honestly say that is what it felt like in the school. It's pretty hard to fake that sort of thing during an all-day visit and I left thinking that the Khourys had indeed created something special and that the school would certainly be worth visiting in the future to see how their transformation programme has progressed.

www.eastwoodcollege.com

'The restrictions on bandwidth in Beirut aren't as much for ideological reasons but because of paralysis within government...'

Eastwood College is a private international school in Beirut comprising two campuses. I visited the campus in Mansourieh, a village situated on one of the lush hillsides on the outskirts of Beirut overlooking the bustle of the city as it reaches the Mediterranean. The school provides education for children from nursery through high school and feels like an oasis of calm, albeit with the buzz of a family gathering.

The school is now in the second generation of family ownership since it opened in 1973 and is undergoing a transformation in the way that it provides its teaching and learning. Eastwood College is the first school in the region to adopt an iPad-per-student strategy where teachers are using advanced tools to create and distribute their lessons whilst engaging with the students in and out of the classroom.

On my visit to Eastwood I was pleased to meet Michel Khoury, a director of the college and one of the most energetically passionate people I've met in a long time.

Graham Brown-Martin: Michel, please tell me about your background and involvement with Eastwood College.

Michel Khoury: I've been here for about three years. I came from the United States after spending 16 years there, first as an investment banker then going into private school education and school leadership. I finally decided that, after years of being there, it was time for me to move back, and move our schools forward in Lebanon, and see how we can become part of the bigger cause.

Graham: I understand that the school was started by your father. What is the history of the college?

Michel: Eastwood College was established in 1973 by my father, Amine Khoury. He started the school when he was 19 years old because he didn't really like the education system he went through and didn't want other students in the future to be going through that same system: the rigid, tough, very militant style of education.

And he wanted a place that was filled with love. At 19 he set out on his goal to build a school, and that is what he's done successfully.

Graham: Lebanon has had a turbulent history. How did this affect the development of the school?

Michel: Lebanon has gone through a lot of changes in the past 40 years: predominately the civil war, that lasted 16 years. So Eastwood College has been demolished three times over the past 40 years, and we've been rebuilt and we've had the same foundations —so you know, those foundations of love and caring and understanding, but also making sure that we treat each student as an individual. But the progress has been very beautiful, it's been very enlightening. What Eastwood College has given back to the community, given back to Lebanon, has been very profound. We've brought in a certain standard of academia, and that's been trickled down to a lot of other private and state schools as well.

So 'Children, our Purpose, and our Future' was the motto that my father had put down back in 1973. He wanted something very thoughtful for the school motto, and what better thought than children: they are our purpose, and that's who we live for, and they are our future. And that trickles down to everything that we do in this school: How are we preparing our students to become the future leaders of the world? Whether they want to be artists or nuclear physicists, how can they be the best at that? And it's about really pertaining to each child, educating every single child in the way they love to be taught.

Graham: What do you think the future that your students are approaching looks like?

Michel: Well, we don't really know where the future lies. Over the past ten years we've gone through incredible change. From my father not knowing how to use a PC and not even touching a laptop, I gave him an iPad two years ago, and he can't live without it.

So the world has changed dramatically over the past few years —especially over the past three years— and all that we can do is teach our students learning models of how to progress with the future: not necessarily the information we need right now, but prepare them to be self-reliant, prepare them to be very thoughtful, prepare them to be very inquisitive, asking the right questions in order for them to get the right answers. That's what we're preparing our children for. I don't think we'll really figure out what's happening in the next five years or ten years, but what we're doing now is preparing our children to be ready for that when it does come.

Systems deployed over the past 30 years have needed to change, and unfortunately they haven't changed or haven't kept up to date with what's happening technologically around the world. Standardised tests have changed a little bit, but we pose the questions: Are standardised tests the right type of tests for our children? Are they producing the higher order of thinking that students really need?

Life has become very complicated. Life has become very connected to where there needs to be more collaboration, a lot more sense of self-reliance, in order to ask the essential questions of: Are we doing the best we can to be able to live for the next 50 to 60 years? Are we keeping a better eco-system for our future children? Are we keeping a better environment for our great-grandchildren? These are all essential questions that we have to ask today.

Graham: A lot of the challenges faced by these children will also be ideological. What are your thoughts on that?

Michel: We're operating under really extreme conditions here in Lebanon. Geopolitically it's been a nightmare. I mean with what's happening around the world, and around our region. We've had refugees come to the country, we've helped Syrian families, we've helped families that have been evacuated with no homes, with no clothing left but the clothes on their backs. And we've been operating under circumstances —also religious circumstances— where there's been so much animosity between different factions.

'What we do teach is world religion, the three monotheistic religions plus Buddhism, Daoism and Hinduism, all of the major religions of the world, because students need to be aware of their surroundings.'

But at the end of the day, Eastwood College is a safe haven, and that's what our culture is about: it's about being one family, it's about appreciating, being aware of all of the different needs and wants of our families and of our students, to be able to give them that sense of security. Kids now come from broken homes: the sense of security in their home is very little, so we try to create that safe haven for them now.

We don't preach politics or religion – that's actually one of the things that isn't allowed at Eastwood College. But what we do teach is world religion, the three monotheistic religions plus Buddhism, Daoism and Hinduism, all of the major religions of the world, because students need to be aware of their surroundings. We're no longer living in a very individualistic world. We're living in a global world where flying to Los Angeles is only an 11-hour flight; where flying to Saudi Arabia is a five-hour flight; flying to Brazil, to Latin America, is another ten-hour flight. So we've become very connected. We've become very dependent on the rest of the world by the products we use. It doesn't mean that if we live in Lebanon we don't use products from China or from the United States, or get education from England, or get resources from Australia. So that's the connectedness that we live under, that we live with right now.

Graham: You have a very international cohort of students here. What are the challenges of bringing together such a mixed group?

Michel: At Eastwood College we cater to 23 embassies, and we're one of the three schools that cater to the children of United Nations employees. That brings in a lot of different cultures, a lot of different values, a lot of different beliefs.

I would say that there isn't anything negative about that. I would say that's all a learning experience for each and every single child. A Korean child could be sitting next to an Indian, or could be sitting also next to an American child. Putting these three children together creates magic: it creates a sense of appreciation for each of the children. It's also about learning how to live with one another because, at the end of the day, we live on a very small globe, and it's all about collaboration and how we interact with one another.

When we push them off to university, a lot of our kids, about 12 percent, go to Ivy League schools, and 78 percent of our children get to the universities that they actually choose. And these children are competing for those spots. Someone applying to Columbia is competing with about 12,000 other applicants from all over the world – it's not just American students who are going to Columbia, or Italian students who are attending Italian universities. So the world has become such a global place, such a small global place, where they need to learn how to live. Students need to learn how to interact with one another in a civilised democratic way. And what's happening at Eastwood College is that sense of democracy, that sense of living with one another, of relying on each other for questions to solve world problems. Or even not solving them, even just thinking about them.

Graham: Tell me about the technological changes that you've been deploying at Eastwood.

Michel: We started three years ago with one question in mind: we wanted to revamp our system, to revamp our curriculum. So we sat down as a leadership team and started asking questions about what we wanted to do, what was our goal in doing this little exercise. And the one question that we all came up with was: Are we preparing students for future jobs that haven't been created yet?

And this is something that I haven't asked by myself. I know there have been hundreds of thousands of people, especially education leaders worldwide, who have asked those questions.

So we went and took a look at curricula around the world, and we said that since technology is available, it should be used as an enabler, as something that's going to provide added value to a student's life. The world has become so connected now that it's just immature not to use technology. It's the route to go, whether you use an iPad or a tablet or an iPhone – it really doesn't matter. It gives students access.

Graham: So what do you believe is the unique thing about digital technology that potentially changes education?

Michel: Well, the transformational nature of digital is that we no longer need to memorise: everything is available at your fingertips. We're in the digital world where everything is available online, and it's about making your students understand the learning model and not necessarily memorising. Technology's been a great enabler for that. We use technology in our classrooms for everything from math to science to art to drama. But in the essential core subjects of math and English and language and the sciences, it's more about research, it's more about being an independent thinker, about having a more self-analytical style, of preparing students to answer the bigger questions.

Collaboration is very important. We see a lot of schools. We go into a lot of schools around the region, and there is no collaboration between students, or among students and teachers. We see that classical classroom being taught where the teacher is at the front and the students are all learning from that teacher. But with the use of technology, the students are able to find out and have the same amount of knowledge as that teacher. The only difference is the years of experience, the fact that the teacher has been trained in that particular subject. But give any educated well-informed student the knowledge and the resources, and they'll probably know as much as the teacher.

Graham: How are you recruiting teachers and what ongoing development do you think they need?

Michel: A lot of schools that have opened in the region during the past ten years act as a business, where it's just purely a business. So because of our history, our culture and our success rates in developing excellent independent thoughtful leaders, we get a lot of applications from teachers. We get teachers from all over the world wanting to apply to Eastwood College. We work with a lot of universities that want to send their students that are training to be teachers to come and teach or do internships for six months or a year.

We also acquire teachers through a word-of-mouth strategy. To become a teacher at Eastwood College is not easy at all, not an easy task. You first have

'With the use of technology, the students are able to find out and have the same amount of knowledge as that teacher. The only difference is the years of experience, the fact that the teacher has been trained in that particular subject.'

to go through an interview with me, which is hell. And then you have to give two or three lesson plans, and then after the two or three lesson plans you have to write an essay, and then after the essay you have to make sure that you speak with the academic dean and write a structured course, and then, after that, if we accept you, you'll have to go through an emotional intelligence test, and an IQ test — just to make sure that you're the type of person that we want.

It's difficult getting the best teachers, but at the end of the day, there is no best teacher: there is a teacher that just fits with our core values, who we are. And the first thing that they need to really understand is that children are our purpose and are our future.

Graham: What obstacles have you encountered introducing these technologies into your school?

Michel: It's been a very tough challenge over the past three years. One of our major challenges is the Internet, the bandwidth. Trying to deploy 400 iPads on an eight-megabit-per-second Internet connection is impossible. We have all our logistics set up properly. We deal with corporations like Apple and Cisco and HP and so on and so forth to make sure that we have the proper infrastructure. We deal with companies like LightSpeed in California for our proper hardware and our software to be able to deploy the necessary firewalls. But there's no bandwidth, and we've really been suffering from that, and we've spoken to the ministries, and we've spoken to ministers, and we've spoken to parents, and we've lobbied the government, and still nothing. And the government doesn't really realise that the number-one most important variable of economic growth of a country is education.

Graham: What are your plans for scaling up Eastwood College?

Michel: One of our goals is to expand Eastwood College into the Middle East, specifically into Qatar, Abu Dhabi, Saudi Arabia and Jordan, because we want to share the knowledge that we've accumulated over the past 40 years, and

create a new standard of education — a new standard of education that is pertinent to this region, that is focused for this region... I don't think our kids can compete with the rest of the world, with Indian, Korean and Singaporean children. What are we doing to be able to compete?

'...data
is the
new oil'

When viewed through the prism of 'network capitalism', the acquisition of the WhatsApp instant messaging service for $19 billion by Facebook looks like good value in 2014. Time will tell, of course.

The consensus at the time was that Facebook acquired the company because it was fearful of losing its grip on the youth market that favoured mobile communications and a system that apparently their parents didn't use. As the world shifts to mobile Internet, it only makes sense, the theory goes, for Facebook to demonstrate its chops in the mobile world, which may also account for why it acquired Instagram. Facebook recently announced an initiative to provide access to the Internet for those in developing nations. SocialEDU, in partnership with mobile operators, will provide free mobile Internet access and educational content, initially to citizens living in Rwanda but the plan is to roll the Internet out to the entire planet. Facebook hired Deloitte to prepare a research report that demonstrated the economic and social benefits of expanding Internet access. Facebook lost out to Google to acquire Titan Aerospace, a manufacturer of sub-orbital drones that could be used to provide Internet access across remote or rural areas of developing countries. These acquisitions are more likely to be a statement about business than altruism, however.

Facebook, like our other great digital mega-corporations including Google, Amazon, Apple and even Netflix, has genuinely figured out how the new world works, providing salient lessons that other potential global megalomaniacs would be wise to follow. These corporations understand the value of data. Not just any old data but *your* data. Personal data is the global currency of network capitalism and these organisations are playing in a high-stakes game.

Google was probably the first company to really understand network capitalism and properly exploit it. There were many search engines before Google but their genius was first in their PageRank algorithm and second in their ability to tune it to advertising. They were smart and surrounded themselves with the right people. The understanding that data, and lots of it, could be turned into something extremely valuable was the secret sauce. So to expand the quantity and quality of this data, as well as provide context, Google has built an empire of applications that nearly all of the connected world uses, including maps, video, mail, education, chat and much more. Each application provides further data points that tell Google more about us, data that can be used by algorithms to customise our experience of the digital world whether we like it or not. A search on one of their tools will mean that suddenly the blogs and newspaper sites you visit are populated with relevant advertising.

Google's investments in mobile and wearable platforms are just another form of data acquisition, but with much higher granularity. We, the connected citizens, leak astounding amounts of data which Google vacuums up for analysis by its algorithms. The world and its shareholders are anticipating Apple's move into wearable computing any day now. You may even be reading this on the much-anticipated iWatch.

Google and Facebook are true embodiments of the oft-quoted 'if the product is free then you're probably the product' statement. The problem is that we, as individuals, haven't figured out a value for our own data beyond giving it away in exchange for communicating with our friends and the convenience that Google's apps provide us. There is a lack of understanding of exactly what data we are giving away. But let's return to the valuation of WhatsApp and we'll start to get an idea. The $19 billion for 450 million users means that each user's data is worth about $42. OK, there's an argument that suggests WhatsApp users pay for their service but is Facebook going to really give up on all that location and content-sharing metadata?

I'm not suggesting that any of these companies are evil; I'm simply pointing out their genius in capturing all our data and monetising it. One only has to see the actions of Microsoft buying Skype and Nokia, Apple's activities around iPhone, iTunes, AppleTV and its own mapping systems, Amazon's investment in hardware platforms, or the valuation of Twitter, to see that data is the new oil. The great industrial capitalists of our times are the leaders of these mega corps. *Plus ça change…*

Big data, like the web, was originally an idea based around scientific advancement. Facilities like CERN would provide huge dollops of data that would require fast and unbiased analysis via sophisticated algorithms running on networked computer farms to reveal the secrets of the universe. This, of course, can still happen, and who knows what might be possible if we have sufficient computing power and algorithmic sophistication to sequence everyone's DNA. Cures for cancer, perhaps?

The flipside is what this might do to human consciousness. There is a raft of social and political theory, from Marx through Gramsci to Adorno, concerned about the consequences of domination by one social group, creating a hegemony where power is constituted in the realm of ideas and knowledge. Under such domination, popular culture is akin to a factory producing standardised cultural goods used to manipulate mass society into passivity. Consumption of pop culture's easy pleasures made available by the mass communications media renders people docile and content, no matter how difficult their circumstances.

Take Netflix for example. Its average user leaks an impressive amount of data, including location, devices and viewing habits at a granular level. Never before have television operators had access to such precise information. Jonathan Friedland, Communications Director for Netflix, said, 'We know what people watch on Netflix and we're able with a high degree of confidence to understand how big a likely audience is for a given show based on people's viewing habits.'[18] As a result Netflix was able to analyse viewing data that showed

an overlap between circles of viewers who enjoyed films starring Kevin Spacey, films directed by David Fincher, and lovers of the 1990s BBC series *House of Cards*. This insight led to its decision to commission a remake of the series to wide acclaim. Think of this as data-driven creativity.

Renaissance Learning, a US-based assessment and learning analytics company, was acquired for $1.1 billion in 2014. This was a staggering figure for an educational technology firm, even one that had been in business for 30 years. Started as a software company with a software-based reading assessment tool, the company developed a range of products centred around computer-based literacy and maths learning and assessment. As the world shifted to cloud-based computing, the company was able to scan all of the assessment data from over 30,000 participating schools to improve teachers' lesson plans and how they track their students' performance. The company handles 45 million online assessments of student progress each year and these inform the development of their learning analytics software that is designed to serve up relevant learning experiences to keep learners on track to meet state examinations.

Across every spectrum of society we can see the easy wins afforded by the tsunami of data that is upon us and rapidly increasing computing power which, if we are to believe our futurology pundits, will create supercomputers 1,000 times faster than the human brain by 2030. Unbridled network capitalism will ensure that no stone is left unturned in the reinvention of education, healthcare, science, media, employment, entertainment and even governance, creating a society that is not unlike the one Aldous Huxley predicted in his novel *Brave New World*.

As Neil Postman maintains in his book *Amusing Ourselves to Death*, it was Orwell who feared that the truth would be hidden from us whereas Huxley feared that the truth would be hidden in plain sight in a sea of irrelevance. Orwell feared we would become a captive culture, while Huxley feared we would become a trivial culture. Huxley remarked that the civil libertarians and rationalists that oppose tyranny failed to take into account mankind's insatiable appetite for distractions. In summary, Orwell feared that what we hate would ruin us, whereas Huxley feared that what we love would ruin us.

When Edward Snowden revealed that government agencies had identified and were exploiting the opportunities afforded by big data, algorithms and ever-increasing computing power, many of us assumed that Orwell's nightmare had come to pass. But perhaps this is only the beginning. Perhaps an algorithmic society based on big data that tells us the *what* rather than the *why* is much more like Huxley's *Brave New World*.

After all, the numbers don't lie. Or do they?

Cambridge
Providence
New York City

San Francisco

Los Angeles
San Diego

United States of America

A question we asked ourselves in editorial pre-production meetings was how we might write a book about the global impact of digital technology on learning without constantly referring to developments in the US or at least without ending up with a section in the book that was noticeably thicker than other countries we visited as part of the research. This wasn't out of a prejudice towards the US but because we didn't want to travel over the ground that has been exhaustively documented elsewhere by educational technology evangelists and in promotional material masquerading as white papers. We didn't want this book to overlook the structural changes and contextual issues that need to be taken into account before real transformation in learning and teaching can occur, with or without technology, anywhere in the world. That is, we didn't want our book to tell a story that to transform learning all you needed was an Internet connection and a smartphone or different variations thereof.

In a way, as one might describe the UK as the cradle of the Industrial Revolution, one could describe the US as the cradle of the Digital Revolution. We can debate where the computer, web, or other components of this revolution were invented, but it is America and American corporations that are really beating the drum to which we dance in today's digital world. Even where dominance has been held elsewhere in the world, it hasn't taken the US long to challenge and surpass it. Europe was, for many years, the dominant leader in mobile telephony. We positively basked in the sophistication of our fancy handsets, roaming charges, SMS messaging, phones that we talked through and network operators as gatekeepers for our digital content. Apple made its first

phone and the rest is history. American science fiction writer Bruce Sterling said in 2012 that it made less sense to talk about the Internet as a culture or an infrastructure any more, given that today what we usually mean is something shaped by one or all of five corporations: Apple, Google, Amazon, Facebook or Microsoft. Our digital technologies will work perfectly well within any one of these industrial silos and their temporary allies, but will be broken between them and their competitors.

This could be a bigger problem than we imagine given that we're not simply talking about the inconvenience of incompatible plugs and sockets that we fix with an adaptor when we travel between countries. These corporations are empires in their own right, some even wealthier and some might say even more influential, than their country of origin. The oil fuelling this third phase of the Industrial Revolution is personal data. That's your data, my data, your neighbours' data and your children's data. It is the ability to capture as much of this global data as possible and make sense of it that determines the market value of these corporations and the ones they acquire. Every digital device you own or use is a potential data point and, to succeed, these digital empires have spread from the desktop to the home to the pocket to the point where, as a result, almost everything we do is recorded in some form.

At the time of writing, Facebook just acquired the phone messaging company WhatsApp, a two-year-old company with 33 employees, for a staggering $19 billion. That's more money than the entire global music industry makes in a year. The reason that this acquisition made sense to Facebook was the value of the continuous stream of data from WhatsApp's 450 million subscribers who send one billion messages a day, and how it believes that population will grow.

This technology uses computer-based statistical analysis of the data to understand how a student is performing and matches its learning provision accordingly.

The sheer volume of data combined with the right algorithms has the potential to improve our lives, from discovering cures for cancer to predicting the things we need even before we know we need them. They might even help students learn better according to the standards that we assess, or believe are important. Such capability means that our window into the digital universe can be personalised and mediated so that it remains constantly relevant. That window used to be the web browser on the screen of your desktop PC or laptop but today it is your mobile phone and the systems that mediate your books, news, communications and entertainment. Tomorrow you may be wearing it on your body, seeing it through your glasses and interacting with it via everyday domestic appliances from refrigerators to vehicles. The more granular this data is, the more seamless – or 'frictionless' as they say in Silicon Valley – our engagement with the world will appear. As long as we remain within one of the silos mentioned earlier.

Personally I wonder if the world is ready to accept this level of digital globalisation, or even if we have really thought it through. It's proven very hard for nations to resist the seduction of convenience that these leading digital corporations provide. Where governments do resist they are accused of being sinister, anti-freedom or anti-democratic, when it could be argued that the hegemony represented by these corporations is in itself all of these things. When we consider a connected society that, as the title of this book suggests, is transforming learning, what do we imagine this means? What is it transforming into if access and equity within the digital world is far from evenly distributed?

Our schedule for the US was always going to be challenging, since within a little over a week we had meetings and visits planned for New York, Cambridge, Providence, Los Angeles, San Francisco, San Diego and then back to New York. With a mixture of trains, planes and automobiles we managed, with only one of us missing a flight (me), receiving a speeding ticket (me again) and losing his sense of humour over a first-world problem concerning a hotel room (yours truly). We visited two impressive schools: Quest to Learn in New York and High Tech High in San Diego. We met with Sir Ken Robinson in Los Angeles, Professors Noam Chomsky and Mitch Resnick at MIT, and visited edX, TED-Ed and IDEO.

It was breathtaking.

'I wonder if the world is ready to accept this level of digital globalisation, or even if we have really thought it through. It's proven very hard for nations to resist the seduction of convenience that these leading digital corporations provide.'

'…as one might describe the UK as the cradle of the Industrial Revolution, one could describe the US as the cradle of the Digital Revolution.'

'It doesn't matter
what we cover.
It matters what
you discover.'

Noam Chomsky is one of today's greatest living intellectuals. Born in 1928 in Pennsylvania, he is himself the product of a progressive education. As a child, he attended Oak Lane Day School, regarded as experimental when it was founded in 1916 upon the principles of honouring a child's individuality in a setting that fosters intellectual, creative, academic and personal growth in the Dewey tradition.

Chomsky has been an influential academic for his entire career. He has been called the father of modern linguistics for his groundbreaking work in human language acquisition. He is a prominent figure in analytic philosophy, a tradition characterised by an emphasis on clarity and argument. Chomsky has worked within MIT since 1955 and is now Professor Emeritus. He has authored more than 100 books and influenced fields including artificial intelligence, cognitive science, computer science, logic, mathematics, music theory and analysis, political science, programming language theory and psychology.

Regarded as a figure of enlightenment and an inspiration for political dissenters, Chomsky has been arrested on multiple occasions for his anti-war activism. He asserts that authority, unless justified, is inherently illegitimate, and that the burden of proof is on those in authority. If this burden can't be met, the authority in question should be dismantled. Critical of both the American state capitalist system and the authoritarian branches of socialism, he argues that libertarian socialist values are the proper extension of classical liberalism to an advanced industrial context, and that society should be highly organised and based on democratic control of communities and workplaces.

Having been influenced by Chomsky myself, I was keen to learn his insights about how we educate ourselves and met him in his office at MIT for this interview.

Graham Brown-Martin: What is the purpose of education?

Noam Chomsky: Well, we can ask ourselves what the purpose of an educational system is, and,

'The purpose of education then, from that point of view, is just to help people determine how to learn on their own.'

of course, there are sharp differences on this matter. There's the traditional interpretation that comes from the Enlightenment, which holds that the highest goal in life is to inquire and create, to search the riches of the past to try to internalise the parts of them that are significant to you and carry that quest for understanding further in your own way.

The purpose of education then, from that point view, is just to help people determine how to learn on their own. It's you, the learner, who is going to achieve in the course of education and it's really up to you what you'll master, where you'll go, how you'll use it, how you'll go on to produce something new and exciting for yourself, maybe for others. That's one concept of education.

The other concept is simply indoctrination. People have taken the idea that from childhood, young people have to be placed into a framework in which they'll follow orders, accept existing frameworks, not challenge and so on, and this is often quite explicit. For example, after the activism of the 1960s, there was a great concern across much of the educated spectrum that young people were just getting too free and independent, that the country was becoming too democratic and so on. In fact, there's an important study. It was called 'The Crisis of Democracy',[19] meaning too much democracy, claiming that there are certain institutions responsible for the indoctrination of the young, so [to paraphrase]: They're not doing their job properly, that is schools, universities, churches. We have to change them so that they carry out the job of indoctrination and control more effectively. That's actually coming from the liberal interna-

tionalist spectrum of educated opinion. In fact, since that time, there have been many measures taken to try to turn the educational system towards more control, more indoctrination, more vocational training, imposing a debt which traps students, young people, into a life of conformity and so on. That's the exact opposite of what I referred to as it traditionally comes out of the Enlightenment. There's a constant struggle between those.

In the colleges and the schools, do you train for passing tests or do you train for creative inquiry, pursuing interests that are aroused by material that's presented and you want to pursue either on your own or with cooperation with others? And this goes all the way through up to graduate school and research, just two different ways of looking at the world when you get to it. Take a research institution like the one we're now in [MIT], at the graduate level. It essentially follows the Enlightenment tradition. In fact, science couldn't progress unless it was based on inculcation of the urge to challenge, to question a doctrine, question authority, to search for alternatives, use your imagination, act freely under your own impulses, cooperatively work with others. You can see this just by walking down the halls.

That's my view of what an educational system should be like down to kindergarten, but there certainly are powerful structures in society which would prefer people to be indoctrinated, conform, not ask too many questions, be obedient, fulfil the roles that are assigned to them and don't try to shake systems of power and authority. Those are choices we have to make either as people —wherever we stand in the educational system— as students, as teachers, as people on the outside trying to help shape the direction in which we think it ought to go.

Graham: What are your views on the kind of standardised testing that we use in schools today to measure student performance and ability?

Chomsky: There is, in the recent period particularly, an increasing shaping of education from the early years on towards passing examinations. Taking tests can be of some use, both for the person just taking the test to see what I know and where I am, what I've achieved, what I haven't. Now for instructors, what should be changed and improved in developing the course of instruction?

Beyond that, they don't really tell you very much. I know for many, many years, I've been on admissions committees for entry to an advanced graduate programme, maybe one of the most advanced anywhere, and we, of course, pay some attention to test results, but really not too much. A person can do magnificently on every test and understand very little. All of us who have been through schools and colleges and universities are very familiar with this. You can be in some, say, course that you have no interest in and there's demand that you pass a test, and you can study hard for the test and you can ace it and do fine, and a couple of weeks later, you forgot what the topic was. I'm sure we've all had that experience. I know I have.

It can be a useful device if it contributes to the constructive purposes of education. If it's just a set of hurdles you have to cross, it can turn out to be not only meaningless, but it can divert you away from things you want to be doing. I see this regularly when I talk to teachers. Just to give you one experience from a couple of weeks ago, but there's plenty like it. I have been talking to a group which included many school teachers, and one of them was a sixth-grade teacher, teaches kids, I guess ten or 11, or something like that. She came up to me afterwards, and I've been talking about these things, and she told me about one experience that she just had in her class, after one of the classes. A little girl came up to her and said she was really interested in something that came up and she asked how she could get the teacher to give her some ideas about how to look into it further, and the teacher was compelled to tell her, 'I'm sorry, but you can't do that. You have to study to pass this national exam that's coming. That's going to determine your future.' The teacher didn't say it, but it's going to determine [her] future like whether [she] may be hired, and so on.

The system is geared to getting the children to pass hurdles, but not to learn and understand and explore. That child would have been better off if she had been allowed to explore what she was interested in and maybe not do so well in the test about things she wasn't interested in. Not that they'll come along when they fit into her interest and concerns. I don't say that tests should be eliminated. They can be a useful educational tool, but ancillary, something that's just helping improve for ourselves, for instructors and others, what we're doing and tell us where we're going to be moving.

Passing tests doesn't begin to compare with searching and inquiring and pursuing topics that engage and excite us. That's far more significant than passing tests. In fact, if that's the kind of educational career that you're given the opportunity to pursue, you will remember what you've discovered. There's a famous physicist, a world-famous physicist right here at MIT who, like a lot of the senior faculty, was teaching freshmen courses. He once said that in his freshmen course, students will ask, 'What are we going to cover this semester?' His standard answer was, 'It doesn't matter what we cover. It matters what you discover.'

That's what teaching ought to be: inspiring students to discover on their own, to challenge if

'...the highest goal in life is to inquire and create, to search the riches of the past to try to internalise the parts of them that are significant to you and carry that quest for understanding further in your own way.'

they don't agree, to look for alternatives if they think there are better ones, to work through the great achievements of the past and try to master them on their own because they're interested in them. If that's the way teaching is done, students will really gain from it and will not really remember what they studied, but will be able to use it as a basis for growing on, on their own. Again, education is really aimed at just helping students get to the point where they can learn on their own because that's what you're going to do for your life, not just to absorb materials given to you from the outside and repeat them.

Graham: How do you believe that new digital technology can play a role in education?

Chomsky: Well, there certainly has been a very substantial growth in new technology, technology of communication, information access, interchange. It's truly a major change in the nature of the culture and society, but we should bear in mind that the technological changes that are taking place now, while they're significant, probably come nowhere near having as much impact as technological advances, let's say, a century ago, plus or minus.

The shift from a typewriter to a computer or a telephone to the email is significant, but I'm beginning to compare it with the shift from a sailing vessel to a telegraph. The time that it cut down in communication between, say, England the United States was extraordinary as compared with the changes taking place now. The same is true with other kinds of technology, like the introduction of, say, widespread plumbing in the city. It's had a huge effect on health, much more than the discovery of antibiotics. The changes are real and significant, but we should recognise that others have taken place, which in many ways are more dramatic.

As far as the technology itself and education are concerned, technology is basically neutral. It's like a hammer. The hammer doesn't care whether you use it to build a house or to torture someone, using it to crush somebody's skull. The hammer can do either. Same with the modern technology – the Internet and so on. The Internet

'As far as the technology itself and education are concerned, technology is basically neutral. It's like a hammer. The hammer doesn't care whether you use it to build a house or to torture someone, using it to crush somebody's skull. The hammer can do either.'

is extremely valuable, if you know what you're looking for. I use it all the time for research. I'm sure everyone does. If you know what you're looking for, you have a framework of understanding which directs you to particular things and lets you sideline lots of others, then this can be a very valuable tool. Of course, you always have to be willing to ask, 'Is my framework the right one? Maybe I ought to modify it, if there's something I look at that questions if I should rethink. How am I looking at things?'

You can't pursue any kind of inquiry without a relatively clear framework that's directing your search and helping you choose what's significant and what isn't, what can be put aside, what are to be pursued, what are to be challenged, what are to be developed, and so on. You can't expect somebody to become a biologist, say, by giving them access to the Harvard University biology library and saying, 'Just look through it.' That will give them nothing. The Internet is the same except magnified enormously. If you don't understand but know what you're looking for, if you don't have some conception of what matters —always, of course, with the proviso that you're willing to question it if it seems to be going

in the wrong direction— if you don't have that, [then] exploring the Internet is just picking out the random factoids that don't mean anything. So behind any significant use of contemporary technology —the Internet, communication systems, the web, whatever it may be— if there isn't some well-constructed directive, a conceptual apparatus, it is very unlikely to be helpful. It may turn out to be harmful. For example, a random exploration through the Internet turns out to be a cult generator. You pick out a factoid here and a factoid there, and somebody else reinforces it and all of a sudden you have a picture which has some factual basis, but nothing to do with the world.

You have to know how to evaluate, interpret and understand. Let's say biology, again. The person who wins the Nobel Prize in biology is not the person who read the most journal articles and those notes on them. He's a person who knew what to look for, cultivating that capacity to seek what's significant, always willing to question whether you're on the right track. That's what education is going to be about, whether it's using computers and the Internet or pencil and paper or books.

Graham: Do you think society should view education provision as an investment or a cost?

Chomsky: Well, education is discussed in terms of whether it's a worthwhile investment, [whether it creates] human capital that can be used for economic growth and so on. That's a very strange and very distorting way to even pose the question, I think.

Do we want to have a society of free, creative, independent individuals, able to appreciate and gain from the cultural achievements of the past and to act to on them? Do we want that or do we want people who can increase GDP? That's not the same thing as an education of the kind that, say, Bertrand Russell, John Dewey and others talked about. That's a value in itself. Whatever impact it has in society, it's a value because it helps create better human beings. After all, that's what an education system should be for.

On the other hand, if you want to look at it in terms of cost and benefits, take the new technology that we were just talking about. Where did that come from? Well, actually a lot of it was developed right where we're sitting. Down below where we now are, it was a major laboratory back in the 1950s —when I was employed, in fact— which had lots of scientists, engineers, people of all kinds of interests, philosophers, others, who were working on developing the basic character of, and even the basics of, the technology that is now common in computers and the Internet, for example.

We were pretty much in the public sector for decades. They just fund it in places like this where people were exploring the possibilities that were mostly unthought-of, unheard-of at that time, and some of them worked, some didn't. The ones that worked were finally converted into tools that people can use. That's the way scientific progress takes place. That's the way cultural progress takes place generally.

A classical artist, for example, came out of a tradition of craftsmanship that was developed over long periods with the master artisans, with others, and sometimes, you can rise on their shoulders and create new marvellous things, but it doesn't come from nowhere. If there isn't a lively cultural and educational system, which is geared towards encouraging creative exploration, independence of thought, the willingness to cross frontiers, to challenge accepted beliefs, and so on, if you don't have that, you're not going to get the technology that can lead to economic gains, though I don't see that as the prime purpose. Cultural enrichment and education, that's a part of it.

'I really do think the technologies, used the right way, can extend the ways that people experiment and explore and express themselves.'

The Lifelong Kindergarten, led by Mitch Resnick, is a research group within the MIT Media Lab which develops technologies that, in the spirit of the blocks and finger-paint of kindergarten, engage people in creative learning experiences. The group's objective is a world full of playfully creative people, who are constantly inventing new possibilities for themselves and their communities.

Resnick's group is the birthplace of numerous learning platforms that many now take for granted. LEGO's Mindstorms, an innovative robotics kit for children, was the result of an early collaboration with MIT. Scratch, a computer-game programming environment for children based on the principles of building blocks, is another widely used tool that was born from the Lifelong Kindergarten. Recent projects such as MaKey MaKey, the do-it-yourself cell phone and app inventor, are all being developed within this leading learning think tank.

I met with Mitch to learn more about the spirit of the Kindergarten and its value for lifelong learning.

Graham Brown-Martin: Mitch, tell me about the Lifelong Kindergarten.

Mitch Resnick: We call it that because I've always been inspired by the way children learn in kindergarten. At least, in the traditional kindergarten, kids spend a lot of time playfully designing and creating things, in collaboration with one another. In one corner of the room, there might be kids building towers out of wooden blocks. Somewhere else, they might be making pictures with finger paints. In the process they learn a lot. As they design and create, they learn about the stability of making a tower, how colours mix together.

Maybe what's even more important is they learn about the creative process, how to start with an idea and carry it out in collaboration with one another, and to make a final product. In the process, they start to develop as creative thinkers. I think that nothing is more important in the world today than learning to think and act

creatively. We're in a world that's changing more rapidly than ever before. Things we learn today may be obsolete tomorrow. People will be facing an uncertain future, so it would be so important for them to learn to come up with creative approaches to the unexpected things that they'll confront in the future.

I think in kindergarten kids get a good start. They start to develop as creative thinkers. Unfortunately, after kindergarten kids go into the traditional classroom, where they spend a lot of time listening to lectures, filling out worksheets. They really don't continue to develop as creative thinkers. I find the school system really isn't preparing young people for what's most needed today to be able to enter the world as a creative thinker that's ready to take on new challenges all of the time.

In fact, I'm worried because today's kindergartens are actually becoming more like the rest of school. You go into many kindergartens today, and kids are filling out phonics worksheets or looking at spelling flashcards. What we want to do is exactly the opposite. We want to make the rest of school, and the rest of life, more like kindergarten. That's why we call our group the Lifelong Kindergarten Group.

Graham: A schools minister in the UK recently complained that she thought children in kindergarten were 'running around with no sense of purpose' and that there should be more 'school-like' discipline for two-year-olds.[20] Why do you suppose there are calls from the political spectrum for kindergarten to mirror school life in this way?

'...the most important part of learning is being able to understand how to make sense of a new situation.'

Mitch: I think there are a few reasons why the schools we see today are the way they are. Some of it is historical, that some of the schools were set up hundreds of years ago, preparing young people for a very different society. If you're preparing young people for society where economically you are going to go and work in a factory and do things repetitively, that might call for a different type of education. I hope if I was living back then, I would have argued against that education. We could at least see some rationale for it if they really were set up to prepare people for what was needed in the workplace at the time.

I think one reason schools haven't changed much is because there's partly some inertia to stay that way. Also, when people want to evaluate, and hold schools accountable, it's pretty easy to evaluate how well students can come back with specific facts that they were taught. The things that are important in today's society, learning to think creatively, to work collaboratively, to reason analytically, to be able to learn continuously, those are much more difficult to evaluate.

Schools end up teaching the things they know how to evaluate. They know how to evaluate people reciting back facts. They end up valuing the things that they can assess, whereas I think instead they should be assessing the things that they value, but it's hard. The things that I value most help people learn to think creatively or collaboratively. Those are difficult things to assess. Since schools don't know how to assess them, they end up focusing on the things that they do know how to assess.

Graham: Comparison of academic performance testing —for example PISA scores— against creative thinking metrics such as entrepreneurship appear to show a negative correlation. What do you think is happening here?

Mitch: I remember a number of years ago I visited some schools in Singapore. Because I had been involved in developing the LEGO Mindstorms Robotics kit, they took me to a school where they introduced me to the National Junior Robotics champion, a 13-year-old, and he showed me the robot he had built out of LEGO. He showed me everything it could do. I was impressed. I even suggested some other questions. What would you need to change to make it do this? Actually, he was very creative in coming up with different solutions to it.

I was impressed with him and his friends. I asked the teacher, 'This is great. How did you integrate this into the school day?' She looked at me like I was crazy. She said, 'We would never do this during the school day. During the school day, they must do their math exercises. This is for after school.' It was really striking to me. Obviously, in some way they recognised that this was important, and it's great that they made space after school, but during the school day, you had to do your math exercises.

I think it was because Singapore is one of those countries which has performed very well on the international math and science exams, and they are very proud of their performance, so they really didn't want to change anything in the school day that harmed that performance. Yet, there is an irony. I was invited to Singapore by the Ministry of Education because they knew that the schools weren't performing well in terms of preparing young people for their lives and society. The companies in Singapore had started to complain to the government saying that the young people, when they graduated from high school, weren't prepared for the workplace. They knew how to do very specific things, but a new issue arose. The students wouldn't know what to do, so the Ministry of Education invited me to come to talk about ways of bringing creativity into the school system so that young people would be better prepared for life and the workplace and society. You could still see the resistance from the school system because they were so proud of their performance in the international exams.

It's really challenging to make these changes when people still value so highly the scores on these exams, even though, in some parts of society, they know it's not doing the right job for young people, helping them prepare for their lives in the future.

'...teachers should be model learners, that kids should come and learn to become good learners from their teachers who show them some of the best tricks of the trade of how to approach a problem when you're puzzled by it.'

Graham: Do you see a time when what and how we assess will change?

Mitch: I certainly hope that the way that we do exams and assessments in the future will change. It is crazy today that they have to cut themselves off from the rest of the world during those two or three hours while they're taking the exam. That's not the way anybody does things in the world, so what are we examining? What are we assessing? It's certainly not preparation for life in the world. Life in the world was never like that.

When I have a question, I look something up online, I call a friend. How resourceful I am in finding out the information I need, that's what's going to help me succeed in the world and thrive in the world, yet exams are testing something very different. They are testing something, but not something which we really will make use of in the world. I certainly hope that this will change over time because it really doesn't fit the needs of society. There's a real disconnect. Hopefully, it will change over time.

Even the idea of sitting down for an exam – I probably would push that away as well. Even if you allowed people to be connected and talk to other people, examining people for what they can do in a certain fixed period of time, that's a thin slice of what you really need in the world. I'd much prefer that people get evaluated by the things that they've created, to have a portfolio assessment approach, where people create a portfolio of their different creations that they do in different subject areas. Then someone can assess that portfolio.

In many ways, that's the way I'm evaluated here as a professor at MIT. When I get promoted at MIT, which is clearly a very distinguished university in the world, they don't give me an exam. I don't take any exam to get my promotion at MIT. They take a look at what I've produced, the papers I produce, the products I produce, the lectures I've given. Then they ask people, they look at my portfolio. Is he making an important contribution? Is he a leader in the field that he's in? No one ever tries to quantify that.

Somehow we trust MIT to make these very important decisions. Who gets promoted to be a professor at MIT is a very important decision for the university, and yet they don't try to give an exam or have a quantification. They look at my portfolio. Why can't we do that with third graders or sixth graders? If it's good enough for MIT, why isn't it good enough for third graders?

Graham: How do you see technology being introduced into the learning process successfully as an act of liberation rather than automation?

Mitch: Since I'm a professor here at MIT, and I'm at the MIT Media Lab, which is a world leader in the creation of innovative technologies, some people might expect that I'd be a proponent of all uses of technology in education and learning, but that's far from the truth. In fact, when I look around, and I see the way that most technology is used in schools today, I shudder, I get very frustrated by it, and I think many of the uses of technologies in schools are counterproductive because they're sustaining and perpetuating a traditional approach to education, which is really no longer relevant for today's students.

'...nothing is more important in the world today than learning to think and act creatively.'

Too often, technology just gets used to perpetuate the pedagogy that's in place. For many, many years, schools have been organised around a teacher delivering information to students. In many classrooms now, they just put a piece of technology that delivers information to the students. Nothing has really changed except you've replaced who's delivering the information. I think what we need to do is rethink our whole approach to learning and education. It's not about delivering information.

Of course sometimes it's useful to get information, but we know that the most important part of learning is being able to understand how to make sense of a new situation, how to create things in the world, how to experiment, how to explore, how to express yourself, communicate ideas. For me, when I look to see if a piece of technology is being used effectively, I ask whether it is enabling the learners to explore, to experiment, to express themselves. Because those are the core important learning experiences.

I'm excited about the potential of technology because I really do think the technologies, used the right way, can extend the ways that people experiment and explore and express themselves. I'm very hopeful about the potential, but then often frustrated that the technology doesn't get used in that way.

Graham: With an emphasis on play and the sorts of things that aren't happening within our existing schooling system, do you think that school is the best place for learning to occur?

Mitch: Unfortunately, schools, as they are today, generally aren't the best places for learning to occur, but I do think there is a value in bringing people together to learn. The idea of having an institution where people get together to learn, I think is a great idea. The problem is how many of today's schools are organised. If a school is set up in order to just deliver a fixed set of information to the kids who come, I don't think that's going to prepare them very well for the future.

On the other hand, if it's a place for kids to come to learn from one another, to share ideas with one another, to collaborate on projects, to work with teachers and mentors who can help share their experiences and their expertise, that's a great opportunity. We've created some after-school centres, like the computer clubhouses, where young people come and learn to design and create an experiment with new technologies.

We think those are great places for kids to come, and they learn a lot when they're there, not just about the technology, and not just about mathematical or scientific ideas, but about the process of learning and about the creative process.

I think that's what a school should be as well. When kids come to school, it should be an opportunity for them to learn to become better learners, and that teachers should be model learners, that kids should come and learn to become good learners from their teachers who show them some of the best tricks of the trade of how to approach a problem when you're puzzled by it, how to persist when you become frustrated. Those are things that good learners know how to do. Kids, by working with others, can get a much better idea of how they too can develop to become creative learners.

llk.media.mit.edu

Quest to Learn, one of their 14-year-old students told me, is a school that everyone has heard of, apart from the people of New York City. By this she meant that Quest to Learn receives a constant stream of visitors, like me, from all over the world and yet many of her neighbourhood friends outside of the school haven't heard of it. Designed from the ground up by a team of teachers and game designers based on 30 years of learning research, it is a bold initiative that redesigns the curriculum and teaching practice, taking influence from the way young people engage with games.

By games they don't specifically mean video games and indeed, despite being known as the 'game-based learning school' in the popular media, there is little evidence of what we typically might think of when we think games. As Co-director Arana Shapiro tells me, 'People expect to see our students sitting around playing video or board games and while we do use such games from time to time, the reference to games is in the mechanics we deploy within our teaching and learning strategy.' To get an idea of what's happening here I visit their Mission Lab, which is an embedded learning design studio within the school where teachers work alongside game and curriculum designers to design flexible learning experiences for their classes.

One of the principles of the teaching style draws heavily on the gaming concept of simulation in which learning is placed in an applied context, rather than simply memorising things by rote, while employing cross-disciplinary skills to solve a particular problem or challenge. Students are actively encouraged to work in collaborative teams which effectively act as self-organising learning environments in between teacher-directed segments of a given class. The self-organising approach is something that has also been recently championed by Professor Sugata Mitra *(see interview on page 308)* although these principles were adopted by Quest to Learn since it opened.

The school has developed a unique standards-based, integrated curriculum designed to mimic the action and design principles of games by generating what they describe as a compelling 'need to know' in the classroom. Each school term, students encounter a series of increasingly complex narrative challenges, games or quests, where learning, knowledge sharing, feedback, reflection and next steps emerge as a natural function of play.

In one example, over the course of one term in the integrated science and math learning domain, 'The Way Things Work', sixth graders help a shrunken mad scientist, lost inside the human body, navigate the systems he encounters and report back to his research lab.

Ross Flatt is one of the Being, Space and Place teachers at Quest to Learn which means that he teaches history, English language and humanities in a way that makes them relevant to the present day. He tells me that the benefits of bringing game-like approaches to teaching is that 'it means we're putting people in some sort of a situation. For example, when students are working on seventh-grade Being, Space and Place, they are spies for King George III and the British Empire. They're scoping out the New World to see if it would be habitable, to see if they should go there, to see if it's worth colonising and then, later on, when this colonisation is unhappy, how should England deal with this. They're like agents, they're secret agents working there. The game-like experiences immediately make it narrative-based and it gives the kids this phenomenal entry point and what we called a "need to know". It gives them a good reason why they should be learning this stuff, doing their readings, doing their homework and coming to class ready to go, and ready to be engaged. That game, a lot of the time, will hook the kids in.'

Liam, a 15-year-old tenth grader, enjoys this way of learning. 'The idea of making education not just a simple "learn this, regurgitate this, answer this question, and do this test", but instead, have it be a fluent conversation, and have it be more engaging, using game design, and using game-like thinking, was something that really attracted me to the school,' he explained.

The designers and directors of the school have learned a lot since it opened in 2009 and an important lesson has been about the role of the teacher. Arana is candid when she explains, 'Initially we imagined that teachers would essentially be content specialists supported by designers, but it soon became clear that there was far more to teaching than simply knowing the subject, specifically their ability to engage learners by being engaged themselves.'

Perhaps inevitably, there is a frustration with standardised testing. The Quest to Learn school, however progressive it is within current teaching practice and curriculum design, is ultimately measured by its test scores which weren't what they'd hoped in the first instance, despite falling within local averages. These scores have since improved and the thinking at the school is that the emphasis on new ways of learning neglected the training that students required to perform well in tests.

Rebecca Gardner, a Point of View teacher for sixth grade, doesn't think standardised testing is such an issue in itself. Rather it is the prominence that it now takes within the teaching profession. She tells me, 'I think standardised testing serves a purpose. If you look at Finland's education system, they still have standardised testing but it's not used as the only thing to drive education. There's also a lot of authentic assessment. I don't think we have to do away with standardised testing. I don't think we have to do away with standards, but what I think we need to do is stop treating them like they're the be-all-end-all of learning. They are not the only measure and they should never be treated as the only measure. Moreover, if we focus on them, and we only focus on them, the more we raise a generation of kids who don't want to learn because learning means taking a test. Learning means learning to do a conformist thing. If we want a society that gets ahead, we need to teach children not to conform but to experiment and to figure things out and to problem solve.'

Research is under way, conducted by the Institute of Play, who designed Quest to Learn, to generate comparative data on student proficiency in 21st-century skills like systems thinking, creative problem-solving, collaboration, time management and identity formation. Preliminary results are promising and today students from the school are performing at or above New York City public school averages on standardised tests.

Emony, a 15-year-old Quest to Learn student, tells me that she has to be careful when she describes her school to her friends who don't attend. 'I have to talk about it in a specific way, because if I say the wrong thing, they'll think we're only playing games, and we're only on computers, but we're really not. We take notes in a classroom, just like everybody else, for those people that do like to take notes, but we also play the games for the people that need that extra push… I have to explain to [my friends] really carefully that we're learning in different forms.'

www.q2l.org

'People expect to see our students sitting around playing video or board games and while we do use such games from time to time, the reference to games is in the mechanics we deploy within our teaching and learning strategy.'

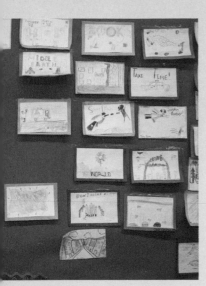

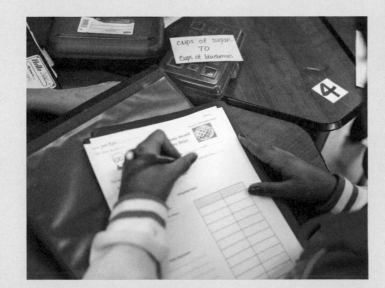

'The school has developed a unique standards-based integrated curriculum designed to mimic the action and design principles of games.'

Arana Shapiro is a member of the founding team that created Quest to Learn, a New York City public (state) school for 6th to 12th graders in the Chelsea neighbourhood of Manhattan.

Founded in 2009 in partnership with the Gates Foundation and the MacArthur backed non-profit Institute of Play, the entire school is organised around principles of games and connected learning. The students are constantly challenged to incorporate 21st-century literacies like iteration and systems thinking into their learning, to follow their own interests, to reach beyond the boundaries of the school, and to work together.

I met with Arana, who first started teaching in 1999, whilst spending a day at Quest to Learn and these are some of the things we discussed.

Graham Brown-Martin: What is the background to Quest to Learn?

Arana Shapiro: Quest to Learn started as an answer to the question of engagement in middle school. Research shows that when kids move from elementary school to middle school, there's a drop in engagement. Quest to Learn was started to see if it would be possible to take the structure of games and what is great about them, and what engages kids, and move that into a school space to see if it helps to engage kids within a classroom.

Graham: What is it about games that you think is so engaging and how can they relate to learning?

Arana: If you think about any game, it is a space where you're learning something. In order to progress and to play a game, you need to learn the skills that the game believes are important for you to be able to play. The thing about games that makes them engaging learning spaces is really that things are very clear. The goal is very clear. You are constantly getting this feedback that is immediate and ongoing. There's something very immersive about a game, there's a suspension of disbelief. You step into the space of a game and you take on the role that the game asks you to take on and then you behave the way that role asks you to behave.

There's also a very clear need to know. There's a reason why you're learning all the things that you're learning. You're asked very immediately to apply that learning and that skill to some kind of a context or problem. Those kinds of things are the reasons why games are engaging for players. Quest to Learn looks at whether or not you could take the things that make games engaging, move them into a school space, and then make the school space engaging for the learners.

Graham: Does that suggest that students are playing video games all day?

Arana: Oftentimes people think that because we talk about games a lot at Quest to Learn, kids are going to be sitting around, playing games, goofing off or playing a game really unintentionally and learning through that experience. That's not what it means. Kids do play games at Quest to Learn. Sometimes they're digital. Oftentimes they're analogue games. What we're more interested in is something that we call game-like learning. It's more about kids, about creating a curriculum that will engage kids the way that games engage kids.

So we may come up with these complex challenges, then move kids through a curriculum with a trajectory that asks them to solve little pieces of the challenge with game skills and expertise along the way so that they are then able to solve a bigger challenge that they wouldn't have previously been able to solve had they not moved through the curriculum or through the game-like experience.

Graham: Some might say this is like chocolate-coating broccoli. Don't the students still have to take the state's standardised tests at the end?

Arana: Kids at Quest to Learn do need to get through the tests. For us the tests are sort of a baseline experience. We are standards-based but there's more than that. It is about getting the kids the skills and knowledge that this kind of curriculum will offer. We think about things like collaboration, complex problem solving and systems thinking. If kids are exposed to challenges that don't have easy solutions or problems that can only be solved by really digging in and trying different ways of solving them, they gain skills that are applicable to the real world in ways that gaming content and understanding facts about something alone aren't.

It's really about this kind of solving of complex problems and collaboration and teamwork and empathy and design. All the things that you need to be able to exist in the real world. These kinds of immersive spaces are able to give them experience with that.

Graham: What is your approach to designing and creating your curriculum with game designers?

Arana: The curriculum at Quest to Learn is co-created by teachers, game designers and curriculum experts who are experts in learning and what it means to learn something deeply. When teachers come in, they come as content and pedagogy experts and game designers come in as experts in realising, engaging and creating engaging spaces for learning. Then we have a curriculum designer who really behaves as an intermediary who can speak the language of the game designer and the language of the teacher and help to move the collaboration forward.

The curriculum is always created starting with what we want kids to learn and then thinking about what the bigger ideas are, what the teams are, what the essential questions that we want kids to be asking are. Then we think about what kind of immersive engaging spaces and problems we can give kids that will engage them in a game-like way.

'It's more about kids, about creating a curriculum that will engage kids the way that games engage kids.'

Graham: You mentioned the teacher as content specialist. Do we really need teachers?

Arana: For us at Quest to Learn the role of the teacher is so important. When we began the school, we thought to ourselves, if we create this really engaging curriculum, if we just write the curriculum and it's game-like, maybe it doesn't matter who teaches it. Maybe it can be anybody and maybe these teachers are just coming in as content experts and that's all. What we found out very quickly was that the teacher actually makes a huge difference in the engagement of the kids and in the success of the curriculum. Teachers come in, in a lot of schools, and are given curriculum that they need to teach. They just teach their curriculum year after year.

What we think is really special about class is that teachers come in with content that they know needs to be taught to kids but then they are also able to add. They're creating curriculums so they're able to add what they feel is important. They're able to add their interest into the curriculum. They're able to mould it and shape it so it becomes something that they are really interested in teaching. Then it's really about the delivery. Teachers are the ones who are facilitating this game-like learning and their enthusiasm and expertise in how to engage kids and run a classroom, making sure that kids feel heard and special and important and facilitating collaboration, are so important to the success of the curriculum at Quest to Learn.

Graham: How do you recruit your teaching staff and prepare them for this style of teaching and curriculum?

Arana: We have a pretty intense recruitment process for teachers that includes a lot of interviews and demo lessons and coming to open houses and learning about the school. We actually really believe that just as much as we're interviewing teachers, we want them to be interviewing us. We don't want teachers to be here unless they're buying into this way of teaching. It's a different way of teaching. For us it's important that they really want to be here. We're also looking for teachers who are really open to

'There's something very immersive about a game, there's a suspension of disbelief.'

learning new things, who are risk takers, who are passionate about kids learning, not just passionate about them passing the test.

We know that teachers aren't going to come in knowing how to teach this way but there's an openness and a risk-taking way of being and, if we believe you have those things, we can turn you into a fantastic Quest to Learn teacher. If you don't have those things then it's hard to do.

Graham: Do your teachers need to be good video gamers?

Arana: No. In fact, I don't even know if we have very many teachers who are gamers *per se*. For us, it really is about dedication, a passion about how kids learn and what you're feeling is about the best way that kids learn. If that's in line with how we're thinking, and there's an openness to reshaping or refining your practice as a teacher, then we're good to go. But if you're not interested in developing your practice as a teacher then this would not be the right place for you.

There are teachers who are out there in the world and interested in Quest to Learn or just thinking about games and learning or game-like learning. You have to be a really reflective person. You have to be able to look at your teaching and be self-critical and uncomfortable and a little bit willing to not know how something is going to go. That's really important.

Graham: Do you think that Quest to Learn can be scaled up through the New York or US education system?

Arana: I think Quest to Learn is unique because of the people who are a part of it. It's not some-

thing that I think can be separated from that. It exists the way it exists because of the people who are a part of it. Each time a teacher leaves or each time a new teacher comes, it becomes a different thing. In order to move it somewhere else, I think that needs to be understood so that if we try to take this model and place it somewhere else the probability that it's going to look very different, based on the people who are involved in it, is high.

That's OK, right? It's about understanding that that's OK and then really trying to figure out what pieces of the model you can take and implement somewhere else and then what pieces can be modified and customised based on the people who are there.

Graham: Whilst students' skills in many areas improved, I understand that scores on the skills that were being tested dropped. What happened?

Arana: This was early on in our tenure as a school. In the first year we had the sixth graders who were doing all these really amazing math things. They were solving all these problems and they were very much in this real-world context. Then they took these standardised math tests and they weren't terrible but they didn't do as well as we had expected them to do based on the kind of work that they were doing throughout the year. We talked to the kids about it, we talked to parents about it and we looked at the test scores and where they were struggling.

What we concluded at the end of all that looking, was that we had taught them how to think and use math in a very applied way but we hadn't actually taught them how to do math in a test-taking way. The truth is, for better or for worse, the tests are here and test taking is a skill in itself. That was something that we had to grapple with. We didn't actually prepare them to take the test. We prepared them with context but we didn't prepare them to take the test.

We started to do some work just with how you answer questions like this. You know how to apply all this stuff in context, and that's wonderful, but if somebody just asks you to use this computational skill, how do we prepare you to just do that? There's a reality. We exist in reality and test taking is part of it. It's a skill just like any other skill. Now we do spend some time just preparing kids to take a test which we don't actually think is wasted time because in the world you have to do things like that.

Graham: What do you think your students' future looks like and how do you think Quest to Learn helps them?

Arana: I think the thing about the future of the kids at Quest to Learn that we are trying to remind ourselves of all the time is that we actually don't know what their future is going to look like, right? Things are changing so fast. We have no idea what sixth graders' future is going to look like when they leave us, let alone graduate from college if they go to college. College may not even be something kids are going to. We don't know what's going to happen. It's the responsibility of the school to then think about what kinds of skills we can give kids that will help them succeed, even if we don't know what the context is that they're going to have to succeed in.

A lot of other competencies —besides the state standards, besides the real-life context stuff— are focused on the kinds of skills that we can give kids to succeed in, no matter what kinds of jobs are out there and what kind of world they're living in. Things like solving complex problems, systems thinking, collaboration and teamwork. Really, the skills that allow you to be successful in any subject matter are the things that kids who graduate from Quest to Learn will take with them. Those are the trademarks of a Quest kid. Those are the things that are really important to us.

'If kids are exposed to challenges that don't have easy solutions or problems that can only be solved by really digging in and trying different ways of solving them, they gain skills that are applicable to the real world.'

'I think our understanding of technology is naive for many reasons. It's because we are still in that drunken, sort of leftover New Year's Eve party of the dot-com boom and all the Internet this, that, whatever, which is not dissimilar to when electricity was invented.'

I met John Maeda while he was President of the Rhode Island School of Design, shortly before he left to join Silicon Valley venture capital firm Kleiner Perkins Caufield & Byers, as its first design partner.

Maeda started out as a software engineering student at MIT, completing Bachelor's and Master's degrees before studying in Japan at Tsukuba University's Institute of Art and Design to complete his PhD in design. As an artist, Maeda's early work redefined the use of electronic media as a tool for expression by combining computer programming with traditional artistic techniques, laying the groundwork for the interactive motion graphics that are taken for granted on the web today.

During his six years at RISD, Maeda led the 'STEM to STEAM' movement to transform the traditional STEM subjects (science, technology, engineering and maths) to STEAM by adding art as a core subject, championing its inclusion in research policy, business and core education from kindergarten to graduation. Under his leadership the number of students applying to study at RISD increased along with the number of financial aid packages offered; tuition fee increases were their lowest in decades.

Graham Brown-Martin: There's a lot of emphasis globally around STEM subjects with the result that creative and design subjects are being sidelined. Is this a problem?

John Maeda: STEM has become an imperative. It's because we believe that technology innovation creates new opportunities, new economic opportunities. Think about the moon shot. We talk about it as an abstract idea, but there was a real moon shot which required a lot of physics and math and everything to make that rocket get there. It didn't require art or design of course, no creativity, just technology. But in reality it was influenced by creativity, even the dream to go to the moon. We have always thought of it as human beings, and so somehow we think that the *what* is more important than the *why*, and that's our tendency.

If we think about the dot-com boom, that was all technology and, therefore, that was good for the economy. So we need STEM to do more of that. At the same time, though, STEM as a policy has not played out well for many countries. You can be a test-taking nation and everybody taking a test, but you can't invent or innovate. That's an issue. That's why we are talking about putting art back into the STEM education conversation. By putting art into STEM, we turn it into STEAM.

Graham: But there is a lot of emphasis on standardised test taking, particularly at high school level. Does this bode well for STEAM?

John: The measurement question is a difficult one. If you are an economist, you believe in it. If you are backing the national policy as an economist, you are going to say that. If you are a businessperson or your metric is money, a simple metric, something measurable, you want to see how it impacts the money equation. Creativity has no good measurable, no good metric, and that's why we think that it is not important. Well, it isn't that we don't think that it's important. It's just not measurable and therefore it's hard to see how you're doing. Every country knows how happy it is. Every country knows how prosperous it is. It's a feeling. It's an emotion. Can you measure that? You bet. It's in the grain of a society, how you feel. The arts are that measure of the power of a society.

Graham: It seems that school curricula separate creativity from disciplines in an attempt to silo them. Do you think that we should rethink this approach?

John: Sure. Well, there is the interpretive silos versus going cross-curriculum. We have David Kelley's good example of the T-shaped person, a person who has depth and breadth. I like to say that you couldn't have a good banana split if you had ice cream that was all the same flavour. You like to have the strawberry and the vanilla and the chocolate and the banana. So there is something about having things singled out so we understand them. The question is: How easy is it to mix them? That is something that academia traditionally does not enable. How to make that easier is the question. But if you make it too easy, then it becomes a flavour unto itself. So there needs to be friction in that structure.

Graham: How do you think we can implement those sorts of structures? Do we need to start work on that at a younger age rather than in higher education?

John: Well, that's a great question. The question of do you start young on acquainting people who are interdisciplinary, or do you wait until they are older after they have mastered a discipline? I don't know the answer. All I know is that not just instilling but sustaining curiosity seems to be the key, because it begins when you are a child. You know nothing about danger, so, 'Yeah I'll walk in the street. Yeah I'm fine. I'll go over there. Nothing is going to happen to me.' As you get older, you're like, 'No, you don't go there, or you don't move your arm backwards.' So our curiosity just goes away because we need to survive.

I think that aside from the questions, Will you be curious inside your field? or, Will you be curious across your field?, the question is how to keep that curiosity. Any of the arts helps to keep that curious spirit alive. You don't get curious when you ask: 'What's four plus five?' or whatever. You don't get to be curious. 'Is it 9.1?' I had a friend who had a campaign speech. It was like, 'If I'm president, I will make Pi into three.' Of course, 'Yeah, let's vote for him.' You know what I mean? So staying curious, that's the question.

Graham: It's an interesting one because you imply a distinction between formal and informal learning.

John: Whether curiosity exists in the informal or formal space, I don't know. But I would say that in the formal space, we are counting on teachers to enable that curiosity, and I know that in my own life, my teachers have enabled that curiosity many times. Now wait, did some try to kill it? Yes. Perhaps for good reason. But some encouraged it. Teachers are in the unique position versus machines or MOOCs or whatever, in that they can believe in you in a way that the animated paper-clip guy who says, 'You wrote a great essay!' can't. You know, like OK, you kind of feel, but if someone says, 'That's a really great essay!' that's going to be important some day. That one little comment, no matter what age you are, is the key to maybe 'I think I can, I think I can' kind of thing.

Graham: How do you see the role of the teacher changing in the digital world?

John: I think we have to ask the inverse question: Is the role of the student changing? The role of the students is changing vastly, and that isn't just a student that's in school. It's a student of life. People our age. We don't know what to learn any more. Remember that we used to die in our mid-40s. We used to go to school, go to college, we would gorge on information. We would work and we would die. Now we are living until we are 80 and 100. So now that model of gorging on information doesn't have momentum in our later life. So we are still students of life living longer. That's a question for learning. Not the question: Oh, those teachers here. The question is: Oh, us students. How do we exist now?

Graham: Do you think that digital technology has a role to play in transforming our learning?

John: I think our understanding of technology is naive for many reasons. It's because we are still in that drunken, sort of leftover New Year's Eve party of the dot-com boom and all the Internet this, that, whatever, which is not dissimilar to when electricity was invented. When electricity came on the scene in the early 1900s, it was like, 'This is amazing! You know, this lightbulb thing. I can stay up late and do stuff, and I can, like, make this stuff happen.' That was magical, and then eventually it became part of the culture.

The computer thing is different because it has to do with the mind versus the physical space. You know, like Steve Jobs said, the computer is like a bicycle for the mind. Well that's a powerful statement, and, thinking about a bicycle, at some point, if you had a thousand-gear bicycle, you couldn't use it. So the computer today is like a million-gear bicycle. You know, Moore's Law is just a powerful thought. Doubling the number of transistors every 18 months. Great. So every time things get faster and stay the same price or cheaper. You live that decades and decades and decades. It was amazing. But now, we don't care.

Ten years ago, you got Pentium 100 Megahertz versus a Pentium 120. You were going to go out and buy the 120 because you had to have it. It became 140. 'I gotta have it.' It's 160. It's a Pro Pentium. 'I gotta have it.' But now you are like, 'It's quad core, you know, Opticore, super cool.' You're like, 'I kinda have enough gears on my bicycle I think.' So we are transitioning from a technology as a *raison d'etre* to something else. We are returning to a kind of normalised state where technology matters less. What it is, why it is, how it exists, matters more. It's why now. In the past it would be two technologists and you would hire a designer. Now you have two designers, you will hire a technologist.

Graham: So would you say that technology amplifies or dulls creativity?

John: I don't know. I've thought a lot about the question of whether technology makes you more or less creative. Just yesterday I opened a mail from Tiffany Shlain, who founded the Webby Awards, and she has a new thing about like fasting from technology, and oh my gosh, it's like the best thing. You know, turn off the technology, it's fantastic. You have *The Shallows* book that says technology, the Internet, makes you dumb, etc. And you have people who say that it is making you smarter than ever. It gets a bit confusing. I think at least, for myself, what I do know is that technology has created a mass delusional-like fog for us all to talk about it. But eventually we will stop talking about it. It will just be a normal thing, and that era will eventually come, so we will wait for that to make sense of it. I'm not in a rush right now to understand it.

'technology
has created a mass
delusional-like
fog for us all to talk
about it. But eventually
we will stop talking
about it. It will just
be a normal thing'

'A human-centred approach
to designing change and education
acknowledges that we have to
meet people where they are and help
them take the next step.'

IDEO is a design and innovation consultancy that was born in Palo Alto in 1991 out of a merger between one American and three British design companies. Today the company employs over 550 people in the disciplines of human factors; mechanical, electrical and software engineering; and industrial, interaction and communication design. A global organisation, it has offices in San Francisco, Chicago, New York, Boston, London, Munich, Shanghai, Singapore, Mumbai, Seoul and Tokyo.

The company has numerous blue-chip clients across many sectors including the food, retail, technology, medical and automotive industries, and is famed for designing Apple's first mouse.

More recently, IDEO has become increasingly involved in management consulting and organisational design, taking what it calls a 'design thinking' approach to helping organisations in the public and private sectors innovate and grow.

Sandy Speicher leads IDEO's education practice, using human-centred methodologies and multi-disciplinary teams, focused on developing tools, environments or curricula that enable more engaging learning experiences; transforming schools, programmes and organisations; or addressing systemic challenges that affect education at large.

I met with Sandy at IDEO's San Francisco studios.

Graham Brown-Martin: Sandy, please would tell me about your background and your work at IDEO?

Sandy Speicher: My background is in graphic design, visual communications. Over time I've found a strong affinity with our education systems and we wondered how design could help our systems evolve. At IDEO, we help organisations and systems find new answers for the future based specifically around the people that we're designing for. We take a human-centred approach to answering questions.

Graham: What do you mean by 'human-centred'?

Sandy: A lot of times we think about how we might re-design something and we start with a lot of assumptions about what should be. When we say 'human-centred design', it's about taking a process that begins with people and what they really care about, starting with what people desire and then looking at how we can quickly make a solution that feels right for the needs of the system, but that we don't forget to understand what people really care about.

Graham: IDEO apply a design approach to public services such as education. But hasn't education as a system always been designed?

Sandy: When we think about an education system or classroom even, as you point out, at some point it has been designed. If we start to realise it's been designed then we can choose to design it anew for modern times.

Graham: What were the education systems that we have today designed for?

Sandy: Our current education systems have really come out of the industrial time. They were beautifully designed to make sense of the time. We have a lot of children. We have a country. We want to raise citizens and we want to actually help bring them to the predominant mindset of the times so that they can be successful and that everything can thrive... Of course, we're living in a really different world now and so we're seeing that that system is starting to feel outdated, not just conceptually... It just doesn't fit the way that the world is moving today.

Graham: Could you be specific about how you see the world being different from our parents' generation?

Sandy: I had a professor in college and he used to say to us, 'If aliens came down and came right into our classrooms, what would they think is actually happening?' They've no context. They've no understanding. If you think about all that's observable in our classrooms today, what would they think we were trying to prepare people to do? Well, they'd probably think we're being trained to rotate spaces in 48-minute incre-

ments. They'd probably think that we were being trained to move at the sound of the bell or to sit still or to override our bodily functions so that we're maintaining order. All these things you could certainly look at that are observable about schools. None of those things feel inherently human. You don't necessarily feel that they're designed around the ways that we relate to each other. They feel they're designed around the ways we'd like people to behave.

I think one of the biggest changes we're seeing today is that this is a very enabled time. We have so much choice. We have so much control over the choices that we're able to make. We can go on a website. We can search through the Internet and find many different offerings for the same thing. We can choose to purchase it. It can appear at our house the next day. We can then write comments on the product, on the service, on the shipper, on everything. We are in an enabled world that is very connected. It is primarily asking us to be very responsible for ourselves, our medical records, even our own education. We're asked to have a lot of responsibility for who we are and what we care about and our future trajectory. If we're not actually helping kids know how to navigate that world, then we're not going to prepare them well to succeed within it.

Graham: Are you saying that there are new demands on present and future generations that are not being addressed by today's education systems?

Sandy: Yes, definitely. Although I think it's tricky to speak about education systems as a whole. To be honest, the reason I got into the work that I'm doing these days is because I was working with a group of students right around the time that Bush declared war. They were struggling to understand their role in it. They understood that it was so much more complex and that they didn't want to be at war. They didn't want people dying. They understood that there were so many different layers of complexity, yet they didn't necessarily feel that they knew how to navigate the range of information that they had access to.

One of the things that I realised in that interaction was that our education systems have a great opportunity to help our youth navigate the complexity of information they have access to and we're not necessarily designing our systems to help them know that they have a role in creating that in the long term. We have global challenges that we're aware of every day on hundreds of news channels and sources that everyone has access to. We need to be able to learn how to navigate that. That is an overwhelming feeling for everyone. That's a new state of possibility in the world. I see this as a major opportunity for our education systems to help prepare youth to navigate the complexity of all this information in the world but also know they can do something about it.

Graham: Can you explain what IDEO means by 'design thinking for education'?

Sandy: Design thinking is really about an approach to problem solving. It's saying that as a designer of many things in this world around us I believe I can help make a difference in it. Design thinking is an approach to problem solving that's very much about what people care about, all the different players in the system, and finding new solutions to help make the world a better place.

We are often looking at the question of how to apply design thinking to challenges in education. Very quickly, with the level of complexity of these questions, we get to what I call the world peace problem. It all of a sudden becomes so big. As we start to look at questions of education, we get into how people are learning, what people are learning. We get into what is a very political conversation about the future of a country, the future of people within it, the stances and the things that they believe in. It becomes very difficult to know how to move anything forward, when a problem becomes so big.

What we are often doing here at IDEO is helping to prise apart the questions. There are a lot of different conversations that are happening around what people are learning. We could talk about a lot of the trends in the world, the skills that are needed for future employability,

and then I think a lot of the things that we all feel might be missing from the assessment mentality of our culture here in the US, for instance. I feel like then we're caught in a world peace conversation. Those questions are actually interdependent.

Because it's so hard to move forward on all of them together, we start to prise them apart and we start to ask, for instance: What are the needs of higher education classrooms? We hear students and we hear faculty demanding a more dynamic environment. They feel stuck in the dialogue. They feel like they're sitting in chairs, that they have to conform, and people are talking at them and they're not able to actively engage though they're wanting to, as a way to learn. To respond to that question, we can start to say how we might rethink the way the environment is designed, the way the interactions are designed, in order to produce the ends that we're looking for.

The chair I'm sitting on is an example of that. It is a very cool story to me about change that we might think may not make that big of an impact. For example, if you put something as simple as a chair that has wheels in a room, you allow people to move around more easily. You start to create a whole different dynamic for how people interact. That determines the way they interact with faculty and that starts to evolve the curriculum, and then we have found the needs that correspond to what people really care about, and started to make a change in institutions. We can look at the question from so many different angles and I feel that prising it apart actually helps to do that.

Graham: That sounds like a design fix to an existing problem within an environment that had already been designed for something else. What happens when you design a completely new system?

Sandy: Yeah, I love the question. How can design thinking be used to transform an education system, to design a transformational education system? One of the things that I've been learning is that everything always builds off with

something else. We recently had a collaboration with an organisation in Peru which is one of the lowest-ranking countries in the PISA survey, consistently over time. As their economy is consistently growing, the country is stabilising. Their education system is struggling and we had a client who approached us to think about a school model that could actually help build the next generation of leaders, a future generation from the emerging middle class of Peru. The brief was: 'We need it affordable, we need it scalable and we need it excellent.' We are using those words as the mantra.

The challenge was a from-scratch question. There were existing schools but they were not necessarily meeting the needs of scale and so the client told us to start from scratch. Design a model that will work from scratch that is affordable, scalable and excellent. Now, that's an amazing challenge and kind of frightening because there are so many diverse possibilities. If we take a human-centred approach, you start to see all the conflicts across what students, teachers, governments and businesses care about and, of course, as you're designing a school model it has to start to reconcile all of these conflicting needs.

Now, we could start to imagine radically new ways of learning. We could take away grade-based classifications. We could create entirely new assessments. We could have learning goals that are not necessarily in the standard government agenda. The truth is that parents have expectations about the way learning can happen, the way learning should happen. A lot of that is built off from the way that they learned. One of the things that we have to do is to look at how to meet people where they are and make sure we're designing in ways that they can understand so that they can still relate to and care about their children in the way their children are growing. We're never really starting from scratch. A human-centred approach to designing change and education acknowledges that we have to meet people where they are and help them take the next step.

Graham: Are you suggesting that we must accept a certain amount of the *status quo*?

Sandy: I'm not necessarily suggesting that. I think that every innovation comes from a context and that what we have to do is understand the context well enough to understand how to make that innovation successful, to make those goals that we have behind them successful. Generally, what we look to do is to enable people. That's how IDEO has always innovated.

Graham: We've discussed how the design thinking methodology might be applied to an education system, but how might it be, for example, embedded as an approach to learning?

Sandy: IDEO's role in the world is to help organisations innovate. That means that no matter what the engagement, whatever conversation that we begin, we never know where we're going to get. The outcomes are not predictable. We could talk about measures. We could talk about what success would look like, but we don't know where we're going to get. Our job is to learn along the way and not just learn but actually create as a result of what we've learned. I'd like to point out that what design thinking is in its core is a learning process. It is a learning process that is inherently tied to active creation. You don't learn it just to learn it. You learn it to then create for the context that you've been learning about.

When we look at education, we've had to say, well, this fits on so many levels that it becomes incredibly confusing. Designing is a very powerful way to learn. This is a great curricular tool.

'...every innovation comes from a context and that what we have to do is understand the context well enough to understand how to make that innovation successful.'

It's a powerful way to learn many things, not just design in itself. Teachers who have to think in the moment all the time and design in immediate ways are actually designers of their environments. Every day, a new question comes to them and they have to very quickly find new solutions.

Design is an incredibly powerful way to learn because it helps people make meaning of the information that they're learning. As we get input, we can learn about history, we can learn about people's desires and then we can create from it. Teachers need to constantly be thinking about the context that they're creating and that is an act of design. The more they're in touch with design processes and methods, the more we start to see relevance in the context that they're designing.

Graham: Would you agree that any design decisions around education are limited by the end goal of assessment?

Sandy: Yes. We have a global testing climate right now where it feels as if the tone of our education systems is about assessing our kids, and that word is directly correlated to testing, whereas the heart of what we wish for it to be about is learning, personal growth, the ability to thrive in the future. As I've looked closer and closer into the questions of education, I believe that the people who are running our systems have come to it from a perspective of great responsibility. We are now in a developmental phase. The system began just as the distribution of information and it has underneath it a promise to help all students thrive in the future.

I'm not so keen on blaming the system for having an assessment tone. What I do feel is that it's really important for us to have a feedback loop on what we have made the promise to do. I just think we need to mature our methods about how we do that. When we look at, for instance, portfolio-based approaches, I think there are a lot of interesting assessments that exist out there and are being developed that are about youth demonstrating what they understand through essay writing or through creating projects where they're applying their knowledge. Those are

actually assessments. They're not tests. Those are a much more sophisticated way to understand what students know and do and believe.

Graham: As an employer, how does IDEO recruit? Does it look at applicants' grades or does it look at something else?

Sandy: The way IDEO hires talent is really about the people themselves. We generally hire for design disciplines. We look for T-shaped people that have depth in a particular design skill and demonstrate awareness of a lot of different disciplines so that they can act together as multi-disciplinary teams. Basically, they have a great skill to deliver and they know how to collaborate.

The truth is, our work is getting increasingly complex and so, I think, are our people. What we're looking for is an extreme quality of craft in design fields when we look at people's portfolios. We're not looking at grades. In fact, we're not really looking at a resume but at the body of work that they have created.

They're brought in to have a conversation with us based on that, but they're hired because of who they are and how they show up, how ready they are to be learning. Do they demonstrate that they would actually help bring out greatness in others? That's one of the qualities that we look for. We're in an interview process. It's a very long journey of actually understanding people and what they're going to be bringing to our culture.

'I would argue that even in the future online education should not and will not replace physical education.'

EdX is a non-profit online initiative created by founding partners Harvard University and MIT, offering interactive online classes and MOOCs from the world's best universities, including MIT, Harvard and the University of California, Berkeley. Topics include biology, business, chemistry, computer science, economics, finance, electronics, engineering, food and nutrition, history, humanities, law, literature, maths, medicine, music, philosophy, physics, science, statistics and more.

Started in prototype form in 2011 as MITx, today edX has nearly two million users and over 30 schools that offer or plan to offer courses on their platform. Students are awarded certificates of successful completion, but edX does not offer course credit. Participating universities may offer credit for an online course within their sole discretion. The platform offers students a variety of ways to take courses, including verified courses in which students have the option to audit the course for free or to work toward a fee-based edX-verified certificate.

Professors deliver course material, via the platform, that typically comprise interactive learning sequences composed of short videos, averaging ten minutes in length, combined with active learning exercises for students to practise concepts. Courses often include tutorial videos that resemble small on-campus discussion groups where students can engage with each other and teaching staff.

The edX learning platform has been developed as open-source software and made available to other institutions of higher learning that want to make similar offerings. The code is available free of charge online via GitHub where major contributors to the platform include Stanford University and Google under the name of Open edX. EdX, in collaboration with Google, is developing a further site, MOOC.org, for non-xConsortium universities, institutions, teachers, businesses and governments to build and host their courses for a global audience. Powered by the jointly developed Open edX platform, the site will open during 2014.

I visited the offices of edX in Cambridge, Massachusetts, to find out more from Johannes Heinlein, edX's Senior Director of Strategic Partnerships.

Graham Brown-Martin: What was the inspiration that led to the creation of edX?

Johannes Heinlein: EdX was established by Harvard-MIT to fulfil a dual mission. On the one hand, to fulfil an altruistic mode of bringing quality education to the world, providing access to learners irrespective of their location. That is the first part of our mission. The second part of our mission is to improve learning outcomes both on-campus and off-campus. So that is to engage universities in the transformation of using technology to improve learning outcomes for the individual. EdX was established about a year and a half ago and now has 30 world-leading partner institutions that deliver their content via our destination portal, edx.org.

We started out providing access through what has become known as a MOOC, a massive open online course. That term has evolved to some extent now and people are also using SPOCs, meaning small private online courses. What we allow now is that institutions or individual organisations provide access to content in a contained environment or as a massive open experiment to learners worldwide.

The MOOC phenomenon is driven by enabling technologies that have evolved towards personalised learning. That's our goal and, I think, our opportunity going forward, providing personalised learning paths for individuals.

Graham: Do you see a commercial business model based around MOOCs and accreditation?

Johannes: Let me start with accreditation. Accreditation is likely to be in the future of at least some MOOCs. There are already organisations that are offering credits for taking MOOC courses from any institution. So learners can take a MOOC class and, if they have successfully completed that class and achieved a certificate at the end, that will be used for accreditation at that educational institution.

That also then translates directly into a commercialisation aspect. There is a charge for that. There is a charge both for learners to receive that certificate and then the universities will charge a much-reduced fee, but they're often likely to charge learners a fee for receiving that accreditation.

The last aspect –and I think that's probably where the future is likely to go with regards to commercialisation– is that you have the unbundling of content and the opportunity for students to build their own learning paths together with experts from within the universities. What we found in many other industries is that people are willing to pay for customised content that meets their needs. That is one opportunity, I believe, going forward.

Graham: It was the unbundling of albums in the music industry that led to the success and later domination of iTunes. Do you think that we might see a dominant commercial player in the MOOC arena and would that be a problem?

Johannes: EdX was really formed to focus on the future of universities and the transformation of a variety of educational institutions in different locations with different emphases. So I do believe there is a danger in one prominent player controlling to that extent educational access. Our goal at edX is very much to counter that through making our platform available as an open-source platform to anyone to use, providing learners with content that is individualised or as a set of bundled information. What we've done is to open our platform up to be open source so that whole countries or individual organisations can continue to use it. We will continue to improve it, together with our partners, and we work in partnership with all of the organisations that are part of the edX infrastructure and ecosystem to really drive individualised learning that isn't necessarily focused on one prominent player.

So our hope is that collectively we're much stronger than an individual, and we provide a much greater degree of diversity in learning, which we believe is important.

Graham: With courseware and accreditation available online, what do you imagine the future role of universities in society to be?

Johannes: The true value of a university education isn't necessarily just in the paper and delivery of content. The true value of any education should be in the peers that you engage with, in the individual engagement you have with your teacher and with other people. You're being exposed to a wide variety of different formats and content.

We believe at edX that the future of successful universities will be in transforming themselves to be much broader places for people to come together and take more individualised learning paths and really engage in ways that involve what I call 'learning to learn'. That's really what we believe the future of universities is about.

Graham: So do you see a blending between what people will do in the digital world and the physical world of the university?

Johannes: I love that you used the term 'blending' because one of our focus areas, as I mentioned, is improving educational outcomes within organisations. What we call that is 'blended learning'. Blended learning is really about combining the best of a traditional in-classroom, or a physical coming together, with the technology to support learning outcomes.

So the future is likely to be that students will access and continue to access material through technology, be it tablets, smartphones or computers, but then find a physical place where they get together. At edX, we've established get-togethers. In over 100 countries and cities, students and learners have formed their own individual groups where they physically get together to exchange thoughts on the material and learn together as a group.

In actual fact, one of the interesting things we found from studies of the outcomes of the first courses, is that there is one primary component that drives successful outcomes for a student. That is: Do they have peers that they can engage with throughout the programme? So we build that peer component very much into the technologies, through wikis, discussion forums and technology, but we also strongly believe in the ongoing need and desire for people to come together in a physical format.

Graham: Do you think, historically, that lack of having that peer support and people doing similar courses together has led to a higher-than-expected dropout rate with the digital courses?

Johannes: I think the dropout rate has been driven by the lack of engagement that was offered to individuals. I remember the first online universities. They would still send you hard copies of the material. You would read that at home, go, 'OK, I've got it.' Then you'd send something back, but that physical engagement with a teacher you didn't have.

Now what you have is the gamification of learning. You have true interactive engagement. Our goal is to improve both the access but also the outcome for students. Right now the dropout rate is still relatively high. To some extent, we believe that's driven by the low barrier of entry. Our courses and any MOOC course, generally speaking, are open to anyone. They're free. There are no barriers. So many people take it as a menu sampler and there's nothing wrong with that, because often the menu sampler whets your appetite for future learning and that's our hope.

Graham: What effect do you think that providing free access to higher education courses without academic entrance requirements might have on the role of secondary schools?

Johannes: I think there's an arbitrary line of distinction right now between what happens in high schools and what happens in university. In high school, you're driven to complete certain subjects and certain standardised tests to a certain result to get you into the university of your choice. There often isn't a consistent path of what you learn.

We often find that many students really experience difficulty when they start university studies because what they learned in high school doesn't really translate into what they need to learn at university.

So that blending, hopefully, will occur. In actual fact, at edX about 30 percent of our learners are high school students. So there's clearly a desire and, dare I call it a market opportunity here, for people to tap into that group of learners who seek to learn something that goes beyond standardised tests in the typical high school.

Graham: Whilst there are no entrance requirements at edX there is a requirement for students to have access via broadband Internet with a good laptop or tablet. Is edX looking at these access issues?

Johannes: Access is one of the primary things that we're looking at and trying to solve together with our partners. There are a variety of ways that we think this can be solved and only the future will tell whether we're right or not.

For one, we think providing access at the source where people access the information is important, whether that's hosting content within China or somewhere within Africa. Providing and engaging with communities and governments to provide access in libraries, for example. We are piloting a number of programmes where we want to provide access together with towns and cities in libraries and community centres where there are, perhaps, faster access opportunities.

Then lastly, we've implemented into our platform the ability to download the videos. So if you have access issues, all of our videos have a transcript and you can download just the source file at a much lower bandwidth requirement. We've compressed it so that you can download the material onto your computer or your phone or tablet, then review it without incurring any bandwidth charges.

Those are some starting points. I think technology, hopefully, will evolve to the extent where the bandwidth issue will become less of a concern. We're not there yet.

Graham: Do you think high school students today might prefer to take an edX course rather than attend a university with its attendant costs?

Johannes: Because physical university education continues to provide value-added activities that no online platform, at this point, is able to deliver, I would argue that even in the future online education should not and will not replace physical education: that is, the engagement with your peers, the face-to-face engagement you have with a teacher, the conversations and arguments that you can have via wiki or an online platform with a MOOC immersion, and so on.

But it's very different to look into someone's face and see them smile or get angry and argue with you. That's the value of universities going forward, to provide not just the delivery and dissemination of content, but the active exchange with your peers and teachers and also, in many instances, to provide a place, a home, a being and identifying with something [like] I went to the university of ... whatever it might be. I studied in Edinburgh. I went to the University of Edinburgh. I can identify with that place. I feel proud to have gone there. That is, I think, something that will continue to be important.

www.edx.org

'The true value of a university education isn't necessarily just in the paper and delivery of content. The true value of any education should be in the peers that you engage with, in the individual engagement you have with your teacher and with other people.'

Case study

'The school looks, and even smells, more like a craft space where things are designed, made and exhibited. Lessons are taking place but it's not obvious where a class ends and a common area begins.'

High Tech High is a progressive school development organisation based in San Diego, California, comprising 11 schools, a teacher certification programme and a graduate school of education. The schools operate on the US charter school system which means that they receive public funding, usually a fixed amount per pupil, but run independently. Students attending charter schools sit the state-mandated examinations but the schools are subject to fewer rules, regulations and statutes than traditional state schools. Charter schools are non-profit organisations and can receive donations from private sources. These schools may be set up by groups of parents, teachers or other activists as well as universities, government entities or non-profit groups and, subject to district, corporations may be permitted to manage multiple charter schools. The approach is similar to movements in other countries, such as Sweden and more recently the UK, with what are known as 'free schools' that encourage market forces to improve public or state education provision and close national achievement gaps.

Charter schools, as well as their international equivalents, have proved almost universally controversial, with critics suggesting that they compete with traditional state schools in a destructive manner rather than work in harmony. The market-driven approaches of some charter schools, it is suggested, are unsustainable in the wider catchment: for example, where a charter school's solution to deficient schooling and the underwhelming outcomes of the disad-vantaged is more school or longer hours, terms, etc. may be pitched against the static provision of state education to the advantaged, creating a new inequality in the system. The result of market forces suggests that a correction will take place and the achievement gaps reappear. It becomes an increasingly complex issue when traditional state schools have insufficient tax dollars to meet a correction that requires schools to stay open longer and teachers to work more hours whilst operating within a more restrictive set of regulations.

There have been a number of scandals as well as notable failures in the world of charter and free schools that range from reports of Dickensian disciplinary measures taken against young disruptive children to the 'privatisation by the back door' of state education by nationwide chains of education management organisations. Driven to improve the test scores of low-income students in state examinations, organisations such as the KIPP chain have deployed what some commentators describe as military-style behaviour where, for example, the public humiliation of students for minor transgressions is a standard method of behaviour control. This treat-ment of children, who typically come from poor urban communities, may increase grade scores to the nodding approval of communities who would not accept the same treatment for their own children. Inevitably, this raises huge moral and social questions that have yet to be fully reconciled within a nation that has an unenviable history of racial inequality. It might be better education, but on what terms?

On the flipside, many charter schools have demonstrated significant improvements in the achievement of their students without resorting to boot-camp style policies or grotesquely extended school days. High Tech High is one of those schools.

I spent a day at the Gary and Jerri-Ann Jacobs High Tech High, the original and first High Tech High school, and if I'm honest I was blown away. A personal yardstick I use when visiting schools is whether I would want to send my kids there and this one would definitely be on my list. For me, the combination of the environment, a holistic blended curriculum, engaged teachers and learners plus an inspired CEO points the direction for a transformative learning experience.

The school was established in 2000 as the result of a coalition between industry and educators with a mission to 'prepare a diverse range of students for post-secondary education, citizenship, and leadership in the high-technology industry'. Enrolment is non-selective via a zip-code-based lottery, where there is no tracking of students by perceived academic ability. It serves approximately 570 students in grades nine to 12 within a single-floor building that is reminiscent of a warehouse space for a design company. I'm struck by how similar the interior of this school is to the San Francisco offices of the renowned design company IDEO that I'd visited a few days earlier. It's easy to see how a student leaving this school would make a seamless transition to the kind of workplaces popular amongst the leading Silicon Valley technology firms or the kind of design companies that surround me in my Shoreditch studio in London. What this school isn't doing is preparing its students for jobs in call centres or industrial manufacturing sweatshops. What it is doing, as we'll come to later, is what their CEO and Founding Principal Larry Rosenstock describes as 'nurturing creative non-compliance'.

Despite the school's name and its stated mission, technology isn't a focal point when walking around the school. There are no grand displays of Jetson-style classrooms with holographic displays or kids permanently glued to iPads. The technology is there but just blended in and it's neither super-advanced nor the focal point of learning. If anything, the school looks, and even smells, more like a craft space where things are designed, made and exhibited. Lessons are taking place but it's not obvious where a class ends and a common area begins.

This integration is at the heart of what the school is about, from integrating with the community to integrating kids from diverse social and cultural backgrounds with the public and private enterprise. And it goes further. The influence of the 19th- and 20th-century American education reformer John Dewey permeates the philosophy of the school with its integration of head and hand, thinking and doing. It seems contradictory to be considering thinkers from the 19th century when the negative impact of that time is still being felt in many of the education factories that our schools have become. However, Dewey's

advocacy of hands-on learning or experiential education remains influential today, even if it is at odds with the educational systems that came out of the Victorian era. There's an irony that, at a time when the US and other Western nations are trying to transform their education systems to meet the challenges of the 21st century, the key to this transformation should be found in the thinking of 19th-century reformers. Perhaps non-compliant critical thinkers were deemed less valuable in the 19th and 20th centuries, but certainly it appears that their time has come.

Project-based learning is an approach deeply rooted in Dewey's thinking *[see thought piece page 254]* and is a foundation block for the practice at High Tech High, where learning is encouraged through active inquiry. Projects based in reality, where problems are creatively solved, provide the opportunity for students to apply their multiple intelligences, or modalities, to complete a project that they can be rightly proud of. One of the big guns in the world of project-based learning is Jeff Robin, who also happens to be High Tech High's art teacher. Like all the teaching faculty I met at the school, Jeff is a passionate educator who cares deeply about his students' work. He also has the demeanour and candour of a mischievous pirate in the Captain Jack Sparrow tradition. I would argue these are great qualities in an educator and I would certainly recommend his website for those looking for the skinny on project-based learning with plenty of free resources *[jeffrobin.com]*.

High Tech High deploys an innovative approach to curriculum design that has its origins in Rosenstock's earlier work with New Urban High School Project, a US Department of Education Office of Vocational and Adult Education initiative from the late 1990s. It takes four design principles – personalisation, adult world connection, common intellectual mission, and teacher as designer – which it directs towards preparation of the student for the adult world. The result is small-sized schools, openness of facilities, personalisation through advisory, learners as producers, emphasis on integrated, project-based learning and student exhibitions, the requirement for all students to complete internships in the community, and the provision of ample planning time for teacher teams during the work day.

Teachers at High Tech High are programme and curriculum designers. Working in interdisciplinary teams, they design the courses they teach. They take the lead in staff meetings and action groups addressing school issues. They are involved in critical decisions regarding curriculum, assessment, professional development, hiring and other significant areas of the school. The school timetable supports team teaching, often with mixed disciplines, and teachers have plenty of planning time to devise integrated projects, common rubrics for assessment, and common rituals by which all students demonstrate their learning and progress toward graduation.

There is a massive commitment to the role of learners as producers, demonstrating their learning and achievement by creating something that can be exhibited to their peers, family and community. This leads to another function of the school environment: it is also a gallery for student work where every wall, common area and walkway is a living exhibition of learning. It has to be said that much of the work that is exhibited – and every student exhibits – is really first-rate and wouldn't be out of place in a traditional gallery or science exhibition. The students also create books and other publications, some of which are available via outlets including Amazon and local bookstores. Rosenstock is bullish when he tells me, 'High-quality work equals high-quality teaching. We let practice speak through exhibitions of student work.'

Under Rosenstock, High Tech High has eschewed much of what is outdated and self-defeating about traditional schooling: classroom design, divisions between subjects, isolation from the community, limiting belief systems about student potential, assessments that only one teacher ever sees, a model of school that fails to inspire and develop staff. Rosenstock is ruthlessly against standardisation and considers that the necessary evil of state examinations that the school is compelled to subject their students to 'sucks the oxygen out of the system'. Yet 100 percent of the students who graduate from the school have been accepted into a college or university. High Tech High, which has a comprehensive intake from a disadvantaged area, is outperforming schools that are selective.

High Tech High's significant achievement demonstrates that there is another way of approaching education where mixing pedagogies in a purposeful way delivers results that are hard to beat or argue with. It flies in the face of what some policymakers might believe is the inevitable, logical and best way of doing things with no serious alternative. The current Western model of learning has been productised from a vision in which students make clear learning progress in every lesson. Thus, we potentially lose the model in which learning is experiential and developmental, achieved through being and doing. High Tech High reflects this long-fuse model of learning, which places more emphasis on competence and authenticity.

I ask Rosenstock how other schools could follow the example of High Tech High. His advice is to keep schools small, around 500 students, identify outstanding teachers to lead the schools with a small design team, agree defining values and key principles, then liberate them to design and define their curriculum and pedagogy. As I leave his office near the end of the day, a visitor from Japan has arrived. He has also come to learn the High Tech High story. This, Rosenstock tells me, is a typical day: it seems that much of the world, at least those with an interest in radical transformation of their education systems, is keen to find out more.

www.hightechhigh.org

'Rosenstock is ruthlessly against standardisation and considers that the necessary evil of state examinations that the school is compelled to subject their students to "sucks the oxygen out of the system".'

'We don't have to worry about factoids in quite the same way. We can look at the big strands rather than the minutiae and I think that that's kind of liberating in some way.'

It has to be said that I was not prepared for Larry Rosenstock. Not from the point of view of whether I was ready to interview him, you'll understand. Rather, I wasn't prepared for the infectious positive energy force that strapped me into his spacecraft at face-changing velocity, with Larry in the driving seat taking me on his fantastic voyage. I'd say that Rosenstock is six parts genius, two parts inspiration, one part pirate and one part maniac. The most important thing is that it works and I want to learn more from him and his colleagues.

His expansive office-cum-playroom is festooned with memorabilia, books and art, ranging from works by graffiti artist Banksy to baseball paraphernalia to photographs of Larry with US presidents. Pride of place amongst the collection is Rosenstock's certificates that show him to be a member of the Massachusetts and US Supreme Court Bars. In addition to having been a lecturer at the Harvard Graduate School of Education, he also served as an attorney at the Harvard Center for Law and Education.

Larry Rosenstock and his work have been featured on Oprah and in *Forbes*, *Newsweek* and other publications. He is a winner of the Ford Foundation Innovations in State and Local Government Award, is an Ashoka Fellow and won the McGraw Prize in Education.

He drinks his coffee from a cup that is inscribed 'Class of 2013, Cultivating Creative Noncompliance'. This, Larry tells me, was a gift from his colleagues following a recent meeting of the school's teaching and leadership team. It's as if he positively goads everyone about him to question traditional practices and see if they can be changed for the better. As the school's principal, he certainly gives his team permission to try. Not especially technology-based, despite the name, a sense of the transformation of the learning and teaching process is palpable throughout the school. It's his passionate and well-reasoned arguments about his school's purpose to nurture creative thinkers who can solve complex problems that have me captivated until the end of my visit.

I had the opportunity to ask Larry some questions, then he does the rest.

Graham Brown-Martin: Larry, what is the background story to High Tech High?

Larry Rosenstock: High Tech High was actually incubated by a group of leaders in the tech sector in San Diego in the late '90s when there was a dearth of visas to bring in people from other countries. They were not xenophobic about other people from other countries. They cherished them but they couldn't get enough of them.

At the same time there was no 'return on investment', in their language, in giving money to the school district. So they had this impulse to stick a flag in the ground and start some schools which might have an engineering focus and that's how we got started in the year 2000.

Graham: And today what do you think makes High Tech High different and special?

Larry: One of them is that we have social class integration as a deep ethos. So we use postal codes to select students blindly. There's no information. It's not selective other than that whatever percent of kids reside in every postal code is the percent of kids that we take because postal codes predict socioeconomic status and ethnicity quite well. That's the good and bad news about them. They are just a five-digit number. So that's how the kids get here. And yet they're doing very interesting and sophisticated work. And we have decided that going to college is a very important outcome and that even if someone might not go to college, they're not going to be segregated from those who are, and they're not going to be segregated from a programme that expects that they will be and prepares them so that they might be.

And it turns out that we have double the national average of kids who do go to college, majoring in science, technology, engineering and math. And I think it's because they're in a school in which they're actually doing science, technology, engineering and math and not just studying it. They're doing fieldwork. They're building and making things.

Graham: The school's name is misleading as there isn't much evidence of a reliance on high technology within the learning and teaching practice. What is your position on digital platforms for learning?

Larry: The use of digital platforms being integrated in the student life is kind of a quizzical question in a lot of ways. I mean someone who I knew that I thought highly of was Neil Postman. In his book *Technopoly* he said [that] any time we get excited about a new technology the question we have to first ask ourselves is what is the problem that this technology is intended to remediate?

So there's a lot of technology. I taught carpentry. A hammer is technology. And there's a lot of technology that we want kids doing, creating books. Drawing is technology. As far as digital technology is concerned, sometimes people are surprised to find out that we don't have a canned curriculum that comes via some supplier or something like that.

Now at the same time the world has really changed. I'm going to reach in my pocket. We all have this thing [a smartphone]. It sees you. It hears you. It feels you. It knows where you are. And so now if I need to know some factoid I can find it out instantly which I think is a relief for a lot of us. We don't have to worry about factoids in quite the same way. We can look at the big strands rather than the minutiae and I think that that's kind of liberating in some way.

So the use of technology in a school like this is for production rather than consumption and I emphasise production because when you're producing, you're also consuming. When you're consuming, you're not necessarily producing. If you're producing you get both. So our kids have published 64 books.

Our kids have gotten patents and they've made films. I'm not into competition but our girls, the Holy Cows, won the international FIRST Robotics Competition last year against 10,000 entrants. And they spent the week that they were there in St Louis with teams from all over the country.

Their robot was so tight before they got there that they spent the whole week helping other teams work on their robots. So this whole spirit of cooperation is really a new one.

And of those girls, all of them are going to college and more than half are majoring in science, technology or engineering or math. I'm not saying that's what they should be doing. I'm just saying that is what they are doing. And that's very different.

Graham: Part of the philosophy of your school is the role of teachers as designers. What is meant by this and how is it different from the role of teachers in the past?

Larry: The idea of teacher as designer means that the teacher has control over what they're basically doing. There's nothing canned about it. And it has not only teacher voice and choice but student voice and choice. What I want to see kids doing is creating new knowledge and I want teachers creating new knowledge, and doing so means that basically the teacher is the designer. Now yesterday morning we were meeting with some teachers and one teacher said, 'Well, if it's teacher as designer what if I think that things should be done more traditionally than we're doing here? May I design that?'

So that's a really interesting question. It depends. If you want to design something which said that we're going to put the smart kids in this room and the not-so-smart kids in that room, that's something that we wouldn't allow you to do because with freedom comes responsibility.

And basically we have a responsibility to stay with our strongest ethos which is that we are not going to mis-predict as society does. We are not going to mis-predict who can and who can't do what. We're not going to mis-predict based on gender. We're not going to mis-predict based on ethnicity. We're not going to mis-predict based on race. And we're not going to mis-predict based on standardised test scores, which is just a more sophisticated or less sophisticated way of making mis-predictions about who can and who

can't do what. So I want teachers that are actually doing really interesting things.

Graham: How does what you're doing here reflect your status as a charter school versus the requirement for your students to perform to existing testing practices?

Larry: OK, so first of all we are a public independent school which is called a charter school in the United States, so we're a public school that happens to be free of 85 percent of this big thick book of regulations called the California Education Code. And there are some superintendents in this state who say it's not fair that you're free of all those regulations and we're bogged down.

And I say you're right and if you get me bogged down again, you're still bogged down. You should be under the mega-waiver for yourself. And in fact if all of the schools in the state were under the mega-waiver it would be like the prisons where they open the doors and most of the prisoners stay in their cells because they've got no place to go.

I don't think we're going to have the rampant inventing that we should be having even if we didn't have these regulations. Nevertheless the regulations suck the oxygen out of the system in my opinion. I'm saying that, having been principal of the oldest high school in the United States, where every time someone did something stupid, including me, they made another rule and they never take rules away, they just add rules.

So we decided when we opened as a charter school —which is a public school— that there was some number that we had to have. And we decided it was our college completion rate. If that number was very high and it is —I've got it right in here from the National Student Clearinghouse, and by subgroup of black students, of Latino students, of Asians, of poverty— then people can't say to us, 'Well, this isn't good college preparation.' We have evidence that it is. Do you have evidence that it isn't? We're going to be evidence-based here.

I remember when the conversation about stand-

ards first happened and I was talking with some others who were there then and we actually said, 'Why don't we call them expectations rather than standards?' And someone said, 'What's wrong with the word "standards"?' Well because if you add a few letters to the word 'standards', you get 'standardisation' and standardisation is the death mill of innovation and the opposite of innovation. That's really the problem I think with this idea about standards and standardising.

So now we've got a new thing called the new common core. We'll see how it goes. It's supposed to be fewer, higher, better. I'm not excited yet. You know what I mean? So that's how we do it. We just picked a number. That was our start. And we hit those numbers and that gives us cover.

Graham: A feature of what you do here is to integrate your students in the adult world. How does that work?

Larry: We began with high schools and, of course, even with younger kids it's sort of paradoxical to segregate kids from the adult world that they're preparing to enter, right? So let's go back to the beginning of schools. I think it's worth spending a minute on that.

Socrates in 400 BC did something new which we still use, the Socratic method. We use the Socratic method here. If you were in a village and you wanted to learn how to make a fishing line, you would learn at the foot of a master or weave a basket, you'd sit at the foot of a master.

It was one-on-one and it was very connected and it was very, very familial. And then the first schools were really around 1,000 years ago when basically across every continent they were for males to be isolated from the community in citadels and study religious texts.

We're not too far from that right now. The high school that I was part of back east in the United States was opened in 1630 for males to study religious texts. It wasn't until 1820 that Thomas Jefferson created the first non-sectarian public university on the whole planet. That's relatively recent.

So this whole question of schools and schooling and the bureaucratisation of schooling is a significant issue. When we first had the public schools —all that was brought to us by Horace Mann around 1820 in New England— there were conservative farmers in New England who didn't want their money to be spent this way. They said, 'OK, we will allow you to do this if we have boards that watch how you're spending our money.' Hence the origination of publicly elected school boards. So if you look at this sort of history of education from the very beginning, a lot of what we're doing is really *déjà vu* all over again.

We're going back to the one-on-one relationship at the foot of a master by basically having the kids go out on internships where they're with somebody who does something well and they're with them for a period of time. They are not predicting their future occupation. In fact, this is the void of life where they're deciding the things they want to be and the things they don't want to be, right?

Graham: Your school uses a project-based learning approach within its teaching practice. Can you explain what this means in practice?

Larry: Anytime you put a label on something, then a lot of people do a lot different things and call it that. Sometimes it gets confused with 'project-oriented' which means that you're doing something for a whole semester and then you've got two days to put a project together for an exhibition. That's not what we mean.

I had a visitor from India. He came here because he has made a lot of money and he wants to do several schools in a low-income area there and he spent a few days here. I was driving him to the airport and he said, 'Very, very interesting' just before he got to the airport. 'But how can I explain project-based learning to everyone when I get back there? I mean I've seen it and I like it but how...' I said, 'OK look —observation, reflection, documentation, exhibition. Think about that.'

You came halfway around the world because you heard that this would be a good place to observe

'We're going back to the one-on-one relationship at the foot of a master by basically having the kids go out on internships where they're with somebody who does something well and they're with them for a period of time.'

and learn a few things from. You're going to reflect on the flight back. You're going to talk to your wife. You're going to talk to your colleagues. You're going to use various media to document your observations and your reflections of your observations and then when the school opens, that's your exhibition.

A lot of people don't do the extra piece. When I had built houses ... observation, reflection, documentation, exhibition. I've made documentary films like you. It's exactly what you're doing right here. You're coming, you're observing, you're reflecting, you're documenting and this is going to be exhibited.

People are going to be watching and reading this thing and this was a project. This is mostly how people work in the world. It's not doctrinaire. It's like a way of being that's very, very commonplace basically. Let kids do it and then there are benefits to it. They get to make something that wasn't there before.

This whole idea is like the book that you're writing, like the books the kids have made, like the houses I have built, like when we have children. There's a great satisfaction in life. I mean, making something that wasn't here before is one of the greatest joys on earth.

Graham: How does that affect the pedagogical practice within the school?

Larry: It affects the practice and also staff development in several ways. Let's assume that I'm a new teacher and I'm not really getting how project-based kind of stuff works. Well, serial exhibitions are going to happen here in which the place will be jammed with parents, uncles, aunts, neighbours, sisters and brothers, cousins, not because we told them to come, but because the kids said, 'You have to come see what I did.'

You can't even park within seven or eight blocks of here on those nights. And I'm a new teacher. And everyone is looking at your work. And everyone is looking at her work. And they're not really looking at my kids' work and I'm a human being. And I'm thinking: What are they doing that I'm not and what is she doing that I'm not? Next cycle, I'm going to start to do more of what they're doing.

So if you think about it, schooling is mostly individuals working in the autonomous isolation of their classroom. Now when you make it a group effort and you make it public, it gives new meaning to transparency, new meaning to family participation, certainly new meaning to accountability of public dollars, right?

Graham: The environment of the school feels very much like an open-plan design consultancy. How did that come about?

Larry: Well the environment is really, really important. There are three characteristics that we really seek in a building: height, light and structure. Those are the iconic pieces that we want. And that's why it feels like a start-up in certain ways, like you would see in Silicon Valley, for example.

So by height obviously the fact that it's 35 feet tall and we've got saw-toothed skylights. Light, having the light come bathing in has a great effect. Photosynthesis is not just for plants. It's for human beings as well. And structure, like kids' museums today, they reveal the structure of the building. You see the bones of the building so you see how the building works.

Then there's the cultural feel of the environment. We don't have a public address system. I have lived in a school with, 'Will Mary please come to the main office.' It's like 50 classes just got interrupted. Mary will make it to the main office. It's not a bus station. It's a school, OK? And it's a different feel. There's something very sacred about a school, right?

If you want to go to the bathroom here, you go to the bathroom. You don't have to curtsy. You just go to the bathroom, right? And so this particular building has 39,000 square feet and instead of having about 300 kids, which is what it should have, it has 572 and it's very, very calm, and we don't have fights.

Graham: Do you think it would be possible to scale High Tech High to a national level?

Larry: We've grown quite a bit in terms of the fact that we now have as many kids as the 300-year-old district I used to work in, and we did it in 13 years. Five thousand kids and 600 employees is a lot now, right? We have two schools in creation and that might be it. We created a graduate school of education as a vehicle to work with adults from around the country and around the world.

We have a visitors' programme where about 3,000 people a year visit. You're here from some place, someone else just came from Japan, there are other people here from all over the place every single day. We used to say to people to go up to the kids and ask them what they're working on but now the kids will just go up to you and start saying, 'Do you want to know what I'm working on?' So there are impediments to doing this which is the negative side of it all.

The narrative when I first taught, 37 years ago, was school reform and the narrative today is school reform. And the narrative every day in between has been school reform. So school reform doesn't mean all that much to me as a term of art but I still —or like to try to— stand on the shoulders of John Dewey who in 1910 said that he'd rather have one school *former* than 100 school reformers. Meaning one school created rather than 100 schools recreated.

I think that what we need is a lot of innovation of a lot of people, not just in schools like this, but doing all kinds of different schools of their own where they take some of the elements from here. It's just people who are realising that what they're doing isn't working anymore and these are our babies, these are our children that we love more than anything in life and we've got to do better by them.

I'm hoping for a renaissance. And we're seeing a bit of a renaissance going on right now but maybe I have a skewed view from the 2,000–3,000 people who come here every year. But I would just say let people go with it. Just let people try it. Don't try to constrain it. Let people experiment. We really need rampant experimentation.

'So the use of technology in a school like this is for production rather than consumption and I emphasise production because when you're producing, you're also consuming. When you're consuming, you're not necessarily producing. If you're producing you get both.'

United States of America

'If you picture that across countless numbers
of students, that's a massively untapped,
unorganised, unfocused group of human
potential and ideas. Students with their
uninhibited creativity. Isn't it motivating
for anyone, not just students, to have their
ideas be seen, be heard, receive oxygen,
grow, change and have an impact?'

The TED conference organisation has, for nearly 30 years, brought together many of the world's leading thinkers to inspire their audiences with new ideas. After bringing their platform to the digital world in 2007, the connected population gained free access to TED's valuable resource of talks, some of which have been viewed millions of times, filling a vacuum left by traditional broadcasters in the science and innovation fields.

With the intention of supporting teachers and sparking the curiosity of learners around the world, TED-Ed is the newest of TED's initiatives. Their mission is to distribute what they call 'lessons worth sharing' via a growing library of curated educational videos, many of which represent collaborations between talented educators and animators nominated through the TED-Ed platform. TED-Ed also allows users to take any useful video and create a customised lesson around it.

Logan Smalley, TED Fellow and former teacher, heads up the initiative in New York, where I met him.

Graham Brown-Martin: What's the background to the TED-Ed initiative?

Logan Smalley: We're about 18 months old as a launched initiative and we really do two things. One is we create original content that features the voice of educators or teachers that we work with, that is recorded and brought to life by professional animators in video form, and we also develop a website that supports teachers and students in using that content and their own content in a classroom environment.

TED-Ed works as an open nomination system so you or anyone out there can nominate themselves or can nominate an educator that they love and respect. Our team reviews the nominations and when there's a particularly great one pitching a salient lesson, we move that into production and so we work with that educator to record their voice and, like I said, professionally animate it in video form.

At the 18-month mark, we've done around 300 original animations and —not that views are the only metric that matters but just to put it in perspective— those have been viewed about 36 million times. What we hear from teachers we've worked with is that they felt like they've given a lesson many years as a science teacher or English teacher, for example, and it's reached the people in that room or occasionally sometimes it goes a little bit beyond that. Now their lessons are reaching on average 100,000 learners. It's extremely exciting to see the voices of great teachers amplified. Now I do want to qualify that because we definitely don't have any delusions and I don't think that anyone should think of video as teaching.

These videos are great teaching aids. They're great ways to get the conversation started or to supplement a particularly confusing part of a conversation or a day's lesson and I think we've done a pretty good job at making sure that people understand that that's what the tool is for. It's really not meant to supplant teachers. In fact, it's made by teachers so it's meant to amplify the voice of people who are actually in the classrooms, formal or informal, teaching and learning.

Graham: From an international perspective, are the lessons primarily US-oriented?

Logan: TED-Ed is a global platform and we've worked with teachers from dozens of countries. We certainly are used by students in a lot of countries.

TED has a volunteer translation force called OTP, Open Translators Project, with something like 12,000 volunteers from all around the world translating TED content so that these ideas, or these lessons in our case, can be more easily accessed in both English-speaking countries and non-English-speaking countries. In fact, one of the most accessed forms of transcript is actually the English one.

Graham: Do you think there's a possibility that educational content from one nation may have a cultural bias in an international context?

Logan: Yes, absolutely. There's always a risk of getting an overly Western perspective or overly anything perspective, right? You always try for a balanced approach to content creation, messaging and access. It's incredibly important that the habits, culture and history of every region in the world are included as part of the story because that's where some incredible learning happens through comparing and contrasting, appreciating similarities, appreciating differences, understanding where not to repeat history.

Graham: People are getting very excited about video in the education world as if it could replace teachers. What are your thoughts on this?

Logan: I try to take a sober line of thought when it comes to video. If you just think about video as the medium, it has pros and cons, it has strengths and weaknesses, just like any tool in the teacher's toolbox. I think what video is really good at is capturing a story from one place and moving it to somewhere else and allowing a one-to-many model.

When that's actually the most beneficial way to communicate what's being taught or what students are trying to learn, then use video. When it's not, I would never argue against the value of small groups. In fact we're even optimising our platform in ways so that five people at a time watching a video together is simply a tool to push them towards a small, live physical group.

I'm really excited about when technology enables our humanity, not when it causes it to decline, and I think it's almost always better to learn in a group because that's how you're exposed to different opinions and different perspectives, and that's how your own opinions and perspectives grow.

Video, as it becomes more and more accessible around the world, can help put local problems or global problems in front of everyone and what could be better than providing students with real problems? If they don't solve them, Earth is in trouble and so getting it to them at an earlier age and giving them tools to help start working is, I think, really empowering and naturally motivating because it is their world more than it is ours as we get older.

Graham: There are a number of interactive video systems appearing across the digital spectrum driving the flipped classroom model. Some support the existing curriculum and others are about discovery. What are your thoughts on this?

Logan: At TED-Ed, we really try to focus on the 'why?' of education. Take the Pythagorean theorem, a classic lesson taught in schools. It's one thing to know how to isolate the variables, solve for the hypotenuse and all those things, and that's important if you're going to be doing a job that requires that. What's also important is: Why is the Pythagorean theorem in existence? Why are the pyramids still standing? Why is the triangle the strongest structure that there is? How does it inspire us? Who was Pythagoras? Right?

There are all these incredible things and I actually think that the best education is a combination of both. Whether it's by virtue of your own curiosity or some stimulus, perhaps a video helped you start asking those questions. Why is the triangle important? I can guarantee you that the triangle is important but probably there are as many answers to that question as there are students.

Graham: You've talked about amplifying the voice of teachers. Have you considered how you might do the same for learners?

Logan: When we ask people that question we hear answers like 'Facebook, YouTube, some other platforms' but I don't think anyone actually thinks of Facebook or YouTube or whatever as a sort of platform for student ideas. Then the other answers we get are, 'Well, my best student ideas I put up on my classroom wall,' or mom says, 'My son wrote a great paper and it's hanging on our fridge with an "A" on it underneath the refrigerator magnet,' or, 'We keep all of our children's best work in this box that we keep in the attic.'

If you picture that across countless numbers of students, that's a massively untapped, unorganised, unfocused group of human potential and ideas. Students with their uninhibited creativity. If they do come up with a wonderful idea which happens all the time, by the way, shouldn't it live beyond the classroom? Shouldn't it be spread? Shouldn't it oxygenate? Isn't it motivating for anyone, not just students, to have their ideas be seen, be heard, receive oxygen, grow, change and have an impact?

To answer that question, we've launched a new program called TED-Ed Clubs and the way that it fits into the sort of ecosystem of TED is year one, we focus on amplifying the voice of teachers and the second year, we really want to focus on helping the best student ideas live beyond their class and celebrate them in order to expand opportunity for those students.

What we're really excited about in this next year is the focus on establishing a platform for celebrating student ideas because even if the idea wasn't a good idea, that's not the point. The point is that they went through the process of trying to articulate whatever that idea was. So the next time they do it, it will be a better idea, and the next time, and by the time they're my age or your age, their ideas would trump ours and their opportunity would have been expanded in the process.

ed.ted.com

'I think it's almost always better to learn in a group because that's how you're exposed to different opinions and different perspectives, and that's how your own opinions and perspectives grow.'

'...our technical prowess is running far ahead of our spiritual and ethical capacities. It's not a wild fancy to imagine that we could create the conditions for our own extinction as a species'

Sir Ken Robinson hardly needs any introduction in the world of education. Indeed, his seminal talk about schools and creativity has been viewed more than 30 million times, achieving a much-needed crossover in the discourse between educators, policymakers and the public about what, why and how our children might learn.

Robinson is a British author, raconteur and international advisor on education in the arts to government, non-profits, education and arts bodies. Born in Liverpool in 1950, he was Director of The Arts in Schools Project (1985–89), Professor of Arts Education at the University of Warwick (1989–2001), and was knighted in 2003 by Queen Elizabeth II for services to education. In 1998, he led a UK commission on creativity, education and the economy and his report, 'All Our Futures: Creativity, Culture, and Education' was influential. *The Times* newspaper reported that, 'This report raises some of the most important issues facing business in the 21st century. It should have every CEO and human resources director thumping the table and demanding action.'

In 2001 Robinson relocated to Los Angeles when he was appointed Senior Advisor for Education & Creativity at the Getty Museum, a post he held until 2005. His books on nurturing creativity and finding individual passion have inspired a generation of educators and those who value the arts within our learning.

On a personal note, I've found the times that I've spent in Ken's company to have an energising quality that informs my thinking around creativity as well as finding my own 'element'. That I'm writing this book is an example of his influence, for which I'm grateful.

We met for coffee and conversation in his offices in the Westwood Village district of Los Angeles, a Bohemian area adjacent to the University of California.

Graham Brown-Martin: Do you think technology can have a transformative impact on learning?

Sir Ken Robinson: Well, when you say technology, you presumably mean digital technology because technology's been with us since the dawn of civilisation, of course. The obvious thing to say about it is that it's no more than the design and making of tools, which have always managed to extend our reach. That's one of the great drivers, I think, of human development culturally –that we have had tools that have extended what we're capable, not just of doing, but capable of thinking about.

As soon as you have writing systems, you don't just extend your ability to spread a message. You affect the very nature of the messages you're able to distribute, the messages you're able to conceive of. All great transformative technologies have done that. They've not just been able to do things we could do before but differently. They've enabled us to do things that we probably even couldn't have conceived of before.

That's what's happening with this new wave of digital technology. It's changing the way we think. It's changing how we communicate. It's changing how we access ideas. It's changing how we not just connect to people, but think of ourselves and our capabilities. In so far as educa-

tion is and should be about helping people learn, it seems to me they have to be seen as pivotal to the way education evolves from here on. They're not incidental. They're not embellishments. We shouldn't be thinking, 'Well, we could bring in some digital technology and see if it helps.'

Graham: What do you think the obstacles are at the moment for embracing digital platforms within our formal education settings?

Sir Ken: Well, I think there are all sorts of obstacles. Some of them are transitional. For example, I was born in 1950. I was schooled in the '50s and '60s. In high schools, nobody had computers at all. They were far-fetched devices... It just wasn't on anybody's radar to think of using computers.

It's obvious enough to say it, but it's easy to forget how quickly this particular digital revolution has overtaken us. There are a lot of people in education who ... didn't grow up in a world where these things existed. They still do, to some degree, think of them as exotic. It is one of the ways in which we are often different from the students that we teach because they've grown up with them. They take them for granted.

Somebody once said, 'Technology is something that happened after you were born.' I think that's right. When I was growing up, electricity wasn't a big deal... But my great-grandparents were thrilled that they could flick a switch, and a light would come on. And motorcars were nothing to my generation, but they were to my parents' generation.

'...a really creative idea excites the imaginations of everybody that comes across it, and they try it for themselves and come up with new stuff.'

The digital technologies are second nature, of course, to a lot of our students... [Most] people who are running the education systems, particularly people over 40, have learned [these technologies] in their adulthood. Some of them are really good at them, and some aren't. So some of it's transitional.

It's yet to sink in with people just how revolutionary these devices are likely to prove to the whole concept of the school, for example. The school as a building contained within walls, with parameters and with a regular schedule everyone has to follow, there's no reason for any of that stuff to really happen any more.

I'm not arguing against having learning communities. I think we should have them. I think there's a huge amount to be gained by being in the company of people that you don't get from Facebook or Skype, no matter how good they are. You know that. There's something about sensing the energy of a room.

The institutional implications are huge and so are the pedagogical implications. I think it changes the whole relationship between teachers and students. We know it does. It's a transition that's going to carry on indefinitely because the devices we've got now that seem so funky and kind of leading-edge will be museum pieces soon enough.

I was looking recently at the impact of Kodak's brand new camera in the early 20th century... It was as revolutionary a device as the iPad is now. It transformed how people saw the world around them, how they hung onto the past, how they viewed their loved ones and others close to them. It gave them a capacity they didn't have before. Of course, now it seems like a quaint device that you occasionally pick up in a junk shop.

You can imagine 30 or 40 years from now, you'll get a generation of kids looking back at pictures of you and your iPhone with a patronising smile... People in the field are developing devices that require no physical contact whatever. If you take seriously the arguments of people who are very well qualified to make them, like Ray Kurzweil, there may come a point in the foreseeable future where we'll not just wear digital devices about our persons, but they'll be integrated into our own consciousness. Well, all bets are off at that point in terms of learning and what it is to be a person.

The implications for the sort of industrialised mass-conformative system of education we have so far, organisationally, are huge. They're beginning to roll through, and like most big revolutions, they're happening already but sporadically. People are ahead of the curve, people pulling back away from it, people who hate the whole idea, and other people who are embracing it. It's a very interesting dynamic period just now in education.

> **Graham:** We know that digital technology has the potential to liberate learning but do you think society might just use it to automate?

Sir Ken: There are two observations I want to make about this. One is that as things stand, these tools have no intentions of any sort. I say as things stand because if ultimately information systems become intelligent, if digital devices become in any feasible sense of the word conscious, then that's a change that we all have to try and evaluate when it comes about.

But as things stand, they don't have intentions. They are tools. They're very sophisticated shovels and spades and complicated pencils. It's like the symphony orchestra is a toolkit. A violin is a tool. It doesn't produce music on its own... A music cupboard full of instruments has no music in it until musicians pick them up and breathe life into them.

It's the same way at the moment with cameras, laptops and iPhones... None of them has any clear set of intentions. It depends how we use them... We can use them to make current activities more efficient. We can use them to dispose of people whose roles have become redundant, or we can use them in very different ways imaginatively to kind of crush new horizons entirely.

It's why I don't see technology as the solution to all educational problems. They're just a new and very interesting, expansive toolkit. But we still need to cultivate our own sensibilities about how to use them, our ethical grasp of their implications. We also have to develop our creative capacities so that we can use that potential in a way that benefits us.

Generally, transformative technologies lead to all kinds of unexpected consequences. They always do. Rock and roll was not a government plan... Facebook wasn't a plan except in the mind of Mark Zuckerberg. Nobody anticipated it. When Logie Baird invented the television, or at least as we believe to be the case in Britain, he couldn't have anticipated Fox News... You can get apps now for your iPhone that turn it into a blues harmonica. Well, that wasn't on the mind of Steve Jobs...

What happens is that a really creative idea excites the imaginations of everybody that comes across it, and they try it for themselves and come up with new stuff. That's why I'm saying I think this is a very complicated picture. I don't think it will be either-or. Maybe some trends will become dominant in some areas, but it's an entirely new set of possibilities that people are just waking up to, I think. MOOCs are a very good example of something unexpected.

> **Graham:** Would you argue that nurturing creativity is more important now than it has been historically within our education systems?

Sir Ken: Yes, I'd say it is. Creativity has a bad press, I think, in the sense that it's very rare to find people who want to argue seriously against developing creativity in education. People on the whole think it's a good thing. It's like health. You don't get people saying that we should make people ill... It's one of those goods.

But there's a huge amount of misunderstanding about what it is. I always have had, for as long as I've been arguing on behalf of more creative approaches to education, people presenting me with all kinds of false dichotomies to choose between. They're saying, 'Oh, creativity is fine, but kids have got to learn the basics.' Or, 'Yes, we should get people to have their own ideas, but they really do have to learn about history and tradition', as if there was a conflict. There isn't any conflict between these two things at all, properly conceived.

My argument has been for a long time that creativity is a *portmanteau* term for a whole set of capacities that we all have and can develop. If you think of it, it's our capacity for original ideas and production that has been the engine of human cultural change and achievement. I always hesitate to use the word progress, but you know what I mean. We're in a building here, and we're sitting here with cameras and we're wearing clothes that somebody's designed and made, whereas, most other creatures are living out there in the natural state they've always lived in. Human beings live in a made world. We create a world. We create ideas and values and systems and languages and technologies. We inhabit that space that we create. And we create ideologies, and we fight over them. Animals ... die for food and territory, but not for ideas and belief systems. We do all of that stuff.

So creativity is a complex set of capacities that human beings have to a unique degree, and it's always been important that we should cultivate them, I believe. It's becoming more important, I think, and education is really at the heart of this because of the challenges, ironically, that we've now created for ourselves. I think there are several here. One of them is that the world population is now well over seven billion... We're heading for nine billion, probably ten billion by the end of the century.

It's pretty clear the planet can't sustain the way we currently live... We're getting massive strains on the environment, and for all the good they're bringing, the technologies in some ways are multiplying many of the ancient cultural issues that have divided people since time immemorial. In a way, our technical prowess is running far ahead of our spiritual and ethical capacities. It's not a wild fancy to imagine that we could create the conditions for our own extinction as a species. Certainly we could hobble ourselves very badly. The irony for me is that we have created all these extraordinary possibilities but we still haven't seen far enough, and it's very important that we do now.

There was a very interesting comment in the early 20th century by H. G. Wells, the science fiction writer, who famously said that 'civilisation is in a race between education and catastrophe.' I think it's true. What we do know is we literally can't afford for everyone on earth to consume, eat, behave in the way that those of us who lived in the old industrialised economies, with a very high level of material standards of living, have become used to.

We can't carry on like this. We do have to think very differently. There's the sense in which creativity and imagination and innovation have always been important at the individual level. I think at the global level, they are becoming increasingly urgent and that we have to put them at the heart of our education systems.

Graham: It seems that our education systems are locked into old ideas by a tyranny of testing that drives teaching and learning. What are your thoughts on this?

Sir Ken: Yes, I do think we live under a tyranny of testing. There's no question about that and it's not totally benign. An interesting parallel to me is the drug industry. Depression is now a worldwide epidemic. It's anticipated that within about 20 years, according to the World Health Organisation, I'm told, that depression will be the single largest cause of mortality among human populations.

Well, the drug companies profit hugely from depression... It doesn't seem to me that they're very keen to cure depression. Why would they? They want you to keep taking [their drugs]... and keep buying their products, just like cigarette manufacturers aren't trying to wean you off them.

There's a kind of benign view of testing which is that it fulfils necessary purposes in keeping track of standards, accountability in providing certification and qualifications for progress through the system. There's a way of looking at them and saying, well, it meets those important purposes in education... What's also true is it's a massively profitable enterprise for all publishers. It's one of the engines of the education economy.

'All great transformative technologies have done that. They've not just been able to do things we could do before but differently. They've enabled us to do things that we probably even couldn't have conceived of before.'

The debate isn't about should we get rid of testing, but can we produce more interesting, more expensive forms of it? In America, the states spend billions of dollars on testing systems. It's a big business. It makes it difficult to have a reasoned conversation about it with people because there are lots of vested interests. Like in the environment. A lot of the arguments about oil and coal aren't being held in some neutral, ethical space. In the environment, there are massive vested interests. You don't want to be looking at a clean source of energy, because the profits lie in the existing source of energy. They'd rather keep it this way until they're exhausted. Then they'll look for some other way of making a profit.

That's not being cynical. That's just a matter of fact. It's how the markets work, and there's a market in education for these things. When you talk about testing, it's a rather complicated picture. If you look at it from a purely educational point of view as opposed to an ideological point of view or a commercial point of view, education can function perfectly well without tests of the sort that we're currently used to. It may be able to function even better in the future without them.

One purpose of testing is to monitor students' progress. Well, there are better ways of doing that than from standardised competitive testing. There

are teacher reports, there are peer-group reports, there are portfolios to give them. If we're just interested in making sure that people are making adequate progress, the occasional diagnostic test is fine, but there are better ways of doing it than sitting people down ritually and routinely in sterile conditions and forcing them to answer a set of questions that they may not be in the best space to deal with at the time. We know that. There's a whole psychology around testing.

One of the reasons that we have these tests is because countries are very keen to know how they're getting along competitively with each other. That's what PISA is about. I do think that we end up with the tail wagging the dog, that you get education ministers who judge each other and judge themselves against them according to how their country's getting along on the PISA test. Well, you have professional reputations, personal reputations vested in these processes. Again, it doesn't have much to do with children's educational development. It has a lot to do with international pride. If you look at the success of countries like Finland where they have very little of this regular testing, they take part in the PISA processes, but they're not obsessed culturally with testing.

There's a political purpose that these things fulfil, and commercial purposes. The other purpose is that they're used as the gateway into things like higher education, in particular. Well, what the MOOCs are showing, and what other forms of online data are showing, is you don't really need these gateways to get access to advanced education. All those things are predicated on limited places and physical buildings. But if there are no limits, and the main requirement is if you can do the work or not, and if you have the kind of mettle and the aptitude to do it, then you don't need these gateways any more.

'Far from being neutral and democratic, the web is dominated by whoever has the most servers.'

There's a common belief in digital folklore that the web as a tool is neutral, that the strength of its search engines, reputation and trust maps lack bias and are therefore particularly suited to use in education. Our technocracy would have us believe that the openness, transparency and accessibility of the web are what provide its unique democratising effect.

But is this true? During this century, we are witnessing the decline of traditional broadcast and physical media as digital distribution and discovery systems dominate the mass-media landscape. This is the world in which our children will grow up. One could argue that one form of media is merely changing hands for another and yet, as we know, digital platforms have an amplifying effect that transcends physical borders. Should we be concerned?

Many social and political theorists have recognised that economic exploitation is not the only driver behind capitalism, and that the system is reinforced by a dominance of ruling-class ideas and values. These ideas led to Engels' concern that 'false consciousness' would keep the working class from recognising and rejecting their oppression. Antonio Gramsci saw the state as being divided into two overlapping spheres: the 'political society' that ruled through force and the 'civil society' that ruled through consent. Civil society, according to Gramsci, is a set of institutions through which society represents itself autonomously from the state. Such institutions would include the mass media, education, family and religion. It is argued that it is these institutions that shape our consciousness – what we think and accept as reality.

The domination of one social group over another is known as a hegemony. Gramsci's insights about how power is constituted in the realm of ideas and knowledge have inspired strategies to contest hegemonic legitimacy. Gramsci's ideas have influenced popular education practices, including the adult literacy and consciousness-raising methods of Paulo Freire in his *Pedagogy of the Oppressed* (1974).

Critical theorists Theodor Adorno and Max Horkheimer later expanded on Gramsci in *Dialectic of Enlightenment* (1944), coining the term 'culture industry'. They proposed that popular culture is akin to a factory producing standardised cultural goods used to manipulate mass society into passivity. Consumption, therefore, of the easy pleasures of popular culture made available by the mass communications media renders people docile and content, no matter how difficult their circumstances.

How do these concepts apply to our emergent digital society? The digital world is run by a small number of large multinational corporations, each with their own proprietary special sauce that makes them unique and powerful. Far from being neutral and demo-cratic, the web is dominated by whoever has the most servers.

Sure, it's possible for anyone with a connection to publish a blog or a website and be accessible by the world, but that doesn't mean anybody will find it.

The special sauce is the algorithm, a digital formula created from lines of code that performs functions that make decisions based on certain data. They are used for tasks such as calculation, data processing and automated reasoning. Clever algorithms are put to work by the largest digital corporations to index the web so that when you use a search engine it displays the results it considers most relevant. These engines are so fast and work so well that essentially everyone with an Internet connection relies on them without a second thought.

In principle, the screens of our connected devices are windows into the world's largest library, an expanding ocean of information, but the reality is that we don't open our window very wide and seldom venture beyond the first results. The limitations of algorithms mean that we title books, articles and reports in an attempt to aid discovery. The notion of metaphor is lost on the humble algorithm. Journalists, writers and publishers game search engine algorithms to optimise their work to appear at the top of a search, sometimes even changing the way an article is written. For commercial information sources, getting discovered is big business, especially when advertising revenue is at stake. The result is that those with the most resources are most likely to take the top positions in search; the notion of a neutral, democratic web is diminished.

How can search algorithms be gamed or manipulated? They have biases, a set of preferences that ensure that one source of information is preferred over another. We don't know exactly what these biases are because they are secret and if we knew, we would all game them, defeating the purpose of an unbiased search engine. So, see the problem?

Engineers are constantly trying to reverse-engineer the bias of search engine algorithms and the creators of these algorithms are constantly trying to outsmart them. But in the end it's the organisations with the resources that often do best in the search and discovery world. Commercial digital publishing is typically supported by advertising, sponsorship or paywalls (subscriptions). As we move towards intense personalisation, where information is held in content farms matched by clever algorithms to relevant advertising, unpopular but important stories may no longer appear in your stream, making our news increasingly superficial or sensationalist.

Similarly, in social media items that we think are news and trending may not be what they seem. Twitter uses its own proprietary algorithm to determine what 'trends'. Trending doesn't mean that something is necessarily the most discussed item on that social media platform; rather it is a spike across a community wider than your own. You could have a discussion on the environment with a huge number of followers over a period of months that could fail to trend. But a spike that occurred over a short amount of time across a number of follower communities could trigger the algorithm that looks after trending. The algorithm is optimised to look out for these spikes rather than consistency. Once something begins to trend, the fact that the algorithm identifies it as trending effectively causes it to trend. The algorithm is affecting the outcome.

The reality is that all algorithms can be gamed. Marketing agencies or other forces can hire extremely low-cost labour, via systems like Amazon's Mechanical Turk, to enter enough search terms, back links or mention certain subjects on social platforms to create the illusion of trends or appearance in search requests.

Even memes, those digital items that seem to appear as a result of the crowd, are more often than not manipulated by advertising and marketing agencies leaking information to smaller independent blog writers and social media influencers before it is eventually picked up by the mainstream. That collection of funny pictures from what looks like an indie site that you share on social media is filling someone's boots with advertising revenue. It's all about the clicks.

If we believe that in the future we'll receive most of our information and news from digital sources, would that not be a concern for Gramsci's civil society or for the culture industry of Adorno and Horkheimer? Could the bias in the machine have an unexpected influence over society so that what we write, communicate and learn is unconsciously directed by algorithmic preference?

This raises the spectre of hegemony. Our digital platforms could be used to reinforce the ideas and values of a ruling elite rather than being the open, egalitarian and democratically neutral force that the 'Internet-centrists', as the critic Evgeny Morozov termed them, would have us believe? Today's global digital corporations wield unprecedented power and influence over the world's information and how it is presented. In their quest to make everything efficient, other roads of progress are closed, leading ultimately to an algorithmic society where these corporations, rather than elected governments, determine the shape of the future.

Nothing here is intended to suggest that these corporations are necessarily evil. The consequences may be unintentional, but given that businesses aim to maximise shareholder financial gain, one might at least apply some critical thinking to what is ahead. In our quest for efficiency and fetish for digital innovation it seems that we haven't considered the unintended consequences of digitising our universities into MOOCs and flipping the classroom. It seems remarkable that there is so little dissent in the education community.

Brazil

Brasilia O

São Paulo
O O Rio de Janeiro

Brazil

Brazil is the fifth-largest country in the world, and the largest country in South America, with a population of about 200 million people. Inhabited by indigenous tribal people until it was claimed and colonised by the Portuguese from the 16th century, Brazil remained a colony until the early 19th century before gaining independence in 1822. The nation passed through a number of constitutional changes including a monarchy and parliamentary system before becoming a presidential republic in the late 19th century after the monarchy was overthrown by the military. Brazil was then governed by a series of presidents until 1964 when the left-wing government was removed by the military, leaving the nation under military rule until 1985 when power was returned to civilian hands, albeit with soaring economic inflation. Today, Brazil operates as a federal republic with 26 states and 5,564 municipalities or administrative divisions.

The ebb and flow of the Brazilian economy and the demographics of its population reflect its history of colonisation and turbulent governmental rule.

Slavery was, at least theoretically, abolished in Brazil in 1888, and a period of economic growth known as the *Encilhamento* followed, based on get-rich-quick schemes supported by unrestricted credit associated with banking reforms and late-19th century industrialisation. This economic bubble quickly burst, leading to decades of austerity with social and political unrest that, it could be argued, lasted well into the late 20th century.

The threat of a socialist government in the early 1960s led to a US-supported *coup* that installed military rule over the country. Brazil evolved from a largely rural, agricultural nation to a primarily urban, industrialised nation. A brief period of economic growth known as the Brazilian Miracle coincided with military dictatorship, but with restricted freedoms and political opposition the economy stagnated and the government fell, like others in the region, under the weight of the pro-democracy movements of the mid-1980s.

Today Brazil is the largest economy in Latin America and, at the time of writing, the seventh-largest economy in the world based on market exchange rates. A mixed economy with abundant natural resources, for much of the 21st century Brazil has been regarded as 'white hot' by many commentators, one of four fast-advancing developing countries, along with Russia, India and China. Yet in 2014 these speculations come with words of caution as the Brazilian economy shows signs of slowing down, having become overly dependent on China for its exports. Economists argue that Brazil is under-investing in infrastructure, suggesting that the productivity spurt it experienced under military dictatorship has fallen.

The country invests just 2.2 percent of its GDP in infrastructure, well below the developing-world average of 5.1 percent. Of the 278,000 patents granted last year by the US patent office, just 254 went to inventors from Brazil, which accounts for three percent of the world's output and people. Brazil's spending on education as a share of GDP has risen to rich-world levels, but quality has not, with pupils among the worst-performing in standardised tests.

Huge inequalities exist amongst marginalised ethnic

groups such as the under-represented Afro-Brazilian population, which is extraordinary when you consider that a recent census showed that over 50 percent of the Brazilian population define themselves as black or dual-heritage. Brazil celebrates its 200th year of independence in 2022 and this perhaps sets a useful target for its nascent educational transformation programme.

The public education system in Brazil has historically been tragically under-funded and the status of teachers and educators undermined by successive governments. Over recent years there have been many attempts to meet the challenges of transforming the educational system through the use of technology, with a variety of national schemes including the One Laptop Per Child, 1:1 computing with Intel Classmate PC and various mobile phone programmes, none of which could claim to have been successful.

But grassroots activism, social entrepreneurship and public-private partnerships are emerging to meet these challenges. The country is so vast and diverse that 'change must be orchestrated in partnership with the civil society', as one government official told me. By this, he recognised that the creation of a long-term plan that could transcend changes of government in a democracy could only really be achieved if the plan was owned by external social and commercial enterprises. While in Brazil I had the opportunity to visit two such projects.

'Brazil celebrates its 200th year of independence in 2022 and this perhaps sets a useful target for its nascent educational transformation programme.'

'The ebb and flow of the Brazilian economy and the demographics of its population reflect its history of colonisation and turbulent governmental rule.'

Brazil

'Today Brazil is the largest economy in Latin America and, at the time of writing, the seventh-largest economy in the world based on market exchange rates.'

We leave New York early on a Saturday morning and spend the entire day flying to São Paulo. It was one of the longest flights of our tour and my orangutan-like arms and legs were definitely feeling the strain by the time my team and I arrived. A constant diet of economy fish, chicken or pasta while strapped to a seat designed for a Hobbit soon strips away the glamour of air travel. So it was with relief that we disembarked in São Paulo, the largest city of Brazil, and headed to our hotel situated in the Bohemian and trendy Pinheiros district, full of cafés, restaurants and lively nightlife. After freshening up, it was evening before we left the hotel in search of food and refreshments from a local café, negotiated with our non-existent grasp of Portuguese. A nightclub across the street looked promising with its painted sign, in the universal language of good times, that said *1980s Disco*. From what I recall we returned to our hotel just before the sun came up after engaging in a lengthy period of participant research in local socialising rituals. Brazilians, it seems, are a friendly bunch.

Founded in February 2012, Porvir is an initiative of Inspirare, an institute founded by former petrochemical entrepreneur Bernardo Gradin and his family. Inspirare seeks to inspire innovation in entrepreneurial initiatives, public policies, programmes and investments aimed at improving the quality of education in Brazil. I was fortunate to meet Gradin and his interview is included within this book.

One of the challenges in Brazil, I learn, is that there isn't an active public dialogue about education within its mainstream media. As a result, editorial coverage in the newspapers, radio or television is scant with few, if any, of the major Brazilian news outlets employing editors specifically covering education. Gilberto Dimenstein, a supporter of Porvir, is a big name in Brazilian journalism with his own radio show on CBN and a newspaper column in *Folha de S. Paulo*. He tells me, 'Education in Brazil is not a priority even though you hear all of the speeches of the government. It's not a priority.' Dimenstein believes that good journalism can be at the heart of education and that the media can educate rather than sedate its population.

Porvir, meaning 'future well-being for all people', is a not-for-profit editorial office and clearing house for the production of content about global developments around innovations in education that promotes the dissemination and exchange of content across all media platforms in Brazil. This means that it has become the go-to place for informed, unbiased editorial comment and material that is provided to the Brazilian media community on a Creative Commons basis. Its objective is to inspire improvements in the quality of education in Brazil by encouraging social mobilisation and public awareness of global best practice and innovation.

Another Porvir supporter is Maria do Pilar Lacerda, former Director of Basic Education at the Ministry of Education. She suggests that the development of Brazil's education systems has suffered as a result of external intervention and military dictatorship. She explains: 'When Cuba had the socialist revolution in 1969, the Brazilian government was overthrown by the military, so at the same time that the Cubans were having a revolution, when the priority was to provide dignity to all with health and education, we were living under a dictatorship which was very nationalist, allied with the US government, hunting our leaders, living under censorship, and we did not have a commitment to education. So we went through 21 years where the students, intellectuals, singers and writers were severely persecuted, and censorship was very strong. A consequence is that we didn't have a mass of critics like we do today, and that means the country has lost this time in relation to education. The education policies of the military dictatorship in Brazil were privatising and selective. There was a clear conception in the political and economic elite, that supported the military dictatorship, that education definitely was not for all, not everyone needs to study or know how to read and, still influenced by the Cold War, that books and music are dangerous.'

Dimenstein also reflects on Brazil's social pressures in relation to its large Afro-Brazilian population: 'Brazil was the last independent country to get rid of slavery and we pay a lot of debt on this, because we still have an education system which reflects this social apartheid.'

Porvir's idea of education includes different agents and spaces that promote learning processes, including schools, universities, companies, social organisations and governments. They engage a full-time editorial team of journalists who map practices, tools, research and people related to innovations and education in Brazil and overseas, with the collaboration of an international network of volunteers. These volunteers help Porvir identify experiences already tested or at an embryonic stage, capable of inspiring ideas and solutions to educational challenges in Brazil.

The Porvir team disseminates this information via their website and collaborations with the media. Their site offers the 'Garimpo' section, featuring a selection of articles and stories published by 70 international and national news media outlets that provides a valuable resource for domestic journalists. Media professionals wanting to deepen their coverage on an education-related subject can rely on the support of Porvir to identify good stories, sources and different approaches, working as a free news agency that aims to place education improvement at the top of the Brazilian social and political agenda. Porvir works to mobilise decision makers and the general public by facilitating strategic meetings and events to inspire and guide governments, investors, social entrepreneurs, experts, and education and human resources leaders.

Mariana Fonseca, Porvir's editor, is upbeat about their work to assist Brazilian journalists when she says, 'You can call us anytime, if you want. We offer all the journalists all our sources. They're free. So if they call me here and say, "I want to write about MOOCs. Who do you think I should call?" I'll say, "Go talk to edX, go talk to Coursera, go talk to these people here." I'll give him the phone, the email. We're helping them. "Now, which angle should we write about?" We help them with that also!'

www.porvir.org

'...journalism can be at the heart of education and that the media can educate rather than sedate its population.'

Brazil

Porvir is a communication and social mobilisation initiative that promotes the production, dissemination and exchange of content on innovations in education in order to inspire improvements in Brazil's education provision. It achieves this by acting as an editorial production team and clearing house that provides quality reporting on education innovations to Brazil's mainstream media and government. Traditionally, reporting on education within Brazil's newspaper and broadcasting media has been limited. Porvir's objective is to change this and thus increase public awareness and desire for positive change *(see case study on page 238)*.

Porvir is an initiative of the Inspirare Institute whose mission is to inspire innovations in entrepreneurial activities, public policies, programmes and investments that improve the quality of education in Brazil. It is the brainchild of Brazilian businessman Bernardo Gradin, whose family fortune was made in the petrochemical industries before investing in sustainable energy sectors and other social programmes.

I met with Bernardo at Porvir's offices to learn more of his work and inspirations.

Graham Brown-Martin: Bernardo, what was the inspiration for establishing the Inspirare Institute?

Bernardo Gradin: I was born in Bahia, Brazil. I'm an engineer and I have an MBA from the United States. After that I came back to Brazil to work in one of the largest corporations in Brazil [Odebrecht]. My family was a stakeholder in this corporation until 2010. At the beginning of 2011 we left the company and we started our own. Together with the new company we also started the Inspirare Institute.

Our intention in founding the Institute was to finance a direct contribution to support education in Brazil. There are many forms and many effective ways to do so, but we thought of having innovation and technology as a premise in our institute. The other concept we would like to have different from what we were seeing was to

focus on the learning process more than the conventional teaching process. So by doing that we united a number of excellent people and talked to another number of excellent people to get inspired on how to promote the institute goals. In the beginning we didn't know exactly what to focus on first. So we took the risk of developing three realms of action in addition to a social impact front, which will be the fourth realm.

Anna Penido had the idea for Porvir. She brought us this concept of Creative Commons where we could report what everybody was doing to benefit learning by stimulating thoughts through good examples and promoting good debates on what has been done in the world in a very proactive and positive sense. So that's how Porvir was created.

In addition, we decided to have another line of action that we call the territory action: how the theory, the invention, the technology that's available or becoming available could be put in practice. We chose the neighbourhood where we were born in Bahia. So seven public schools in Bahia are united in this project, and it's not just a passive project. It's a project on how to attract the entire population of this neighbourhood to actually participate in bringing the school process and experience out of school. It's kind of an open-door school, trying to make the neighbourhood a learning territory.

And the third area is more on bureaucracy, trying to use our network built in the corporate world and how to contribute to policymakers that are open to listening to what has been done elsewhere with new legislation, resolutions and ways of doing in other states, cities and even countries.

Graham: Is there compatibility between the needs of business within Brazil and the needs of the people in education and does your background as a successful businessman assist you in having an influence in government?

Bernardo: There's a primary need for education in Brazil and such a need is not only, I think, from a citizen perspective. Certainly there is

a direct link, and I think they should be looking to attract more corporate help and aid into fostering education at basic levels. I think one of the mistakes industrialists and businessmen make in Brazil is that they take for granted basic education and try to pour lots of training and money in at a later stage. People without basic education will not perform well at a technical level and at more advanced stages, so productivity may be lower than it could be because of a lack of basic education, despite what business is trying to support in technical education.

But I think our motivation is less related to how to apply education to business and more as a citizenship role, and we try to separate out those two things as much as we can. We think that what we can return to society is how we unite experts and people that can be either volunteers or people who can contribute to the cause of bringing education in Brazil to a better level.

So our concept is: How can we do that without fighting the usual vanity and the usual competition we see in the business world, being as neutral as possible and as cooperative as possible in a game that's not short-term or for profit? Obviously we need to work in the future because it's an endless job, an endless mission. So our concept is how to actually separate what's for profit and what's for the cause, while bearing in mind that we can use some of the experience we

'We think that what we can return to society is how we unite experts and people that can be either volunteers or people who can contribute to the cause of bringing education in Brazil to a better level.'

have in pragmatism and orientation for profit to achieve the goals of our cause.

Graham: Is there something that motivates you in terms of ensuring that we have adequate education so that we can nurture the problemsolvers of tomorrow?

Bernardo: Education can definitely help solve the problems of tomorrow … and the benefits that education brings to a nation are not limited to one niche or one specific realm.

I believe that one of the roles of educated citizens in a country that's in a developing phase is to make sure that all your fellow citizens are at least having the chance to choose freely and to choose freely you must be educated, otherwise your choice will be limited. The discussion about education is not that deep in Brazil or not as passionate as it could be for Latin Americans because there's [an expectation] still in place that this role belongs to government, or that if I play a role with my kids or my specific school, I'm fine...

I believe that if we can, to some extent, cause a kind of revolution to open the appetite of kids and youngsters to learn, independently from school, and to open our horizons so much that the entire neighbourhood becomes the teaching process, then I think we can go for the next step, that the demand for education will come from the customers and not from the policymakers.

Graham: Could you talk me through the rationale behind your investment fund for start-ups, particularly in education?

Bernardo: Our family decided to put together the fund because legislation in Brazil is not friendly for non-profit organisations that invest in companies or to invest in for-profit organisations. So we are trying to combine both efforts. The fund is a for-profit because the legislation demands it to be. But we invest our funds and dividends internally so we call it a social impact fund. So the investors, the shareholders, never see dividends in money form or have capital gains in money form. Everything will be indefinitely reinvested.

The concept is that, by doing so, we try to provide the start-up entrepreneur in education with finance, and the governance we can bring from our background. So this is the goal that we try to combine by making it for-profit. They are free to be profitable. Actually we want them to be profitable so that the fund grows. The concept is that everything will be reinvested, and it's kind of complementary to the institute.

First of all, the criterion is that the entrepreneurs are totally dedicated to the cause of transforming education through innovation and technology. They must be key-person-oriented funds, so the person who founded it and the people who are promoting the business plan must be there for some time. Also, the concept is that we should be able to work in harmony with the other investments that we already made, so we don't have conflict with the governance model. But the concept is to accelerate how we can impact the most Brazilians that could benefit from technology and innovation in education, the sooner the better.

Graham: Do you believe that you and fellow business leaders in Brazil can have a positive impact on the political process in favour of education?

Bernardo: I think business leaders in Brazil are putting their minds and hands to work in favour of education and I believe that we transitioned in the last decade from speech and scattered work to more coordinated work. I have great examples, like All for Education (Todos Pela Educação), which is a group of entrepreneurs, businessmen and industrial leaders that, with government, promotes business approaches to achieving goals and measuring how education improves that. It also gives some clarity on how the new policies could be more effective and listens to the government on how directly or indirectly the business sector could also support education through their own foundations and institutes.

And although it's not a passion yet, and although it's not something like their first priority, I think there's a great wave coming in favour of a Brazilian change of mind on how to be responsible for the education of our young people.

'Education can definitely help solve the problems of tomorrow ... and the benefits that education brings to a nation are not limited to one niche or one specific realm.'

Brazil

José Leite Lopes State College

NAVE School

Rio de Janeiro

Case study

On the outskirts of Rio de Janeiro to the north, hidden away inside a repurposed telephone exchange, is the José Leite Lopes State College, or NAVE Rio. It is one of two Núcleo Avançado em Educação, or Advanced Education Centres, schools that are part of a public-private initiative between Brazil's largest telecommunications company, Oi, and the State Departments of Education of Rio de Janeiro and Pernambuco. NAVE Rio was recognised in 2009 by Microsoft as one of the 30 most innovative schools in the world, the only school in Brazil to have made the list. UNESCO describes it as an innovative model for teaching new technology in public high schools.

Oi Futuro is the social responsibility institute of the Oi company. Its mission is to develop and support ideas capable of building a better future for Brazil with programmes across culture, education and sustainability. The objective of Oi Futuro's education programme is to build innovative templates that serve as a benchmark – scalable to the greatest number of schools, educators and young people – recognising the transformational potential of ICT within the school environment and in the professional and personal development of students. Oi Futuro has two programmes for education, NAVE and the Oi Kabum! Arts and Technology School, that develop educational methodologies which, in addition to promoting professional qualification and digital inclusion, seek to educate critical, independent and open-minded youngsters.

NAVE Rio is a public state school for students aged 16 to 19 and is an exemplar of how public schools could be in Brazil given the necessary level of support and vision from the private as well as the public sector. Competition for one of the 500 places at the school is fierce with some 5,000 applications for the 160 places available each year. But the demands placed on students are also fierce. Given that the school is compelled to meet the statutory demands of the state education department but at the same time is striving to provide students with marketable skills in the digital domain such as web design, video game programming, scripting and design, students work a ten-hour day, five days a week. The long school days are pretty much the only thing that students here complain about. Lisa, a student, tells me, 'It's ten hours per day from Monday to Friday. We don't have long break times. They're really short. We have a lot of projects to do, a lot of homework. You have to want to study here because if not, you're not going to survive, but if you want to, it's good.'

I spent much of my visit with a group of enthusiastic students who showed me their school and took me to lessons. Like High Tech High in San Diego, the school features a strong project-based learning ethos where cross-disciplinary subjects are merged to solve particular challenges with the results being exhibited around the school building. The learning methodologies used by the school are rooted in the Delors Commission's four pillars of learning – learning to know, learning

to do, learning to live together and learning to be – as described in the UNESCO report 'Learning: The Treasure Within', published in 1996 and available from the UNESCO site.

The inside of NAVE Rio is jaw-dropping. Policymakers who assume that architectural enhancements to learning are a folly should take note. The environment at NAVE Rio is one of the keys to its success. Like High Tech High and the creative offices of IDEO in San Francisco, the building is a warehouse-style design space full of collaborative common areas imaginatively decorated and lit. Converted from a former telephone exchange (it still has some of the original analogue switching gear) the inside of NAVE Rio looks more like the inside of a corporation such as Google than the sort of industrialised schools that resemble prisons. In discussing this with the students it's clear that this environment is important. Like employees of Google, they are expected to spend long hours in the building while being able to meet the demands of the day, staying sharp, social and creative. Whilst both the students and teachers would like to see a shorter day, which may actually come to pass, the environment was compelling rather than oppressive and in my mind answers the question about environment when so many policymakers see it as an unnecessary luxury.

The school is a private-public partnership similar to the charter schools in the US and academies in the UK, so I was cautious about the motives behind the investment of Brazil's telecom company Oi in this venture. Was it intended to simply be a training camp for compliant future employees willing to work over 50 hours a week?

I put this question to Oi Futuro's Industry Liaison Head, Carla Branco, who explained that whilst mine was a natural suspicion, the initiative was 'not intended to create future employees for Oi but to stimulate local well-being and independent wealth creation within the community itself. If Brazilians are doing well, then so are our businesses. What is key is that students from NAVE Rio generally gain entry to the state-funded universities which are far better than the private ones.' This statement was also roundly supported by the students who all have ambitions for future careers and not necessarily in the digital industries.

Broad international acclaim from the likes of Microsoft and UNESCO for NAVE Rio is one thing, but meeting the demands of the state examination board is another. Results show that José Leite Lopes State College was in first place among the schools related to the Rio de Janeiro State Department of Education (Secretaria de Estado de Educação), a result which was also attained by the Cicero Dias State Technical School (NAVE Recife), first place among Pernambuco's schools related to the Pernambuco State Department of Education. Whether this can be scaled remains to be seen but clearly the results indicate that the NAVE approach is working. Assuming that private enterprise in Brazil can be encouraged to participate in the public education sector, then the nation's future could look very bright indeed.

www.oifuturo.org.br/educacao/nave

Brazil

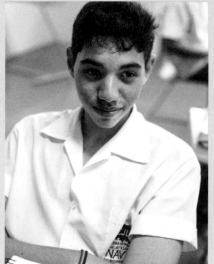

'The school is compelled to meet the statutory demands of the state education department but at the same time is striving to provide students with marketable skills in the digital domain such as webdesign, video game programming, scripting and design.'

'What makes students' eyes shine? What makes them happy and bright?'

Graham Brown-Martin: You work in the private sector in the telecommunications industry. What is your role here in the school and how did it come about?

Carla Branco: I work for the Institute Oi Futuro, which is the partner of the government of the State of Rio de Janeiro in this programme called NAVE, the Advanced Centre of Education. We have two schools. One of them is here in Rio and the other one is in Recife, Pernambuco.

Oi is the biggest telecommunications company of Brazil. The Institute is part of its social responsibility programme. Oi Futuro is more than ten years old. It has projects in education, culture, sports and the environment.

When it started to think about developing projects in education, Oi Futuro began working with the government of the State of Pernambuco and we opened a school there in Recife. The school started working in 2006 as a regular high school in the morning with some courses which were not mandatory, only for the students who wanted, in the afternoon. The courses were all based on IT and video-game design. But here in Rio, it was different because it was, since the beginning, a high school with professional/vocational courses. Later in 2009, Recife also became a regular and technical high school, in what we call in Brazil Integrated Secondary Education.

Graham: So this is a private investment in the public, state education system?

Carla: In Brazil, it is important to have money invested by private institutions in public institutions. This kind of initiative makes the state stronger because it alone cannot afford everything that we do here, for example. So I think it's essential that the civil society participates in this way, or in alternative ways, because, of course, in spite of education having to be public and the responsibility of the government, everyone must participate in order to make education something better.

So, in this way, when we have two actors participating financially, and not only financially,

but with people, I think it's richer, such as the result that we have here. The other thing that we have here is that we work with institutions that are famous for their work in education such as PUC-Rio. We have here a university that is in charge of the multimedia course, for instance. PUC is a very renowned university.

We have a company, C.E.S.A.R., which is responsible for the course of programming here in Rio and the courses of Recife. This company is developing a lot of projects in technology and programming and things like that. So when we decide to have this kind of institution involved in our programme, we are giving the students the best of the best that we have in these areas, in these fields of study.

It's a very good opportunity to have these teachers and professionals that we have here. I am almost sure that most of the public schools in Brazil do not have the same.

Graham: Is there a plan for students that pass through the school to then work for Oi?

Carla: When Oi decided to have this programme of education the idea was not to prepare youngsters to work for the company. The idea was to make students attracted by the school. The idea was to diminish the number of students who give up high school before finishing it.

So the most important thing was to decide the theme of the courses. What makes students' eyes shine? What makes them happy and bright? It is video games. So, video games were not chosen because they are part of the business of the company. Oi is a telecommunications enterprise. It does not sell video games.

Our intention was not to have these students working for us, but it does not mean that they can't work with the company if they want to when they finish school and if there is the opportunity. Oi has good, very good eyes on these guys because we know that they are very talented and we are working to make them good adults, intelligent, articulate, motivated, very good citizens. We believe that we are doing that.

Graham: What success have you seen with the school so far in terms of students going on to higher education or employment?

Carla: We are working on the numbers that we have after our students finish the school. We are very glad to see that most of them keep studying. They enter university. It's good to see that they go to public universities which are very hard to enter in Brazil.

The students say in the research we conducted when they leave school, that they are certain that if they hadn't studied with us, they wouldn't have had the same opportunities. Oi feels good because we are returning something positive to society.

'What nutrition
and reproduction
are to physiological
life, education
is to social life.'

You may regard as somewhat anachronistic the inclusion of a short essay about an early 20th-century thinker in a book about the present and future of 21st-century society and education, but I think it fits. In these days of the Internet with a capital 'I', and Digital with a capital 'D', you could be forgiven for thinking that everything before was quite primitive and that the ideas evangelised today by bearded 20-somethings over their soya flat-white are somehow revolutionary. But little of what is being said today around the transformation of learning hasn't been said before. That's not to diminish our revolutionaries of today – more power to them – but to draw attention to how long this debate has been happening and the heritage of that in which we are participating and adding our voices.

John Dewey (1859-1952) was a well-known public intellectual of the time as well as an inspired education reformer. There has hardly been a case study, organisation or person that I met in the creation of this book whose work or ideas weren't somehow related, consciously or otherwise, to the thinking of Dewey. He believed that a properly functioning democracy demanded the existence of fully formed public opinion in addition to simply extending voting rights. This public opinion would be the result of effective communication amongst citizens, experts and politicians. Thus, without unbiased education there is no democracy. As such, he joins a long tradition of educational philosophers from Plato to Jean-Jacques Rousseau, who consider the developmental process common to all humans.

In his work *Democracy and Education*, published in 1916, Dewey argued that it is simply not enough to physically preserve the immature members of a society. It is the responsibility of the mature members to initiate the young into the interests, purposes, information, skills and practices of the group to prevent the end of its characteristic life. Just physically growing up and learning the bare necessities of subsistence would not reproduce the life of the group. He wrote that 'Deliberate effort and the taking of thoughtful pains are required. Beings who are born not only unaware of, but quite indifferent to, the aims and habits of the social group have to be rendered cognisant of them and actively interested. Education, and education alone, spans the gap.'

In the same work Dewey argued that 'Society exists through a process of transmission quite as much as biological life. This transmission occurs by means of communication of habits of doing, thinking, and feeling from the older to the younger. Without this communication of ideals, hopes, expectations, standards, opinions, from those members of society who are passing out of the group life to those who are coming into it, social life could not survive. If the members who compose a society lived on continuously, they might educate the new-born members, but it would be a task directed by personal interest rather than social need. Now it is a work of necessity.' He summarised that 'What nutrition and reproduction are to physiological life, education is to social life.'

Presciently, given that this was nearly 100 years ago, Dewey reflected that 'As formal teaching and training grow in extent, there is the danger of creating an undesirable split between the experience gained in more direct associations and what is acquired in school. This danger was never greater than at the present time, on account of the rapid growth in the last few centuries of knowledge and technical modes of skill.' And indeed today that is the focus of our discourse around the purpose of schooling and education.

The crux of Dewey's thinking was the changeability of individuals as a result of education and that the philosophy of nature dominant at the time greatly impoverished the human experience, which is the outcome of a range of interacting processes. The challenge to human life, therefore, is to determine how to live well with processes of change, not somehow to transcend them.

In his work *Experience and Education*, published in 1938, Dewey provided a concise and powerful analysis of education emphasising experience, experimentation, purposeful learning and freedom as vital components of a progressive education. He argued that the quality of an educational experience is critical and stressed the importance of the social and interactive processes of learning. Dewey's learning theory is rooted within the concept that people, even young people, aren't sponges waiting to be filled with knowledge from kindergarten through college. Rather, Dewey proposed that students organise fact-based comprehension through meta-cognition, building onto prior experiences, preconceptions and knowledge and, as a result, the educator's role is in creating an educative experience.

Dewey's ideas found difficulty in gaining traction in the American public education systems of the day, though some of his values and terms were widespread. Thinking around progressive education, as proffered by Dewey and others, was essentially scrapped during the Cold War after the dominant concern for education was the creation of a scientific and technological elite for military purposes. Even today, the largest employer of mathematics and STEM graduates in the US is the National Security Agency. But, that said, in the post-Cold War period, new thinking based on old thinking around progressive education is re-emerging and many approaches such as project-based learning, a focus on the experiential aspects of learning, as well as many of the ideas promoted by the case studies and interviews in this book, are rooted in Dewey's theories.

Beijing ○

Chengdu ○
Ya'an ○

Shanghai ○

China

China
◉

The People's Republic of China, the world's most populous country, with more than 1.35 billion people, is a single-party state governed by the Communist Party with its seat of government in Beijing. It holds jurisdiction over 22 provinces, five autonomous regions, four directly controlled municipalities (including Shanghai) and two nearly self-governing special administrative regions (Hong Kong and Macau).

China is home to an ancient civilisation, one of the earliest, that emerged and flourished in the fertile basin created by the Yellow River and the North Region Plain. For thousands of years, China was governed by hereditary dynasties. The Qing Dynasty, China's last, was overthrown in 1911 after a long period of ethnic unrest, the effects of an expansionist Europe and international trade sanctions as a result of the Opium Wars.

The Republic of China replaced the monarchy and was founded on the Three Principles of the People: nationalism, democracy and people's livelihood. These great ideals didn't come to pass as the nation fell to warlordism, foreign invasions, suppression of communists and civil war. China became a single-party dictatorship and, with a weak central government, land reforms and redistribution of wealth proved impossible.

World War II and the death of millions of civilians during the Japanese occupation of the second Sino-Japanese War were followed by an uneasy alliance between the Chinese Nationalist Party (Kuomintang) and the Communists. China was left financially ruined and war-ravaged. Ongoing tensions between the Kuomintang and the Communists soon led to the Chinese Civil War.

In 1949, following the Nationalists' retreat to Taiwan, Communist Party Chairman Mao Zedong proclaimed the establishment of the People's Republic of China.

China's population almost doubled during Mao's tenure (1949-1976) to over 950 million, despite economic and social reform projects that led to mass deaths from starvation in the late 1950s. The Cultural Revolution of the mid-1960s, intended to enforce communism by removing capitalist, traditional and cultural elements from society, paralysed China politically and economically. Millions were persecuted in violent factional struggles and large parts of the population were displaced. Anti-bourgeois thinking forced urban youth to rural regions to learn from the workers and farmers. Millions more suffered a range of abuses.

Following Mao's death in 1976, reformers led by Deng Xiaoping ended the policies associated with the Cultural Revolution. The Communist Party Central Committee admitted that the policies were 'responsible for the most severe setback and the heaviest losses' suffered by the People's Republic. Significant economic reforms followed and were intended to prevent a repeat of the famines of the late-1950s. These led to the opening of markets to foreign investment for the first time since the Kuomintang era. Special economic zones, comparatively free from bureaucratic regulation, were created, and these regions became the engines of growth for the national economy.

Controls on private business and government intervention continued to be reduced through the early

1990s. The reforms began affecting the interests of certain groups and individuals within the state, particularly as town and village enterprises began to gain market share. Despite a backlash following the Tiananmen Square protests of 1989, Deng's reforms continued. The Shanghai Stock Exchange reopened. As economic growth continued financial challenges to the inefficient state sector increased, leading to heavy losses. Privatisations increased and by the mid-1990s China's private sector surpassed the state sector by share of GDP; a sort of free-market socialism emerged.

Ongoing privatisations, the dismantling of the welfare system, and the laying off of workers have provoked discontent. Since 2005, some of Deng's reforms have been modified, and more welfare-oriented policies have been introduced such as increased subsidies for healthcare.

Today, after more than 30 years of economic reform and one the world's biggest boom periods, China is widely seen as an engine of world and regional growth. Its economic growth and GDP have outstripped those of all other developing countries; only India's, post-1990, come close. Some have argued that this is proof of the benefits of globalisation in which China's relatively free economy, with less government intervention and regulation, is cited as an important factor in its superior performance. Others suggest that this growth has increased inequality and that state assets were sold off cheaply to private entrepreneurs. What is clear is that China has become a fierce competitor for the world's natural resources, required to power its industrial engine and whose output Western nations are reliant upon. China's public spending on education reached four percent of GDP in 2012, which is considered a landmark but still remains below the world average. Traditionally, Chinese parents tend to spend heavily on their children's education. Urban Chinese families spend more than 30 percent of their household income on alternative education for their children, [21] compared to two percent in the UK. In line with the Confucian tradition, teachers in China have a high level of public respect compared to other countries. China's education fever is compounded with its one-child generation and while this fever may boost Chinese students' learning outcomes in tests, it is also a cultural obstacle to the diversification of the country's education system, as most parents consider going to college the only goal of a successful education and thus a successful life.

There is unequal access to education between the urban and the rural, the rich and the poor, urban residents and migrants, boys and girls in rural areas, the socially privileged and the underprivileged, and so forth.

The Gaokao, or National Higher Education Entrance Exam, is the nation's single prerequisite entrance test that permits student access to almost all of China's higher education institutes. But the exam remains divisive by amplifying the inequalities within the existing state provision of education. It is a notoriously tough test that some have criticised as 'squeezing creativity out of students' and 'the culmination of a year of cramming, of repeating past papers and in large part, learning by rote.' [22]

Students from Shanghai, with a population of about 24 million, scored at the top of the 2012 OECD PISA rankings. These triennial tests are conducted by the OECD amongst half a million 15-year-old students in 65 countries. They are intended to act as a diagnostic that proves a link between education and economic performance. Shanghai students aced the maths, reading and science scores. In maths they scored 119 points above the global average, which equates to an advantage worth about three years of extra schooling. This sent shivers through the policymakers of Western nations when their respective national media distilled PISA scores as if they were a crude league table. Inevitable knee-jerk reactions followed, with these policymakers booking the next flight to Shanghai to view this miracle with their own eyes. Yet while Shanghai's reputation is well-earned, it doesn't come close to representing China's education system as a whole.

As China's financial capital, Shanghai lies at the forefront of an ambitious reform agenda under which education authorities grant schools an unusual degree of curricular autonomy. Critics suggest that China's education system prioritises test-taking ability over creativity and critical thinking. Shanghai is trying to buck the trend by introducing elective courses and by phasing out multiple-choice tests. But Shanghai's population is less than two percent of the nation and its per-capita GDP is more than twice the national average. Although students from 12 provinces took the PISA test, China only shared the results from Shanghai.

I had the opportunity to visit a high school in Beijing. I then travelled to Ya'an in the Sichuan province, some 1,200 miles southwest of Beijing, to meet the founder of the Free Lunch for Children programme and visit a crisis response school that was set up by the government following a catastrophic earthquake that hit the area some months earlier. The opportunity to visit schools in distinctly different settings provided me with a chance to see the contrast between a leading high-technology school in Beijing against the more typical provision within rural China. Such a large population, much of it in rural, mountainous settings, shows the scale of the challenge that China faces. Financing programmes like Free Lunch for Children might also be adapted to meet these needs or at least draw attention to them *(see interview with Deng Fei on page 272).*

China

'Critics suggest that China's education system prioritises test-taking ability over creativity and critical thinking. Shanghai is trying to buck the trend by introducing elective courses and by phasing out multiple-choice tests.'

Situated on Ring Six in the outskirts of Beijing, about 30 minutes from the main campus of the Renda Fuzhong School (the affiliated high school of Renmin University of China and one of the most prestigious high schools in Beijing), the RDFZ Xishan School is the home of the Future School programme. With a vision of changing the face of education in the country, RDFZ Xishan was the first school in mainland China to participate in a 1:1 computing approach using Apple Mac laptops, followed by iPads, focused on enhancing its students' 21st-century skills. The Chinese government had released a national plan for education reform, acknowledging that its teaching philosophy and methods were out-dated. The government challenged local schools to conduct programmes in education reform, declaring that 'the destiny of our nation rests on education'. The RDFZ Xishan School opened in the summer of 2010 to accept this challenge and currently has 800 seventh- to 12th-grade students.

The school's principal, Shu Dajun, told me that he was charged with launching the school to push the boundaries of traditional Chinese education. I asked him if he thought technology had the potential to transform the learning process or simply reinforce old teaching practices. He replied, 'Because technology may change us, we need to train a new group of people. And technology also changes the shape of our society, the way we work and the way we live. So the requirements that people have for education also change. It changes the way we study. This is a totally new definition.'

Immersed in a complete wireless environment at school, RDFZ Xishan students are engaged in ways of learning designed to encourage their critical thinking, collaborative skills, communication skills and creativity. The school collaborated with researchers at Beijing Normal University in designing the programme. Professor Yu Shengquan, Dean of the School of Educational Technology, explains that although the majority of schools in China already utilise digital media in their classrooms, this technology is mainly used by teachers to present lectures. For RDFZ Xishan, it was important not to simply use technology for technology's sake but as a cognitive tool for students and ultimately to promote learning at a higher level.

The school adopts what it describes as a 21st-century learning framework in its 1:1 pedagogy, with a particular emphasis on building information, media and technology skills. Using mobile platforms such as their iPads, as well as social media sites, the school has implemented a challenge-based learning framework aimed at using digital platforms to create and develop new thinking processes rather than simply using technology. Challenge-based learning is Apple Education's take on problem-based learning, not to be confused with the project-based learning approach notably used by High Tech High in the US and NAVE Rio in Brazil, although all have their roots in John Dewey's thinking. Challenge-based learning is a collaborative learning

'RDFZ Xishan students are engaged in ways of learning designed to encourage their critical thinking, collaborative skills, communication skills and creativity.'

China

experience in which teachers and students work together to learn about compelling issues, propose solutions to real problems and take action. As you'd expect from Apple, it is a technology-dependent approach but like problem- and project-based approaches its aim is to give the learning a real-world context. If you search online you'll find Apple's published white paper on challenge-based learning.

I wondered if the school believed that the role of the teacher would change in China if children were provided with iPads or similar and put this question to Principal Shu. He replied:

> Teachers are no longer the main sources or authorities of knowledge. In [the teacher's] school days, his teacher played the role of the authority of knowledge and the one imparting the knowledge. So when someone becomes a teacher today, he will have to lose the old concepts and reorient himself. For example, as the amount of knowledge on the Internet is far more than his own, and knowledge updates continuously, what is his role? He becomes the one who helps kids to make choices and judgements when faced with the huge mass of information. And how should he guide the kids with his experience? How should he have a good influence with his personality if the task of a teacher changes in this way?

Vice-Principal Liu Yan doesn't believe that teachers are going to be replaced by technology, however. 'In my opinion, just as the robot cannot replace human beings, technology cannot replace teachers in the future... The communication between teachers and students cannot be replaced by technology, because it is emotional, heart-to-heart.'

Professor Yu from Beijing Normal University suggests the RDFZ Xishan School approach is a balance of Eastern and Western teaching philosophies: the Chinese emphasis on the system of knowledge and the Western focus on the student's development.

Since the programme started, the school has seen positive results. Based on surveys and qualitative data, students have shown better independent thinking skills, improved autonomous learning abilities and greater confidence than students not participating in the programme. In the classroom, students are more willing to express themselves and ask questions. And they are completing assignments at a much higher level of complexity compared with the traditional school.

I ask Principal Shu about state test scores.

> We started the 1:1 programme in this school in 2010, and we have just had our first graduates. So if we simply judge their studies by test scores, I can say that some of them have good scores, some of them have so-so scores and some of them have bad scores. But any teaching method can have an effect like this. So it depends on the way you treat this programme.

In China, we judge kids in two ways: the first is to judge by his score, e.g. the mark he gets in exams; the second is to judge by his real abilities. In this way, we may be unable to compare because we cannot make two choices at the same time. We can just see his current condition after the teacher's continuous exploration. But we value [also] ... his abilities in 20 years, including his ability to learn, to adjust, to get along with others, to express himself, to communicate with others, to resist setback and frustration, and of value judgement. We cannot come to any conclusion now about these aspects, but we see a lot of changes happening to our students and that makes us proud.

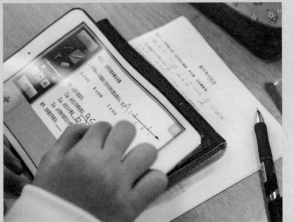

'The teacher becomes the one who helps kids to make choices and judgements when faced with the huge mass of information.'

'The ultimate goal
is to create…'

With more than 20 years' experience in the education sector, Ching Ya's career spans teaching and management at primary and secondary school levels. It reached new heights when she joined the Ministry of Education, Singapore, as Curriculum Planning Officer and National Chief Trainer for primary school education. A core member of the school setup committee of the sixth FutureSchool@Singapore —Science and Technology— and subsequently appointed head of its Mother Tongue Languages Department, Ching Ya led the school's branding and publicity efforts and was heavily involved in ICT curriculum development.

Today Ching Ya is Head of Strategic & Innovation Development at RDFZ Xishan School. On top of managing partnerships with global institutions and organisations, she oversees strategic planning and leads the ICT department and 1:1 learning of its Future School programme. Her latest work involves designing the school's 21st-century skills learning framework. She is a certified Apple Distinguished Educator and also the first certified Apple Professional Development Consultant 2012 for K-12 public schools in China.

Graham Brown-Martin: The RDFZ Xishan School has adopted a 1:1 computing approach based around iPads. Can you tell me about the background to this initiative?

Ching Ya: The school started in 2009. We are one of the satellite schools of the main campus under the Renda Fuzhong High School, affiliated to the Renmin University of China. There are ten schools and every school has its own niche. So, for the Xishan school, our niche is the Future School programme, which is about 1:1 learning and developing the 21st-century skills of the students.

So we started a whole school. When I joined the school in August 2011, we started looking at the whole school again, going through the strategic planning of vision, mission, values and goals. We called it VMVG, for short. That's the entire strategic direction of the school's development.

We looked into one very important matter which is

developing the students' 21st-century skills, and rooting it in China. Our goal is for the students to be 'Global Citizens with a Chinese Heart'.

We developed 21st-century skills that are put into different programmes like the youth entrepreneurship programmes. We have a challenge-based learning programme, and all these different programmes to develop the students' skills.

What is so different? I'm sure when you step into the school, the whole ambience, the look and feel is different. We have been mistakenly called an international school, which we are not. We are a free public school.

I think that this is a very daring, very bold move for the school, especially in the Chinese context, but we are lucky that we are in Beijing. I don't think we could do it elsewhere. Maybe in Guangzhou we can. In Shanghai, we can, but maybe in the western part of the country.

Every student in the Future School programme had to purchase their own Macbook and now many of them have to purchase an iPad Mini, which was actually introduced only this semester.

Graham: You mentioned that the students must buy their own iPad. How do the parents feel about this?

Ya: Prior to students joining, we conduct a parent seminar. We explain to them what this 1:1 programme encapsulates, how we can provide this different mode of learning, what kind of curriculum we're trying to impart to the students.

For the curriculum, we cannot change the content, but what we do change is the mode of learning, which is the pedagogy. Assessment is very important. How do I know my learners have learned when they leave my classroom? So, for assessment, we have two parts. One is the assessment of learning, where every step of learning counts. We also have the final assessment of learning... So we explain this to the parents. They agree to this kind of learning. They participate and we have a whole package for them where they have to purchase their own learning device.

Graham: Although this is a state school, do you think that parents having to purchase computers creates an artificial selection process?

Ya: Actually no, because if you look at students' status and demographics, they live nearby. This is the purpose of the school being set on the outskirts of Beijing on Ring Six. It's a residential area, so it's up to the parents to choose. We are just providing another kind of learning experience for them.

Graham: How do you think China's education system compares to others in the region, such as Singapore's or South Korea's? Is it right that such systems are weighted towards test scores rather than creativity?

Ya: Excellent question. This is a question for every educator, especially in China. I was saying that RDFZ Xishan was one of the satellite schools of the main campus. The headmaster of all ten schools, Madame Liu Pengzhi, advocates being an innovative learner, being a creative learner. So that's what we're wanting to achieve with the ten schools, especially us, RDFZ Xishan School. We try to do this. How can we produce a creative thinker, a creative learner? Ultimately, why are we receiving education? I always ask my team.

The ultimate goal is to create, just like Steve Jobs. He created things. He created iPhones that changed our lives, right? So for learners to change, to have that kind of aspiration, you have to reconsider our curriculum, but as I said very honestly, it's not easy. We try to redesign it, introducing problem-based learning and challenge-based learning approaches. It's very challenging because we have many restrictions.

Actually, it's about the philosophy of the whole school. Our students need to think differently. We always say that we think we are not street-smart, but we are textbook-smart. We are exam-smart. That's why we cannot be so creative.

Graham: What do you think are the tensions between having a progressive approach to learning for the future versus having to pass assessments based in the past?

Ya: Ultimately, when it comes to the testing point, which means we have to assess for the learning, we have to assess them according to grades, if the process is correct – every point, every check, at the end when you take whatever exams. The result should be in proportion to what we have learned.

That's what we are also trying to do. We cannot say, 'Oh, we don't care about the national exam.' They'll go crazy if you say that. No, we don't do that, but having that in mind, we are ultimately going to face a national exam in whichever country, especially in this China context, the middle school exam, the high school, when they have to go for the university entrance exam.

Graham: Do you think they should be allowed to use the same iPads that they use for learning within the examination room?

Ya: That's very interesting. That would depend on your assessment goal. Why are you trying to test them without the iPad? If it's a pen-and-paper test, I think you test them for their knowledge goals. But if I were to bring this iPad in, maybe the assessment goal is for creativity, so you are testing their skills. You could have them both together during the test and tell them it depends on the assessment goals.

'How can we produce a creative thinker, a creative learner? Ultimately, why are we receiving education?'

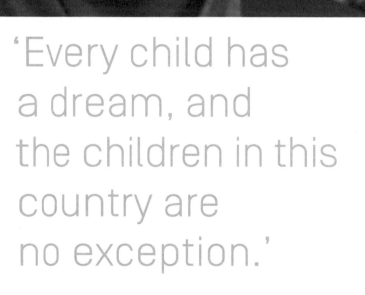

'Every child has
a dream, and
the children in this
country are
no exception.'

Deng Fei is a campaigning investigative journalist who leverages Chinese social media such as the Weibo (a Chinese equivalent of Twitter) to raise awareness of social issues and crowd-source solutions. With more than four million followers, Fei has conducted campaigns around sensitive topics including child trafficking, organ harvesting from death-penalty victims and shoddy school construction.

In 2011 he launched a charity to help provide lunches to rural schoolchildren free of charge. Within six months he had raised $3.7 million from individual donors who knew his reporting work and trusted him with their money. While the public is generally sceptical about government-owned charitable organisations in China, Free Lunch for Children, initiated by Deng Fei, is recognised for its openness and transparency, becoming the new online micro-philanthropic model in China.

I met Deng Fei at an important gathering in Ya'an, the scene of a devastating earthquake in April 2013, about 1,200 miles southwest of Beijing in the province of Sichuan. Here, Fei has been raising awareness and support for the people in the surrounding area since the earthquake; a number of schools in the rural areas surrounding the town benefit from his Free Lunch for Children programme.

Graham Brown-Martin: What was your inspiration for the Free Lunch for Children programme?

Deng Fei: At the beginning of 2011, I became aware of children in the rural mountainous region who suffered from starvation. I decided to change that situation to help them. Because I am a father, I cannot stand such situations where children are suffering from hunger, so I chose to take action.

Graham: How did you achieve the momentum from the public to support this initiative?

Fei: When we initiated the project, we didn't have many resources, but we didn't give up because we had Weibo, a new tool. We demonstrated the children's plight through Weibo. We called for help from citizens to help the children out. We got enormous recognition and support, like a rolling snowball. We got more and more people involved.

Graham: How do you think that social media, like Weibo, differ from traditional media in creating public awareness and engagement?

Fei: We use Weibo because we cannot use the traditional media which belong to the government or business organisations. Weibo is a common media platform for everyone who is connected. Now I have an audience of about four million people. From this point of view, we have our own media. We can express our own ideas and efforts, report on our project and get more people involved.

Graham: What impact has your initiative had on the schools?

Fei: When we started our first project providing free lunch, we only had 20,000 yuan ($3,200), but over the last two years we have received enormous support and an increasing number of people have got involved in it. Now we have collected 70 million yuan ($11.2 million). We provided ten million lunches for children in 300 schools of 18 provinces. Our actions affect our government. Our Premier, Wen Jiabao, announced that our government will allocate 16 billion yuan ($2.6 billion) for the nutrition of children in poverty.

This problem didn't draw much attention from our government, but later it took action quickly after seeing our efforts. Now we work together to deal with this hunger problem.

Graham: Could this approach of social engagement be used to improve other aspects of rural schools?

Fei: Many problems of country schools result from the inequality of investment in education. When we arrive there, we find the number one problem we have to deal with is hunger. If this problem can't be solved, it will jeopardise other aspects. When hunger is not a problem they will have energy to do sports and study. Then we will help them to solve other problems, such as stationery, clothes and medical care. So we have done several projects in addition to the lunch project. We want to unite more people to help children more comprehensively and efficiently.

Graham: What do you believe are the challenges for schools in China?

Fei: Every child has a dream, and the children in this country are no exception. But they are unable to realise their dreams because they are facing huge inequality. Most parents of these children are migrant workers, leaving their children to face many difficulties themselves. The children in this kind of difficulty number up to 62 million. Some areas of the country are in poverty, so the children there have no equal opportunity to gain knowledge no matter how hard they study, that is to say they have only a slim chance of realising their dreams. This is why we want to help them.

There are many factors contributing to this situation. Mainly because they live in remote areas, their local teachers are relatively old and have a lower level of education. And, as we mentioned before, they are suffering from hunger because of the long distance between home and school, which consequently affects their study. In addition, their parents are outside the village, working as migrant workers, so the children have to live together with their grandparents. Under these circumstances, they cannot perform as well as students in cities. They have no ability to compete with students in cities. It is less possible for the children in mountainous regions to change their lives.

Graham: If you could re-imagine learning and education, what would it be?

Fei: I hope that every child can receive quality education, at least equal education. So we want to take some educational resources and material resources to schools in mountainous areas to enable children there to have the same education as children in cities. Finally, they may be able to change their lives through education.

Teacher 2.0:
The information delivery system
Thought piece

'...teaching is an art form. It's not a delivery system.'

That's why I always say that teaching is an art form. It's not a delivery system. I don't know when we started confusing teaching with FedEx. Teaching is an arts practice. It's about connoisseurship and judgement and intuition. We all remember the great teachers in our lives. The ones who kind of woke us up and that we're still thinking about because they said something to us or they gave us an angle on something that we've never forgotten.

Sir Ken Robinson

One of the features of an industrialised society is the way that it deploys technology in processes to make them more efficient, particularly in the field of manufacturing, where it is important to make things to a particular standard with as little variance as possible. By taking measurements at various intervals it is possible to use the resultant data to improve the process both in terms of economy and quality. This is great when you're making cars or spoons or cans of beans. The idea is to remove humans, or at least skilled humans, from the process so that craft production can be transformed into mass production.

Not all technology is used for this purpose however. Some technology is used to amplify the skills of craftspeople or specialists. A microscope greatly amplifies the skill of a scientist searching for clues. The Internet can unite people who have never met but share a passion. And so on.

How we use digital technology to teach and to learn remains a subject of debate and challenges what we think a school or university is for. If we imagine school as a sort of factory that processes kids into the human capital for a master plan of economic growth then it might be possible to automate this process and de-skill those on the production line charged with the job of kid-processing. Teachers in this scenario might be regarded as a kind of delivery system. Their job would be to deliver the curriculum in the prescribed manner then subject the kids to regular tests in order to generate the data that can be analysed by management. The data could be used to diagnose failure in the production line or used in league tables to show performance and see where certain production lines are falling behind. This top-down, data-driven approach has the advantage that it removes the craft from teaching which can then be delivered by less engaged or skilful practitioners who tend to be demanding in terms of their expectations.

In this scenario we could use digital technology to impart the knowledge to kids and check that they have retained it whilst the teacher does the 'human stuff' like encouraging kids or making sure they don't take too many toilet breaks or something. At this point you're either agreeing that this could be a reasonable scenario or shaking your head in disbelief, but let me assure you that I have heard this description of a future school delivered in all seriousness by government policymakers and techno-fetishists alike.

What is it that we dislike about craft?

Personally, I quite like craft. If the law in England says that I must hand my child over to the state to attend school from the age of five, then I would very much like to entrust a craftsperson to the task of their education. The argument against this is that we're then asked to think about the costs and the potential variance in output that might not tally with the state economic development plan, i.e. human capital. But, to be honest, I believe that it is variance and diversity that breeds innovation. One of the reasons that cool stuff has come out of the UK during the last 50 or more years, and especially from the more cosmopolitan cities, is the social and cultural diversity of its inhabitants rather than a mono-cultural standard. I also suggest that when it comes to education we, as a society, pay now or pay later. By this I mean that an investment in craft to ensure a well-educated, well-rounded population with equal opportunities in an equitable society is almost certainly less expensive and more enriched than one that conforms to a mass-produced standard.

That today we are even thinking that schools and universities are places where knowledge is simply delivered and digested, and that this is something that can be automated by digital technology, simply proves how little is understood by those who make policy and those who make well-intentioned gadgets. Such deliverologists are really only solving the problems of politicians whose sole objective is to be re-elected. Thus, we live under a tyranny of data and measurement that is used to neutralise critique and debate. But we must remember that we have agency and we should make claim to it when thinking about the role of teachers. Who do we want teaching our kids, an algorithm, a drone or a craftsperson?

'Who do we want teaching our kids, an algorithm, a drone or a craftsperson?'

New Delhi

Patna

Chennai

India

India

My trip to India was perhaps the most memorable journey of my life. I woke in the morning to breakfast in Chengdu, China. I then boarded a flight that took me across the Himalayas, breathtakingly visible from my plane window, to Kathmandu, Nepal, where I disembarked for lunch. With a stop-over that gave us just about time to leave the airport and find a café, my photographer companion, Newsha Tavakolian, and I mused about how on this project we had visited both the lowest place on Earth, the Dead Sea, as well as the highest place, Mount Everest, as we flew across. After lunch, we left Nepal on a flight for New Delhi, India, where we had dinner. I have no idea how I will ever beat that!

Ashish Rajpal, the founder of the affordable education design firm, XSEED, tells me at breakfast the following day that India is three countries. It is the India of the well-to-do elite, it is the India of the extremely poor and it is the India of the aspiring middle class. It is the last two groups that I had the opportunity to visit, perhaps guided by the first, during my five days spent in this incredibly diverse country with its vast differences in geography, climate, culture, language and ethnicity.

India is the second most populous country in the world, just behind China, with 1.2 billion people. It is the world's largest democracy, militarily strong, a major cultural influence and a powerful, fast-growing economy. It has its own $1 billion-a-year space programme, having recently sent a rocket to Mars. Its people hold some of the highest positions across global technology companies, investment banks and the arts, to name a few. It is home to more than 400 living languages, the birthplace of four major religions, and the site of monuments thousands of years old. Archaeological evidence shows civilisations present in India since before 7000 BCE.

European traders began visiting India from the 16th century, prominent among which were the British, French and Portuguese. In the 17th century, the British East India Company was formed to trade with the East Indies and by the 19th century accounted for half of the world's trade, mainly in basic commodities including cotton, silk, indigo dye, salt, saltpetre, tea and opium. It could almost be regarded as the 19th-century equivalent of Google. The company, only indirectly controlled by the British government, was owned by wealthy British aristocrats and merchants. It employed its own private armies, exercising military control and administrative functions within the country. The Rebellion of 1857, which began as a mutiny against the company, led to the Government of India Act, and the ascendance of the British Raj, as it was known.

India remained under the control of the British Raj until 1947 and the Partition, establishing the two sovereign states, India and Pakistan. An estimated million people lost their lives and several millions were displaced. India emerged with a Hindu majority population and a large Muslim minority while Pakistan had a largely Muslim majority.

India's first Prime Minister, Jawaharlal Nehru, governed India from independence until his death in 1964. He is widely regarded as the architect of the modern Indian nationstate, a sovereign, socialist, secular and democratic republic. The many languages, cultures and religions of India are also reflected in its federal political system; power is shared between the central government and 28 states. Communal, caste and regional tensions continue to haunt Indian politics, sometimes threatening its long-standing democratic and secular ethos.

From independence until the early 1990s India had a largely mixed economy that combined features of capitalism and socialism, inward-looking, interventionist policies that attempted to substitute foreign imports with domestic production. The result was that India missed the post-World War II expansion of trade and experienced widespread inefficiencies and corruption that led to poor implementation. Large-scale infrastructure projects became a burden to the state. The economic reforms of the 1990s, adopting liberal and free-market principles, led to rapid growth and inbound foreign investment. The country has a burgeoning urban middle class and has made great strides in fields such as information technology. Its large, skilled workforce makes it a popular choice for international companies seeking to outsource work. Some forecasters have predicted that India could by 2035 become the third economic superpower along with the US and China.

But against this growth, the vast mass of the rural population remains impoverished, their lives still influenced by the ancient Hindu caste system that assigns each person a place in the social hierarchy. Discrimination on the basis of caste is now illegal and measures have been introduced to empower disadvantaged groups. Poverty alleviation and literacy campaigns have a long way to go to bring a third of the country's population above the poverty line. According to the World Bank, 34 percent of people in rural India live on less than $1.25 a day.

Education is hugely important amongst the Indian population even at the street, everyday person, level. Every place I visited there, whether it was New Delhi, Chennai, Patna or way out into the rural villages, I would find billboards or advertising for educational courses, schools and colleges. Education is regarded as a passport out of poverty and to a better life. Citizens who may have worked long hours for many years in factory conditions are forging their way into India's emerging middle class. They may not have been to school themselves and may be illiterate, but they understand the value of education and they want it for their children.

The Annual Status of Education Report[23]* published by the ASER Centre in 2014 concluded that despite India's Right to Education Act, which increased the enrolment of children into schools from 92 percent to 96 percent and improved facilities, the issues of quality of learning have remained largely neglected over the past nine years. The report indicates that, as a result, there is a dramatic shift to private-school enrolment in rural areas and that there is a crisis of learning affecting both state and private schools where low-income and emerging middle-class families are sending their children. Perhaps ironically, after the government declared it would provide free and compulsory education to all children, the pace of enrolment in private schools increased. The government's failure to deliver fully on basic achievements in learning, combined with the influence of urbanisation and access to a wider world via television and mobile telephony, has led to greater educational aspirations amongst the entire population.

While in India I visited the offices of XSEED in Delhi before visiting an example of a school using their affordable learning programme in Chennai and the offices of BBC Media Action, then heading to Patna and on to a remote village in Bihar to observe a mobile education system in practice.

---

* The original framework of ASER, which is the Hindi word for 'impact', was developed by Pratham, one of the largest NGOs involved with education. The Co-founder and CEO of Pratham, Dr Madhav Chavan, was the 2012 WISE Prize for Education Laureate.

India

'The British East India Company could almost be regarded as the 19th-century equivalent of Google. The company, only indirectly controlled by the British government, was owned by wealthy British aristocrats and merchants.'

'Every place I visited there, whether it was New Delhi, Chennai, Patna or way out in the rural villages, I would find billboards or advertising for educational courses, schools and colleges.'

India

'India isn't a 5.5-million-population monoculture like Finland. It is a country with more than 300 million people of different cultures, religions and languages who live below the poverty line.'

I should confess I have long held a prejudice against private education. Philosophically, it strikes me as divisive, a way to buy into an ideology that says because you're rich you deserve a better standard of education, an advantage over the poor, so much that you must be separated. The option of choice between state and private means that there's a whole segment of society that doesn't have an incentive to improve the provision of the state, the media and political classes being prime examples. There are also examples such as Finland where private education isn't an option and the state provision is amongst the world's best. I could go on but I am writing this from the privileged position of my home in London having enjoyed a state-provided education and a career that has given me access to most things. It's easy being an armchair socialist. Not so easy if you're one of the majority of the world who are genuinely poor. Poor not in the sense of not having a television set, but poor in the sense of having to go to bed hungry on a regular basis.

Thinking about this in India and having it explained to me by Ashish Rajpal, the founder of XSEED, a creator of affordable learning programmes for India, the world became less black and white. After all, we're not talking about Wellington College or Eton here. There is an emergent middle class in India that isn't the *New York Times* or *Guardian*-reading middle class of the US or UK. It is an emergent middle class of people who may not have attended school themselves but can just about save up to $20 per month to fund their child's education. We could have long debates about why it is the state's responsibility to provide this education for all, and indeed many post-colonial societies like India have tried to achieve this. Often, however, the scale of the project is simply too large or it takes too long, or greed blinds people to its mission. Putting myself in the shoes of India's struggling and emerging middle class, would I really, based on political conviction, choose to wait until there was adequate state education rather than buy a place for my child that would continue to lift my family out of poverty?

The reality is that I wouldn't wait. Like most parents I would do all that I could to ensure a better life for my children whilst nurturing their social conscience that would add to society and lead to a socialist utopia where high-quality education is indeed available to all. I recognise the hypocrisy of my thinking but I don't believe in the polarity of such debates. India isn't a 5.5-million-population monoculture like Finland. It is a country with more than 300 million people of different cultures, religions and languages who live below the poverty line. To put that in perspective, it's about the same number of people as the entire US.

The ASER report shows that 29 percent of India's child population attend private school. However, amongst the emerging middle class this figure rises to 44 percent. Even in households in less affluent circumstances, defined by standard of housing, as many as 15 percent of the children are enrolled in private schools, demonstrating that parents are making a conscious choice in favour of private schools. Parents are also investing in private tuition outside of school to get their children extra help, whether they attend a state or private school. While private-school learning levels in India may be higher than state schools, they are generally still below grade competency, with the ASER report showing, for example, that up to one third of children are at least two grades behind in reading ability.

It is the emerging middle class that XSEED is targeting with its affordable learning programmes provided to over 1,000 schools in India that have subscribed to its service. XSEED is a privately funded, for-profit venture headquartered in New Delhi whose programme is currently being used by over 1.3 million children. Returning from his studies at Harvard to his native India, Rajpal developed his company to solve what he saw as an education crisis for the poor and emerging middle classes. He identified that a key problem was a lack of teacher training and curriculum materials that would ensure a high standard of teaching and learning for the children. Working in schools and observing what was happening, he understood that teachers were unprepared, unsupported or relied on broadcasting information to learners, teacher-at-the-front-style, in the hope that some of it would stick. He observed schools with large classes where children were seldom encouraged to ask questions or make enquiries. Thus teachers were overwhelmed, learners were disengaged, struggling parents were unhappy.

Rajpal's solution was to create a programme of materials, lesson plans and workbooks, supported by a training programme that would allow teachers in India to reach a high standard of practice in a way that was engaging for learners. Rajpal studied education at Harvard under Howard Gardner and was influenced by his theory of multiple intelligences. The theory proposes that intelligence is a set of modalities rather than a single general ability. Gardner suggests that intelligence is the ability to create things that have value to society, a set of problem-solving skills, and the potential to find new knowledge to solve problems. In this respect it can be seen that Gardner's work is a direct line from the work of John Dewey, whose thinking, in one form or another, has influenced all of the major transformative work described in this book. Indeed, Rajpal suggests that what he has tried to do is 'productise John Dewey' or perhaps, in an act of heresy, take a MacDonald's approach to distributing a Dewey-inspired educational model to India's affordable private schools *[see interview on page 294]*.

Again, I find my personal thinking around education challenged. My belief is that our education systems have been impoverished by their industrialisation and reduction of teachers to mere delivery systems of education to meet a standardised control quality metric.

India

Large consulting companies like McKinsey even invented a word for this kind of education. They called it 'deliverology' and it seems that the global debate around education is how we can undo this factory approach to learning. Here I am confronted by the challenge of how India solves its crisis of learning that is affecting over half a billion people. Yet Rajpal is successfully marrying two seemingly opposite approaches to teaching and learning though, of course, the reality is more sophisticated than the soundbite. When challenged, Rajpal stretches his fast-food metaphor, telling me that it's important to get the pizza base right before we think about the toppings. And whilst he clearly isn't equating teachers to pizza delivery services, he is making an important point in the context of India. Without achieving a baseline, any hope of raising standards and introducing new ideas and techniques, including digital platforms, will be destined to an endless series of false starts, promises and pilot projects.

I left Delhi and headed 1,300 miles south to Chennai, to visit the Muslim Women's Association school that had adopted the XSEED programme. There I met students, teachers and parents who told me their story of how the school had been transformed as a result. The school was busy with large classes, energetic teachers and engaged learners. Without knowing what it was like before, it was impossible to tell if this had been an under-performing school but what I experienced was a school that was functioning well. Certainly there was a lack of the kind of digital technology and interactive whiteboards we've become accustomed to in most of our school visits, but the sound was the same. The sound of curiosity and learning taking place. I couldn't hum it but I know the tune.

www.xseed.in/index1.html

'It is an emergent middle class of people who may not have attended school themselves but can just about save up to $20 per month to fund their child's education.'

India

'I did an MBA and worked
for a multinational overseas.
I got married young, had kids,
then wanted to return to do
something for children in India.'

XSEED is a private-sector company, focused on leadership and learning programmes, headquartered in Gurgaon, just outside New Delhi in India. Ashish Rajpal, the company's founder, received an MBA from XLRI in Jamshedpur, India's leading private management school, before embarking on a corporate career outside of India.

After providing leadership programmes for corporations for a number of years, today XSEED offers affordable learning programmes based around teacher materials, lesson plans and student learning materials for schools. Presently not based around digital delivery, the programme has been adopted by nearly 1,000 schools at primary and secondary level.

Graham Brown-Martin: Ashish, would you please tell me a little about your background and your inspiration for XSEED?

Ashish Rajpal: I grew up here in Delhi, then lived and worked around the world. I was in Russia. I was in Paris. I was in the United States for a while. For about the last ten years, I've been working in school education in India. I have two lovely children who have been my inspiration.

As a middle-class kid growing up in Delhi I had all the dreams of any young person living in a developing country. I did an MBA and worked for a multinational overseas. I got married young, had kids, then wanted to return to do something for children in India. For about five years, we were in the wilderness. It was like throwing dirty socks on the wall, not knowing which one is going to stick. We tried teacher training. We tried consulting. We tried helping people set up new schools. We did work in leadership but nothing seemed to really work.

After five years, a lot of this inspiration, evangelical energy, belief and wanting to bring change was running down, as was my bank balance. I was almost bankrupt. What little I'd saved up in Europe was gone. It was almost in desperation that I was driven to the classroom. That's when I started teaching children myself in the context of an Indian classroom. This was how the

birth of XSEED took place. I realised how hard it is to teach a lesson well with 45 kids, a temperature of 45 degrees outside, and all kinds of constraints. One kid not shutting up, the other one running out of the class, the third one not opening her mouth. How do you make a good class come to be?

Then came the realisation that unless you have a better mousetrap, you have no right to give speeches and lectures to other people. That's how XSEED was born, to let us give teachers a better mousetrap.

Graham: How would you describe the challenges faced by education in India?

Ashish: It's difficult to talk about challenges in a knowing manner about a country as big and complex as India. Here are the two or three things which I see. I think, in many senses, the problems are similar to what they are elsewhere in the world. How do you attract good people to the domain? How do you get the best people into teaching? How do you take care for the enormous differences between children, and so on and so forth? How do you equip children for 21st-century skills as opposed to industrial-era skills?

Here are few things which are, I think, different. Foremost, there is no one India. India is really three Indias. There's the India here, the one you're interviewing me in, and the one you will perhaps see most of. There is the poorest of the poor India which I call India Three, which is perhaps 65 to 80 percent of our country. Thankfully, there's an emerging middle India, a population of close to 300 million people who haven't quite reached Western standards or even Indian standards of doing well. There's a lot of aspiration, the very basics have been met. Creating an education system which caters to these three Indias is complex. All sense of equity or equality would want you to create one system but can there be one system? I don't know. I think that's an enormous challenge.

The other big challenge, I think, is regulation. It's possibly well-meaning, possibly well-intentioned, but we know that with any domain

that is overly regulated, the only people who thrive are the crooks and the chiefs and the people who know how to work their way through. You don't attract the best people to the domain when there are no fair returns on capital. The right kind of investment doesn't come in. Education is stopped. It's challenged. It's deprived. Then, how do you solve such an enormous problem without the right talent working on it? Super-important, on top of this, is the enormous diversity of India.

If you think Europe is diverse, just multiply that by ten or 20. There is no one India. We are just as Greek and as Dutch and as Spanish and as English. From Kashmir to way down in Tamil Nadu and from Gujarat all the way to Assam, there are four or five distinct ethnic races. There's a history of oppression. There's 10,000 years of caste. The mountains look steep.

Graham: Given such a vast country and diverse population how do you believe education can be transformed? Does it require a private or state-sector initiative?

Ashish: I'm a left-leaning liberal at heart but my considered view now is that the Western model, where the state does it, is not going to happen in poor countries and certainly not in your and my lifetime. I think it'll be in the interest of the privileged, of those who've had a good education and some means to bring about the change. I think it's going to be the role of the entrepreneur, hopefully an enlightened entrepreneur, in the role of social business, to bring about this change. I also recognise the limitations of that. I think there is always going to be a segment, possibly the poorest of the poor, whom only the state will be able to service because it's just not viable to do that. Certainly, a very large part of the responsibility, if not all of it, I think, will need to be shouldered by private enterprise.

Graham: How has your programme scaled and do you adapt to different requirements?

Ashish: XSEED is now in 1,000 schools. It's serving 500,000 children. It works with about 40,000 teachers. What's interesting about it is

'There's an emerging middle India, a population of close to 300 million people who haven't quite reached Western standards or even Indian standards of doing well.'

it serves schools of privilege but, most importantly, the majority of our schools are ordinary, lower-middle-class private schools in India with fee levels ranging typically from $10 to $20 a month. I think it's important, especially for a Western audience, to clarify what a private school may mean.

The insight XSEED is based on is that teaching in classrooms may be of poor quality because perhaps the education of the teacher herself, the motivation of the teacher herself is not up to where it should be. It's also because she doesn't know better. What if you told her that here is the better way?

Not in philosophy, not in grand platitudes but in specifics. If this is how you are going to teach fractions, you will get a better effect in the classroom. If this is how you teach the sinking and floating of objects, you will get a better result in the classroom. This is the way to introduce Mughal history. This is the way you would disseminate it for a particular kind of learner versus one who likes reading and writing more, as opposed to someone who's more talkative. Yes, there may be a shortage of know-how and morale or motivation, but then this insight struck us: What if we just told her?

A traditional daughter-in-law comes into an Indian house and is not able to cook the meal that people expect. The truth is the mother-in-law screams and shouts and complains that she's not a cook. Why don't we just show them how?

To cut a long a story short, XSEED is a programme which has four parts. At the heart of it are micro lesson plans. There's a bank of 8,000 micro lesson plans which cover every topic which is started in primary and middle school. In English, in math, in science, in social science, minute-by-minute lesson plans as to how you could teach that topic really well. Alongside that, it's a professional development and training programme which we roll out to the school so that the teacher knows how to use these micro lesson plans. Along with that, we have student materials. We provide textbooks and workbooks where children do the practice. Finally, very important, is the assessment programme. Now I think it's important to emphasise that the programme is not just packaging all the stuff which exists in mainstream schools and making it available to a larger population. It is based on progressive pedagogy. It emphasises experience. It emphasises differences in children. It emphasises learning outcomes and, in a sense, the kind of education which will perhaps be available only to very privileged Western audiences is now being brought in pencil form to very ordinary schools.

Graham: How do you square what appears to be a productising of teaching and learning with something that is genuinely personal and experiential for the learner?

Ashish: I think a criticism that could be made of XSEED, and several people do make it, is that we've McDonaldsised John Dewey. Is that a good thing or is that a bad thing to do? I live in a country where one billion people are very, very poor. They should have the right and destiny to get the best possible education. Will we stoop to conquer just a little bit? From my whole view, I think XSEED is providing a structure whereby any teacher, a not so fortunate one, a very creative one, will have the skeletal system to provide an education for a 21st-century child.

The Sistine Chapel and the Blue Mosque and the Taj Mahal look very different but they all have a foundation. They all have structures. Just because you weren't born into a rich society where those structures or that philosophical background exists, I don't think you should be deprived of that. I do not for a moment prescribe that this is the only way to do it. I'm saying, 'Just in case you do not know, here is a way to vaccinate for smallpox.' If you can come up with a better way, sure, you teach this lesson plan for a year. You got a better idea, tear it up. Build a better one. Let neither creativity nor diversity become an excuse for not having the right stuff in your portfolio. Let that not become an excuse for someone who is less privileged not having an opportunity to do a good job in the classroom. I think you first need the base of the pizza before we can discuss the toppings and it's a very good base.

Graham: Do you have any evidence of positive outcomes from your programme?

Ashish: We're still in relative infancy. We are five years old now. In a relatively short period, we've reached 500,000 kids. I think we have a long, long way to go. There are over one billion around the world and most of them do not have this kind of education. Having said that, there are some early signs which we are beginning to see. There are two behaviours or outcomes which are almost continuously getting reported. One, there seems to be a visible impact on children's curiosity within six months of this programme coming out. Now, that's not rocket science. The whole programme is built on the premise that children need to experiment. After that, they should be asked what they saw and their part should take primacy over the teacher's role.

Whatever the teacher has to say comes later. Time in classrooms where teacher used to be doing 95 percent of the talking is now down to 40 percent or 50 percent. Children are talking more. They have room to ask questions. That is a very noticeable outcome. Those are the kind of skills you need in the world of tomorrow. You may not have the right answer but you have the right question. In fact, very often, that's all you need.

The second positive outcome is improved spoken English skills, which was not the original intention of the programme but is a very fortunate side effect. These skills manifest themselves again in the six- to nine-month period. Since the vast majority of children do not come from homes where there's any exposure to English, parents are delighted. One thing which unites them, apart from cricket and Bollywood, is the obsession with spoken English, and for good reasons. You tend to get a better job. You tend to be doing better in life if you speak English.

XSEED has become a symbol of 'Hey, these kids are kind of curious. They talk a lot and they talk in English.' I think that's a good thing. That's not the soul of what the programme is about but these are the two visible changes.

'I think it's important, especially for a Western audience, to clarify what a private school may mean.'

In the early 1980s, before the Internet, I had the idea of building a small portable mobile computer for children. A pioneer in the early days of multimedia CD-ROM technology, I imagined a world where children would use these devices to access libraries full of these CD-ROM plastic discs that held the world's knowledge via radio waves. It was a marvellous steam-punk vision of what became the Internet, born from watching too much *Star Trek* as a child. As a young entrepreneur, I was successful in winning a UK government grant to design and create a prototype of this device, which I called Satchel, and a CD-ROM jukebox to go with it that I called Voyager. I even received a visit from His Royal Highness, Prince Charles, to my high-tech offices in Cambridge. Alas, timing is everything, as is location, and my vision died without even a footnote in the history of what today is called mobile learning.

That today, in a world of ubiquitous smartphones and tablet computers, we still have something called mobile learning strikes me as a sort of chronological displacement or demonstration of how the education sector works at a glacial pace. I hosted a huge summit about mobile learning from 2005 to 2009, in fact the world's largest. Smartphone and tablet computer sales were outstripping those of desktop and laptop PCs, yet schools were still banning them. I couldn't see the point of having the same conversation over and over again. It seemed to me that if we were using digital platforms for learning then mobile learning was the default position. Besides, when did learning stop being mobile?

I think there are still conferences and research summits being held today whose sole purpose is navel-gazing and pontificating about learning while staring at a handheld device. Well, good luck with that and may your funding never dry up.

But just when I was ready to forget about mobile learning, because it had already happened to the majority of us who weren't busy talking about it at conferences, the work of BBC Media Action in India shook me out of my complacency. Here in India was a project that made absolute sense and at this point in time could only be achieved using the most basic of mobile phones. Forget feature phones. The feature of these phones was their featureless-ness, apart from the fact that many of them were really bad, black-market knock-offs, with brands like 'NOYIA'.

BBC Media Action is the international development charity of the British Broadcasting Corporation. It is legally, financially and operationally independent of the BBC but builds on the fundamental values of the BBC to guide its work. It shares a joint heritage with

'Supported by the Bill and Melinda Gates Foundation, BBC Media Action has designed a pioneering approach to improve the demand and uptake of life-saving family health behaviours.'

the BBC World Service, enjoying a close relationship through broadcast partnerships that reach millions of people in developing countries, yet the organisations are distinct. BBC Media Action works with multiple media, non-governmental, academic and donor organisations around the world. The organisation uses the power of media and communication to help reduce poverty and assist women, children and men to understand their rights. It is focused on health, governance and rights, and resilience and humanitarian response. I am in India to learn about its work in health education, specifically maternal and child health in the state of Bihar.

Bihar is India's 12th largest state and third largest by population – 104 million people, of which 80 percent live in rural areas and 40 percent live below the poverty line. It borders Nepal to the north and was once the centre of power, learning and culture in ancient and classical India. Since the 1970s, Bihar has fallen behind other Indian states in social and economic development terms, which is blamed on a combination of central government policy, apathy, lack of sub-nationalism and the permanent settlement of the British East India Company there in the late 18th century.

There are 27 million women of childbearing age in Bihar and 18.5 million children under the age of six who are looked after by just 200,000 community health workers or Accredited Social Health Activists. The state's newborn and maternal mortality rates are much higher than the national level and it has among the lowest uptake of health services in the country. Whilst the Bihari government has recently made important advances to improve the state's health infrastructure, awareness of critical family health issues remains low.

Supported by the Bill and Melinda Gates Foundation, BBC Media Action has designed a pioneering approach to improve the demand and uptake of life-saving family health behaviours. Reaching this enormous audience through conventional forms of media is difficult. Only 27 percent of young mothers have access to TV, radio, newspapers or cinema.

Country Director Priyanka Dutt explains: 'You're working in an environment that's incredibly challenging. It's almost media-dark. It's very, very difficult to reach them. When you link that with things like the lack of electricity or just the status of women in the state where mobility is non-existent. So once a girl gets married, until she becomes a mother-in-law, and that's a significant part of her life, she's behind closed doors. She doesn't really have any interaction with the outside world.'

But add mobile phones to the mix and access goes up dramatically to around 90 percent. BBC Media Action has designed and deployed a 360-degree approach to connecting with this population, featuring a combination of face-to-face communication, ICT, mass media and community work, implemented on a scale that makes this the world's largest mobile learning programme.

As part of the project, they have developed two innovative mobile phone services for health workers: a training course called Mobile Academy, and an on-demand service called Mobile Kunji supported by a deck of cards illustrated with life-saving messages. The Mobile Academy is designed to refresh and reinforce the health workers' knowledge of life-saving health behaviours as well as their communication skills. It takes the form of an audio course delivered via Interactive Voice Response, a technology that can be used with even the most basic mobile handset. The result is that health workers can complete the course anywhere, any time at a fraction of the cost of face-to-face training.

Health workers visit the homes of women and families in Bihar and are equipped with Mobile Kunji (meaning 'guide' or 'key' in Hindi), which use an IVR-based service along with a printed deck of cards on a ring. The Kunji cards have been carefully designed to look like a mobile phone, with illustrations supporting key messages about maternal and child health. Each card has a unique mobile shortcode printed on it, corresponding to a specific audio health message. When a visiting health worker dials the number, they can play the health message which is voiced by a character called Dr Anita, an engaging, culturally neutral but authoritative female doctor, to the family via their mobile phone.

The key aspect of this project is that Mobile Kunji and Academy are accessible from any mobile phone handset without any special software. Shortcodes and tariffs are common across six of the biggest mobile operators in India, responsible for 90 percent of the market in Bihar. Calls to Mobile Kunji are toll free, while calls to Mobile Academy are 90 percent less than standard IVR rates. Unlike so many mobile learning projects that stalled after a pilot scheme, the BBC Media Action programme is demonstrably scalable, having already rolled out successfully to 40,000 health workers across eight districts. By the end of 2015 it will have reached the remaining 160,000 ASHAs.

I asked Siddhartha Swarup, Director for Family Health Programmes at BBC Media Action, why he hadn't used modern smartphones or tablets in this programme. His reply was, I think, very important when we are making decisions about technology. He said:
> There are a range of technology solutions that people are experimenting with, starting from tablets to high-end smartphones to be used in rural areas across the developing world. A lot of these are pilots being done with 50 people in four or five villages and what we realised, because we have to go to scale and we're an organisation that works at scale, was that there were two options. We could either wait for these technologies to develop and become ubiquitous in five to ten years time or we could start to save lives immediately. Therefore the solutions we came up with use very simple technologies such as IVR that has existed for the last 15 or 20 years, so it's not about using new technology but using technologies that make a difference today.

www.bbc.co.uk/mediaaction/

'Here in India was a project that made absolute sense and at this point in time could only be achieved using the most basic of mobile phones.'

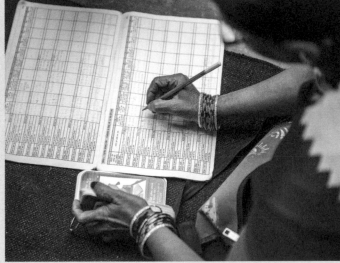

'Technology companies, particularly foreign
tech companies from Silicon Valley or the UK,
are very focused on high-end technology,
the cutting edge, the latest in user-interface
design, touch screens and apps.
What we've discovered in Bihar is that people
don't know how to use that technology.'

BBC Media Action is the BBC's international development charity. It is legally, financially and operationally independent from the BBC, but builds on the values of the BBC to guide its work. The organisation works with multiple media, non-governmental, academic and donor organisations around the world.

BBC Media Action uses various forms of media and communication from street theatre to broadcast media, to tackle poverty and contribute to long-term change in some of the world's poorest places.

I visited the organisation's office in Delhi before travelling to Patna, in the state of Bihar, where I then journeyed several hours by car to a village to see their mobile learning intervention for maternal and child healthcare being deployed *(see case study on page 298)*.

There are numerous technical challenges in the deployment of this kind of project in rural India, so I met with Sara Chamberlain, their head of ICT, to find out more.

Graham Brown-Martin: Sara, please would you tell me about your background and what led you to this project?

Sara Chamberlain: Prior to working in India, I was working in Bangladesh for three-and-a-half years where we developed mobile-based solutions for teaching low-income rural people to learn English. This was an interesting learning experience because we learned how they learn through an approach called the user-centred design where essentially we go through round after round after round of user testing. We take a prototype of the services, the content, the navigation and the functionality out into the places where they're going to be used and interact in sort of a mob environment with the people who are going to be using them, and get their feedback on every aspect of the service.

I think we got through eight months of user testing to develop the Mobile Academy application, which is the application that we've now brought to India and are using to teach community health workers about maternal and child health.

After three-and-a-half years in Bangladesh, I moved with BBC Media Action to India where I'm working on the Ananya Bihar Programme which is an initiative that was created by the government of Bihar, working with the Bill and Melinda Gates Foundation to transform public and private-sector health in the State of Bihar by December 2015, to radically reduce the maternal and infant mortality rate in the state by then. I'm responsible for developing ICT solutions as part of that programme.

Graham: Did your user-centred design work indicate a different style of learning from what you'd experience in Western-centric settings?

Sara: Yes. It's a very humbling experience, because you have your preconceived idea that you worked very hard to develop, you bring it out to the people who are going to be using it and they can't. They don't understand what it's going on about. They can't comprehend the information and they can't use the product is what I have usually found. There are a lot of bright brains involved but it is very hard for people to put themselves in the shoes of say, a 22-year-old rural Bangladeshi man. It's very difficult, I think, to second-guess how they might engage with the service.

We found many, many different things. One is that the approach to information which is based on a library originally — structured information that's hierarchically arranged where you dive down into different aspects of something, organised from an information-hierarchy perspective — is not how people access information. At least not in rural Bangladesh or in rural India, for that matter, in Bihar. People access information much more in terms of a narrative and a storyline and through characters. Really how information needs to be presented is more as a story with a narrative arc as opposed to information shown in a hierarchy. That was a key learning.

The other is less is more. What we found was that the quantity of information that we were trying to communicate in one lesson was far too much. We had to really reduce the amount of

information that was being communicated. Also, we couldn't make assumptions about concepts that would be understood. There are some great examples from Bihar where if you're talking to rural women about iron, they might have never heard of iron before or ambulances, and they don't know what an ambulance is because there aren't any for that matter. Just basic concepts that we assume are going to be understood but are not understood because people aren't familiar with them.

We also discovered that people who are exposed to the mass media, who watch TV and listen to the radio, are much more comfortable with processing recorded information compared to people who have no exposure to mass media or are, essentially, mass-media dark. [To them] listening to recorded information is actually a very alien experience.

Developing the voice of the character, which is what we've done in Bihar, is incredibly important. We developed a character called Dr Anita who is the person who delivers most of the information and we put a lot of effort into ensuring that Dr Anita connected with her audience as somebody who they thought might not be from their village but whom they could relate to and understand — a sympathetic, authoritative, yet engaging person. All the content is developed in this sort of narrative story-based way using local idioms, and poems, and drumbeats to really provide a context that's familiar and to engage people in a way that they're used to, which is storytelling.

Graham: This must be quite a challenging environment for organisations proposing technological solutions that are seemingly more advanced.

Sara: Technology companies, particularly foreign tech companies from Silicon Valley or the UK, are very focused on high-end technology, the cutting edge, the latest in user-interface design, touch screens and apps.

What we've discovered in Bihar is that people don't know how to use that technology. We did a very large piece of quantitative and qualitative research in Bihar before we developed our ser-

India

vices to understand people's mobile usage habits. What we discovered is that only nine percent have ever sent an SMS. The reason that only nine percent have ever sent an SMS is because the majority of the phones that they have are used, second-hand, very poor quality, brick phones. Not even feature phones.

These phones are grey market. They're copycat Nokia and Samsung phones and are coming in over the border and are in foreign languages. They don't support the local Hindi font. They might be in English or Chinese or Arabic but they're not in Hindi. Essentially people have a very basic piece of technology in their hands that's in a foreign language which is really limiting their ability to actually use it for anything other than a voice call. What we found is that the majority can only make and receive voice calls, and that's really it.

That really dictated our choice of technology and the technology that we chose to use is something called IVR, interactive voice response, which is a rather ancient technology that goes back to the '80s. It was developed for handling call-centre calls. It's not even a mobile phone technology, but a really basic old-school kind of technology. We decided to use that because it could be accessed from the basic handsets. That way, we got around the problem of people not being able to use their phone for anything other than a voice call. Essentially, 70 percent of women who are in Bihar are illiterate anyway. They can only understand audio information.

Unless you actually go out and talk to the people who are going to be using your services, and talk to them actually in a pretty significant way —I think we talked to over 1,500 people who are sort of representatives of rural families in Bihar and community health workers in Bihar— you're not going to understand how they engage with technology right here and now.

You see people inventing these apps in Silicon Valley and in other places and bringing those apps over saying, 'Look, let's do a pilot or let's launch a mobile education service here with these apps to teach with videos of this and the

other.' Then they discover, lo and behold, the target population doesn't have the handsets to support the app and couldn't use the app anyway.

Graham: What do you think of the initiatives directed at introducing low-cost Internet-connected devices to rural India?

Sara: I think there are a lot of challenges with the distribution of low-cost devices to large numbers of people. If you're distributing low-cost devices to a small target population of professionals where you can support those devices, then that's fine. In fact, that's really exciting. But if you're looking at somehow distributing low-cost devices to millions of people in rural India, rural Bihar, there are some major challenges.

The first one is electricity. In the majority of villages in rural Bihar, there is no access to electricity through a mainline solution. The only way that they get electricity is through a generator. They pay 100 rupees a month to get two hours of generator electricity per night, which is a single light bulb, and enables them to charge a very basic mobile phone. In a situation where there is no electricity, it's hard to understand how a tablet, for instance, would work in that kind of situation because how are you going to charge the tablet?

I thought a lot about broadband for all and bringing it out to the last mile, to rural villages, but how is that broadband going to run when there is no electricity? Every single sort of Internet community or resource centre would need to be running a generator. Generators are very expensive to run because they require a huge amount of petrol. How are these solutions actually going to be viable in a situation where there's no power to charge and run them and where, at least in Bihar, 70 percent of rural women are illiterate? It's hard to really understand how they would engage with the tablet if they can't read.

Also I think people don't think about the logistics involved in support. What happens when the laptop or the tablet breaks? Tablets, as

we all know, are very delicate creatures. They are designed to fit on coffee tables in Silicon Valley. They're not necessarily designed to sit in hot, rural Bihar where you have monsoons, dust and extreme heat. Who is going to support that laptop or that tablet? Who is going to replace the screen when the child drops it on the floor and the screen breaks? Who is going to reinstall the software when it hangs or when half of the applications are deleted by people who don't know how to use them? Who is going to replace that tablet when it's lost, stolen or sold?

It's really these kinds of ongoing logistics of maintaining and running low-cost solutions that I'm interested in because the reason that we have decided to use the technology that's already in their hands, i.e. the basic handset, is because it's already in their hands and they already know how to support that phone, and how to fix it, and how to power it.

'In a situation where there is no electricity, it's hard to understand how a tablet, for instance, would work in that kind of situation because how are you going to charge the tablet?'

'In places where 70 percent of India lives, where a billion people live, there aren't paved roads, and a third of the schools on a given day don't have teachers.'

Datawind surprised the world when, in 2011, it announced that it would make a tablet computer designed for the Indian education sector that would cost end-users just $35. The device, with a seven-inch touch screen, ARM processor, 256Mb memory, running the Android operating system and manufactured in India, would be sold to the Indian government for distribution to university students.

When I met Suneet Singh Tuli, Datawind's President and CEO, at a conference in 2013 he was already pitching an unreleased third-generation device that he was planning to introduce into the Indian market, also for $35, that included free Internet connectivity over India's 2G network.

I've had the product in my hands and, whilst it's no iPad, it does work and doesn't feel as flimsy as the price tag suggests. When one considers the thinking of Tuli's fellow countryman Sugata Mitra and his work with self-organising learning environments for Internet-connected students *[see interview on page 308]* one wonders whether such a low-cost tablet might not be just the thing to ignite a learning revolution in India.

Graham Brown-Martin: How do you believe that your technology can impact learning in India?

Suneet Singh Tuli: We're big believers that technology can empower students and teachers in a manner that wasn't possible before. And we believe that that opportunity is greatest at the bottom of the pyramid. In places where 70 percent of India lives, where a billion people live, there aren't paved roads, and a third of the schools on a given day don't have teachers.

So in that kind of environment especially, we think that technology, Internet connectivity and the opportunity for collaboration that that provides, offers a great chance to improve education and that's where we're focused.

Graham: You're aiming at a low price point to the end-user. How is that working out?

Suneet: Our entry-level devices are sub-$40. In the US, they'll be available at $37.99 for the average consumer, in the UK, £29, if that. That's sort of the price point that they start at. We believe that the price points will continue coming down. We see them at around $25 a unit within 12 months. The reason that these price points are important is that our studies show that computing adoption in North America and Europe really took off when the average cost of a PC dropped below a weekly salary. So for our target markets, a week of salary is sub-$50. And we want to be able to get into the right price point for that consumer. That kind of price point can make it affordable for anybody who has been able to afford a mobile phone. And that's why we're focused on those price points.

Graham: So you're pricing at a similar point to feature phones that are commonplace in developing countries. What about power requirements and networks?

Suneet: One of the things that people question when you think of mass adoption of Internet com-puting devices is whether there is electricity and networks and so on. And while there's a por-tion of the global population that still doesn't have electricity and still doesn't have access to networks, the disparity between Internet users and cellphone users is very stark. There are over five billion cellphone users globally that use six billion mobile phones. There are two bil-lion people that use the Internet. So there's a three-billion-person gap where they have access to electricity to be able to charge their mobile phones, they have access to networks to be able to use their mobile phones, but they don't have Internet. We believe that if we can get comput-ing and Internet devices to the same price point as what they bought their feature phones for, that three-billion-person market opens up. And that's one of the big reasons that the price point is very important for us and will help drive that adoption.

Graham: How do you plan to achieve free Internet access across India with this tablet?

Suneet: Our target has been to deliver free mobile access to our consumers, and we've done about two or three years of experimentation on this in the UK, where we generated about 150,000 subscribers and we focused on the UK version of the digital divide, which were gener-ally the elderly, the 'silver surfers' as they're referred to, who hadn't been on the Internet. And we wanted to deliver a simple, easy-to-use, cost-effective solution for that consumer. So they would purchase the device and there would be no additional fees for Internet access. The mobile access would be built in.

We've been working on this for a few years in India, and we believe we're a few weeks away from announcing a relationship with a network operator which will allow us to do this. So you'll be able to buy an entry-level device for sub-$50 and it will come with a SIM. And basic browsing and email will be part of the package, so you won't have to pay a monthly fee to be able to access the Internet. And we think that that is another very key element to it. The cost isn't just the hardware. We know that the cost of access in many of these markets in the first couple of years easily exceeds the cost of the hardware. So the cost of access is another area that we had to address.

We've created a technology which is a com-pression-acceleration algorithm on which we received 18 US patents, and it reduces band-width consumption by factors of 30 times. So we consume less data, hence it costs us less, but then we use sponsorship relationships to be able to drive it down to zero. This is similar to how Google offers searches for free. We believe that basic Internet access can also be offered for free, subsidised by advertising.

Graham: But isn't there a problem with most of the digital content being from outside of India?

Suneet: For content and apps, it's a longer-term approach. To a great degree, what we do is we partner with universities to launch courses for app development, and then we run contests and encourage students to develop apps. We run hackathons with the universities to focus on apps that would be relevant to that customer base and relevant to better quality education or social good, the areas that we're passionate about. And we do it not only in India, but in a number of markets.

We continue sponsoring and supporting these so that we can get the next generation of develop-ers thinking about the opportunity of the next three billion consumers and how we can impact them in a positive kind of way. And we think we're having an effect.

Sugata Mitra has no formal background in education and did not study education as a subject. Yet in 2013 he was awarded the $1 million TED Prize to develop his School in the Cloud concept in which children can explore and learn from each other. The project will recruit technology, architecture, creative and educational partners to help design and build the School in the Cloud, a physical building in India that is intended to try out a range of cloud-based, scalable approaches to self-directed learning. Mitra's project will see the creation of seven learning labs, two in the UK and five in India, that are designed as a self-organising learning environment for children to tackle big questions on their own, teaching each other in the process. The project taps into a network of retired teachers who connect to the labs via Skype.

Mitra first came to prominence in the education world as a result of the Hole in the Wall project that saw the installation of Internet-connected computer kiosks in a wall situated in an urban slum area of New Delhi, India. Mitra and his colleagues observed kids from the slum playing with the computer and in the process learning how to use it and how to go online, then teaching each other. The project suggests that, even in the absence of any direct input from a teacher, an environment that stimulates curiosity can cause learning through self-instruction and peer-shared knowledge.

Graham Brown-Martin: Sugata, your background is not in education so I wonder if you could tell me about that?

Sugata Mitra: I was born in West Bengal in India, in Calcutta, and I am a professor of educational technology here at the School of Education, Communication and Language Sciences in Newcastle University, England. I work mostly with learning and particularly how learning happens with children in the presence of the current technical and information infrastructure.

I have not studied education as a subject. What I did study as a subject is theoretical physics. When I sort of bumped into education, which I did somewhat accidentally, I had no choice but to look at what I was doing through the eyes of a physicist which may be good or bad news, I'm not sure. I could have said things about education to which people in education would have replied, 'But this was said years and years ago.' It's entirely possible. So I don't know if what I'm saying is new, but what I can say is that what I am observing about learning and children is through the eyes of a physicist and that seems to lead to certain interesting possibilities of what might be happening.

Graham: The Hole in the Wall project indicated that children were able to organise themselves and learn. What had you expected from this project?

Sugata: Well, we started off with very low expectations. I was working in the private sector at that time. We had very easy access to broadband. I didn't even think of it as an experiment. I just thought of it as something to observe to see if street children with no education and who don't know English would be able to use or show any interest in a computer.

When I did the actual experiment, we saw that they were able to handle the computer and get into the Internet. Every day was a surprise because whatever we thought would be the limit, the children would immediately cross that. That story continued for 14 years all through India into England, into the rest of the world. I think a one-liner would be to say that whatever we think, or wherever we think children will stop when given a computer, is wrong. They don't. They just keep going further and further.

The other important thing to understand is that I'm using the expression self-organising systems in its technical sense, as used in maths and in physics, which is not to be interpreted as organising ourselves. It's not that. Self-organising systems is a technical term which really means that when you have things interacting with things, if you have a sufficiently large number of them, then they start to produce spontaneous order under certain circumstances. That's how clouds and flowers and storms and the stock market work.

What this work seems to show is that learning could be this kind of spontaneous ordering mechanism happening, provided children are allowed to interact with each other. It's not that they're organising each other, just the act of interacting with each other changes their behaviour and when viewed as a group produces these very surprising learning outcomes which I think are what we would describe as spontaneous order.

If that is the case, then we have a somewhat different take on learning. It doesn't necessarily have to be externally imposed and then examined. It can actually happen internally, from the inside, and I later found that actually many people had said this about education up to 150 years ago.

Graham: So are you suggesting that learning follows a similar mechanism to first-language acquisition?

Sugata: It is very much along those lines and I think language acquisition is a really good example of that. The acquisition of many skills has this property that everything falls into place suddenly. It's like learning to ride a bicycle. The first bit is when you're thinking rationally about the whole thing. I'm tipping over to the left so I should now swing myself to the right to keep myself upright and so on and so forth, which only results in your falling several times because you can't do that kind of thinking and reasoning quickly enough. Until one day you just know how to ride a bike. You cannot describe it. I think that's an emergent phenomenon happening from the inside.

Graham: And you see digital technology as an enabler for this kind of self-organised learning?

Sugata: Yes. I think what I have stumbled upon really is that when groups of children interact with a computer in a very low-threat environment it means that their entire energy, their entire brains can focus on this activity. If they can talk to each other, if they can run around, if they can talk to other groups working on other things and so on, then you do get self-organising behaviour and you get emergent learning which seems to go right across all the groups. That seems to happen all the time, I mean again and again.

Graham: So what do you think your work says about the way that we educate, particularly in the Western world, with classrooms and teachers and so on?

Sugata: I got really curious about the existing education system because I thought to myself: If what I am observing in the field appears to be so different, then why was that system made the way it was? It can't be that people were making mistakes for hundreds of years. It's much more probable that I'm making a mistake and they were not. Where did that system come from?

I started investigating and I found a couple of rather interesting things, I think. Firstly, to do with technology. There must have been a time when paper and pencils and things like that were really expensive toys for rich people, so there was no question of children having access to those things. Children were examined orally and the whole system was oral. You needed a sage. You needed a person who knew something because there were no books. If you wanted to learn something, the sage would explain it to you and you would learn it. Then when books became cheaper and easily available the sage was now under threat because the learner might say, 'Whatever you know is there in the book, so I'm going to read the book and I don't need you.'

The sage then had to beat a hasty retreat, saying, 'No, a teacher doesn't have to be a "sage on a stage", but a teacher has to be a "guide on the side".' Because after all the teacher has to direct you to what you have to read and say, 'Go ahead and read that book. Once you finish that book then read the other one. Let me check if you understood the book, so I will examine you.'

This became and continued to be the role of the teacher until the Internet came along and did something that books don't do. Books don't point at each other, at least they don't do that easily. The Internet does that all the time. One link points to another link, and another link, and so on.

Now the guide on the side is also in trouble because the learners are no longer looking for a guide. The Internet is guiding them all over the place. What I discovered was that an individual may get lost inside that huge array of links and go down a badly linked area whereas groups of learners can self-correct.

It would appear that groups interacting with the Internet do not need a guide on the side either. What happens to us teachers? Do we have no role? Well, I did one experiment on testing for the limits of self-organised learning with a really difficult experiment on biotechnology and children. The children were to learn something about biotechnology ten years ahead of their time in a language that they didn't quite understand, English. It's all published.

What we found was that they were able to get to over 30 percent from zero by themselves which is really an absurd thing to say, but they did. They would go from 30 to 50 if they were encouraged to do so by an entirely non-threatening friendly adult such as a grandmother. All this then became a self-organised learning environment where learning is a self-organising system assisted by, or encouraged by, a friendly adult. Now the guide on the side becomes your friend and that's the role I think teachers would have to have in the existing system.

Graham: Do you think that this approach might have an influence on how we might perform assessments in the future?

Sugata: Coming back to technology, now paper and pencils become really cheap. Now you can have all that in the hands of children. Books become really cheap. You can give them to children. The teacher's role starts to change. Then comes technology and, to my surprise, technology wasn't allowed inside the examination hall. You were allowed to use paper. You were allowed to use pencils. You were allowed to use rulers, straight edge, set squares, protractors, compass, everything that the last generation used for solving real-world problems were available to the person being examined. Somewhere along the line we seem to have lost sight of it.

I wonder sometimes, if I were to go back 100 years to the Victorians and show them our world, those same Victorians would say, 'Why on earth aren't you allowing all this inside the examination hall? How are you going to test them for their real-world skills?' Are we actually doing worse than they were 100 years earlier in terms of our thinking about education?

The existing system is based on the last age, the age of empires, so the Spanish Empire, the French Empire, the Russian Empire, the Austro-Hungarian Empire, and of course the last of the lot, the British Empire. All of them needed an education system which would enable them to govern large parts of the planet in an age when there were no computers, no telephones, no ways of data processing other than the human mind. You need people who obviously had to have two or three capabilities or skills. They had to be able to read and understand. They had to have good handwriting so that when one person writes something another person at the other end of the world should be able to read it and understand it. Therefore they had to have good spelling. They had to have good grammar and they had to be able to do arithmetic in their minds, computation in their minds. Hence, they had to learn multiplication tables and how to calculate by hand.

Now these had to be the pillars of primary education in the age of empires. They were engineered carefully by each of the empires and created a schooling system which did its job beautifully. It produced an array of identical clocks where the same abilities were even dressed the same way and were then shipped off to run the show. The British Empire is an example of a humongously large human computer, a brilliant design which the British were able to employ almost over the entire globe and run successfully for hundreds of years.

We should applaud that, but not keep it going when the empire is not there.

Graham: So are you suggesting that we have an education and assessment system that is based around compliance rather than critical thinking?

Sugata: Well, I think yes. Look at the average adolescent. They have their smartphones which have access to every piece of knowledge that humanity has ever had which they have to put away every morning when they come to school. They enter these large school gates which are still made of 19th-century iron. It looks like a jail, actually. They go in there until the bell rings for them to be released and then the doors open and they come out and they whip out their phones. That's the first thing they do.

They show extraordinary amounts of discriminatory and critical thinking in being able to detect a fraud and fraudulent offers. In fact, it's not uncommon for adults to ask children, 'What do you think of that? Do you think it's worth going to? Do you think the price is all right?' It is they who tell us. It is possible that critical thinking has happened in spite of us, in spite of the schooling system in a generation that had to survive in this environment. Whereas what the school was doing was teaching them how to survive in a world that no longer exists.

'What the school was doing was teaching them how to survive in a world that no longer exists.'

Andreas Schleicher

director, Directorate of Education and Skills

OECD, Paris, France

Interview

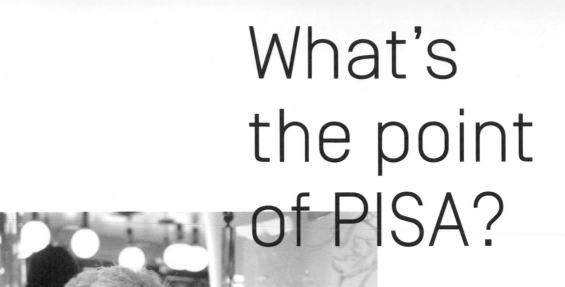

photo credit: Graham Brown-Martin

What's the point of PISA?

From the experiences of my journey it seems that the OECD's PISA (Programme for International Student Assessment) provokes strong emotions from educators the world over. Intended as a diagnostic tool to bring together policymakers into a dialogue about education and improvement, it has become widely criticised as a league table that the very same policymakers use to beat up their respective educators in a kind of 'must do better' end of term report.

Sir Ken Robinson recently criticised PISA for 'squeezing out' other more creative subjects and creating an anxiety around education that was 'grotesque'.

I met with Andreas Schleicher in Paris to learn more about PISA. A German statistician and researcher in the field of education, Schleicher is the Director for the Directorate of Education and Skills at the OECD and the coordinator of PISA. I found my conversation with Andreas illuminating and whilst I have my reservations about the benefits of standardised testing I was left without any doubt that Schleicher was one of the good guys.

Graham Brown-Martin: What is OECD and PISA about?

Andreas Schleicher: OECD is an international organisation of principally industrialised countries, but many more also working to develop better policies for better lives. Actually, in the spheres of public policy, education is just one facet of all of that. When we talk about education it's really about how we can develop the right skills for people, how we can make sure that people get the opportunities to use those skills, and how do we match the emerging skills to the emerging demand in our society. It's a typical way of looking for the OECD: cross-sectoral, cross-government, with all sectors of society. It's all about better policies.

Graham: Am I right in thinking that the OECD is driven towards economic development?

Andreas: Not really, I actually think it's to improve the quality of lives of people. For exam-ple, when we measure development, it's not GDP. GDP is one facet of this, but we look at all facets of what drives the quality of human life: social participation, economic outcome, civic participation, all of those issues are part of the agenda of the OECD. That's why we work in education.

Graham: So would I be wrong to describe OECD as economic determinists?

Andreas: Absolutely. I think actually when you look at the OECD, when you look at the work programme, you're going to find lots of things that look at this in a much broader sense. For example, we have a very big work programme on inclusive growth. It is not about how to regenerate more output, but how do we ensure that we distribute the benefits of economic growth to the widest group in society.

Graham: What do you suggest are the strengths and weaknesses of PISA today?

Andreas: The idea of PISA has always been to create a platform for dialogue among countries, among policymakers, among educators, among researchers. When we look at this, we don't have yet a global outlook on education. Education is still a very domestic inward-looking business. Even schools don't necessarily or are not intuitively looking out to the next school, or the next teacher. They all work in their own field. They don't have this kind of common language across countries, and that was the idea of PISA, and it does that very well.

When we started it, I remember my first meeting of education ministers where we had all of them sitting around the table and everyone telling us, 'I have got the best education system. If I have a little problem left, then last year I put a reform in place to fix it.' There was no real genuine dialogue. Today, people go out to ask: What they have done in Finland? What do they do in China? And so on. It's looking outwards. PISA has shown what's possible in education and it also gives people who are complacent a bit of a reality check.

I think PISA is very strong in measuring problem-solving skills, critical thinking, mathemat-ics, science and literacy. It's just beginning to measure things like social competence that we know are really important for the success of people. Intra-personal competence. It's not about what you know, it's what you do with what you know that determines whether you're successful. I think we're just beginning to actually capture those kind of outcomes. That's one dimension.

The second dimension that PISA needs to become better is to link what students learn to how they actually learn. Now we want to link their learning environment at school, teaching policies, teaching practices to those outcomes. Education is still pretty much a black box, and opening that, I think, is an important mission as well.

Graham: It seems that many educators believe that policymakers use PISA as a sort of league table to beat them up. Is this how you imagined it would be used?

Andreas: No. It's not the purpose and I don't think it's a dominant use of it. It's usually three days after the launch of a PISA round in the media today. But after three days people start to think what they can do. I can tell you in my country, Germany, back in 2000, there was a big PISA result that caused a big shock with the public. It was the first time that the sixteen German ministers of education properly looked outside. They went to Finland. Before, many of them wouldn't know where Finland was on the map. Ask yourself: How many delegations have travelled to countries like Finland, or Ontario, Canada, or Shanghai and China? I think in that respect PISA has achieved its objectives of creating an intensive dialogue that strives for better policies for education. And this league table, I don't think there's anything wrong with it; it's a starting point for discussion. You don't get further just by looking at where you are.

Graham: Do you think that the context of the nation participating in PISA is important?

Andreas: I think so. But at the very same time, we often look at context as an excuse not to look outward. We think we are really different from everybody else, so we can't really work with anybody else. I think that's fundamentally wrong. We need to think. You can't copy and paste in an education system; I think everybody understood that. But you can learn a lot from what makes school systems successful. Why do Asian countries place this high value on education, this aspiration for everyone to succeed? Why are they so successful in overcoming social background? In our countries, if you come from a poor family, you're doing a lot worse in school than someone coming from an impoverished country. That is not the case in South East Asia. We can actually look outward how they achieve this, and I think that's really what PISA does. PISA is not good at telling you what you need to do. But PISA is very good at telling you what everybody else has been doing and with what success, and that can be a good source of inspiration.

Graham: So it seems that there remains a great misunderstanding of what PISA is for, would you agree?

Andreas: Maybe I'm misunderstanding but overall I think the message is right. I'll give you an example. In my own country, Germany, when the results came out there was real devastation. Everybody prior to PISA would have said, 'Well, it's normal that students from disadvantaged families don't do well. That's why we put them in lower tracks of the system.' Suddenly they see, well wow, actually countries do much better with this. And within the last ten years, Germany was able to close half of the achievement gap. The performance of immigrant students improved dramatically and it tells you. You see that you can do better, that's what PISA does. You look at who actually does better. Let's have a look at what they're doing. You try to configure those ideas in your own context, and you can actually leverage a lot of improvement. There are plenty of examples from around the world.

Graham: So really it's a diagnostic tool.

Andreas: Yes.

Graham: How does OECD in terms of PISA define creativity?

Andreas: PISA is not measuring whether students can reproduce what they've learned. The world economy no longer rewards people for what they know —Google knows everything— but for what people do with what they know. To do well on the PISA test you need to be able to extrapolate from what you know, to apply your knowledge in other contexts, to connect the dots. You need to demonstrate that you can think across subject disciplines. Many of our tasks are not physics tasks, or chemistry tasks. You need to link history and physics in a way. Whoever can demonstrate that kind of thinking, out-of-the-box thinking, trans-vessel thinking, will do well on PISA. Then one of the biggest surprises of the PISA test has been [the mistaken assumption] that ... because you're not doing so well in mathematics you must be very creative, [or that] the kids in China, because they do so well in mathematics ... can't be creative. Actually this is another example of the sort of myth that PISA has debunked really. A lot of people would know that: just go to Silicon Valley. Look around [at] how many Chinese you find there.

The challenge of some economies is often that they're not making good use of people's creativity, their most creative minds. They have the kind of labour market that doesn't reward that kind of thinking.

I think creative skills are the differentiator today. The routine cognitive skills are no longer valued. In fact, some of the criticism to PISA goes the other way around. They basically say, 'Well you test some thinking skills, but this is not mathematics. Mathematics are those kind of formulas.'

Graham: Sir Ken Robinson suggests that PISA creates anxiety around education that is grotesque, how do you respond to that?

Andreas: Again, looking back to my own country, yes, PISA created a lot of anxiety in 2000. Performance wasn't good, social disparities were large. But then that anxiety translated very quickly in a very constructive action on the part of educators, on the part of policymakers.

If we are totally confident and complacent with what we have today, we're not going to change. One of the fundamental problems that we see in education is that the world around us changes much faster than our education system. Everybody says reform is too fast and too fast paced. In fact, the demand for skills is evolving much faster than the way we teach, the way we learn in school. I think anxiety is a great starting point. Translating it into a really meaningful action is the purpose of PISA. I do think that it does that, not in all countries, but in some countries, really well.

Graham: Why in China did you test in Shanghai rather than the country?

Andreas: It's simply [a capacity issue] —I mean the demand and exercise of something like PISA in a country like China... Actually I'm quite surprised with the Chinese. They have now started very seriously to expand it to other provinces, but building the infrastructure for this is a multi-year task.

Graham: Perhaps even a generational task?

Andreas: Exactly. In some of the areas, you don't have functioning infrastructures for school, how you can actually dream of mounting an assessment like PISA. It's a beginning, Shanghai, clearly it's not China. It's a very exceptional province in education, but I don't think we should dismiss its success. Shanghai is larger than most European countries. It's a pretty big entity, 25 million people living there, in very challenging circumstances. There are some super-rich people but there are also some very, very poor people, and how the education system has been able to leverage the talent of disadvantaged children is something we can learn a lot from. How it creates the educational aspiration in first-generation children. I think that's very impressive. There's a lot we can learn from it. We shouldn't extrapolate to China. Shanghai doesn't represent China. But it's been a meaningful and useful reference point in the PISA assessment I would think, as the Indian provinces have been, but in both countries it's going to take a lot of time to get it.

'The child is the starting point,
the centre, and the end.
His development, his growth,
is the ideal. It alone furnishes
the standard. To the growth
of the child all studies are
subservient; they are instruments
valued as they serve the needs
of growth. Personality, character,
is more than subject matter.
Not knowledge or information,
but self realisation, is the goal.'

Thank you for making it this far, even if you're one of those people who start at the end. I went on a global journey seeking innovation and transformative practice in how we teach and learn, and I found it, everywhere. My big takeaways are that context is king, digital technologies are a catalyst for change and that the future, rather than a preset destination, is what we, as a society, decide to make it.

The title of this book, *Learning {Re}imagined: How the Connected Society is Transforming Learning*, was something I had been considering for some years before WISE gave me the opportunity to make it a reality. My idea was to document the ways in which our global society is reflecting on the way we learn and, perhaps more importantly, why we learn.

The influence of digital technology was the starting point of my exploration but I believe it would have been a missed opportunity if I had only reported on the what, how and why of digital deployments for learning without reflecting on the social, cultural and historical contexts. I didn't want to add another book to the pile that explains how technology is the solution now what's the problem?

I truly believe digital technology can have a positive role in the transformation of education systems and how we learn. I also think, however, before we race ahead and digitise 19th- and 20th-century practices and beliefs, we need a wider public debate about what it's all for. If we agree that every child has a right to an education then what is that education for? Only when we answer that question can we really decide how our educational establishments can be truly transformed at a global scale using digital platforms.

By public, I really do mean the wider community beyond educators, technologists and policymakers. If we are to accept that there are profound challenges ahead for our society and our species then the decisions taken must engage us all.

But what are these challenges?

It seems to me that we are a remarkable species, blessed with a beautiful home, intent on its own annihilation. Historically the pain we have wrecked on one another and the damage we have caused to our only home, and fellow inhabitants, is an act of global unconsciousness where ideology trumps survival. What can we do to empower our children and future generations to make better decisions than their ancestors?

What will we do when the antibiotics that we believed had won the war on disease just a few decades ago no longer work? Climate change, population, energy, water, food, shelter, sanitation, poverty, peace; these are challenges that will affect every human being on this planet.

What is the purpose of education? I think it is the survival of our species, not just one elite group or culture but all of us in our amazing diversity, for without diversity there will be no innovation, no art, no dreams.

I was asked during the creation of this book if I thought the world has ever been united in a global purpose and it's hard to think beyond the global conflicts of two world wars or the march of industrialisation that is the fountainhead of globalisation. But it also occurs to me that when you connect billions of people via our digital networks and let them explore and share each other's ideas and beliefs that something unexpected and amazing could happen. Of course, unfettered freedom of speech across borders is feared by a great many institutions, nations and corporations. It challenges the *status quo*, challenges the hegemonies of vested interests and societal control. That said, we're already seeing the advance of leaderless, self-organising groups and borderless projects with no vested interest that, for example, place advanced open source technology and software into the hands of the masses. These are characteristics of what happens when you let people talk, share and play. This is the connected society.

It's been my privilege to meet so many inspiring, passionate people who took the time to share their imagination with me. I hope that I have managed to capture and convey the essence of their thinking. We've still got a way to go but we are the first generation in history to begin a genuinely global discourse about our society and about learning. Digital platforms are an enabler for this dialogue but I wonder if technology is really the driver of social change and transformation. Does it shape the dialogue? Is the medium, as Marshall McLuhan once suggested, the message?

McLuhan was a technological determinist. He, like many others of his time, believed and presented convincing arguments that it was technology that shaped and determined society. Whilst this view has been widely discredited in academic circles, it is experiencing a bit of a revival. In fact, one can hardly read a newspaper or attend an educational technology conference without being convinced that there is an implicit causality between advances in technology and society.

The link between technology and society is so embedded in our thinking that we quite often mistake it for common sense. We classify entire civilisations by their tools and instruments, referring to the stone, iron, steam, and now, digital, ages. Marx talked about the windmill and the feudal lord, the steam engine and the industrial capitalist. But the truth is that we got sucked into this linguistic prison by accident. Archaeology and anthropology were amongst the first academic disciplines to treat technological change seriously, where material artefacts are often the sole record in non-literate societies. Thus, we typically name societies by their dominant technological artefacts even where causality isn't explicit. I've even used the term 'connected society' in the title of this book!

So how do I get out of this one?

I would say that ten years ago I had completely bought the determinist argument hook, line and sinker. After all if it wasn't technology determining the shape of society then it was the economy, right?

At any global summit on education or, for example, Davos in Switzerland, organisations from the World Bank to the OECD would have us believe that investment in education will deliver the essential human capital to meet economic development plans and national prosperity. And, of course, they're right. It's just different ways of looking at things and measuring them. We could kick this ball around until the cows come home!

You could make arguments for a host of other determinants such as biology, gender, religion, etc., that shape our society and many of them would, in part, be plausible and may, to some extent, even be right. But one of the key determinants that we should not ignore is social determinism and my belief is that the connected society has the power to amplify human agency, our influence, voice and ownership of our future. And where better to start than with education, one of the world's powerful superstructures that supports the foundation of our society.

This brings me to my first conclusion that context is king and that the nature of transformation is related to context.

In Ghana, for example, providing access to books via inexpensive eReaders, part of the Worldreader programme, has transformed rural schools. The scarce availability of up-to-date books in rural Africa and the costs of distribution in printed form have impoverished many schools. The reduction of cost and distribution of books in digital form via inexpensive readers in places where there is restricted access to the Internet now reach many thousands of children, teachers and parents. Similarly, in rural India, much of which is 'media dark' and with limited electricity, a basic mobile phone is used to save lives through the teaching of maternal healthcare.

In England, America and Lebanon we saw how ubiquitous tablet computing in schools leads to greater efficiencies that allowed the schools to transform their curriculum and timetables to enjoy greater freedom to collaborate and reflect in solving problems, hanging where and when learning could take place. In Singapore, we learned how simulations in the forms of collaborative digital games could provide a safe platform where students could consider citizenship and the formation of societies. In Jordan we learned how students could work together and share their learning with each other using social media platforms. In Qatar we discovered how children's learning that had been challenged by traditional teaching methods, was transformed by assistive technologies which enabled students to participate and exceed earlier expectations that they would be left behind.

My second conclusion, that digital technologies are a catalyst for change, might be self-evident but we must continue to ask what these changes can and should be. Historically, technology has been used in factories, offices and other aspects of our society to gain quality and cost efficiencies. By reducing the possibility of human error, machines and computers have in many circumstances transformed craft production into mass production. Computers and the Internet have been the great disintermediators that have cut out the middlemen between individuals and the provision of products and services. Global enterprises such as Amazon mean that we no longer have to visit physical shops; media streaming providers such as YouTube, Spotify and Netflix mean that we have immediate access to an unprecedented volume of entertainment without stepping out of our homes. With Wikipedia we are building our own body of knowledge and sharing it. But when we consider teaching and learning, is our imagination limited to merely digitising and seeking more efficient ways of distributing and testing a curriculum? Are these platforms simply going to reinforce our 19th-century teaching and assessment processes?

Sugata Mitra wonders what would happen if we made it mandatory that every child had today's technology with them in an examination room and that they were obligated to discuss and share their answers with each other during the test. Surely this is a greater and more useful test of a child's ability in this age than asking them to simply regurgitate facts using a pen and paper?

Contrary to the notion of disintermediating and mass production afforded by industrial processes, we now see the re-emergence of a maker movement whose work reflects our value in the authentic; we encourage our children to design and create rather than merely consume. Perhaps it's not inconceivable that we will witness a re-emergence of the physical economy as it re-aligns itself within this new digital world.

The change that we'll see will no doubt rely on our answer to what we, as a society, re-imagine what education and learning are for, which brings me to my third conclusion: the future is what we make it.

My conversation with Keri Facer recalled that, regardless of what our futurologists and policymakers tell us, the future does not yet exist, and that we, as a society, have a voice in what it can be. Mitch Resnick from MIT believes that our society could be more like a life-long kindergarten, full of wonder and curiosity that allows us to solve challenges in novel ways. And challenges we have in abundance.

For a moment let's re-imagine that the purpose of learning, the purpose of education, is to equip our present and future generations with the skills to solve the big challenges that face humanity. Let's imagine that we can reach a global consensus over these challenges – from population, to equity, to the environment, to our wellbeing. And let's imagine a future where we solve these challenges together. How might that transform the way we learn?

During my journey nearly every person and organisation I met and visited re-imagined learning not just in terms of technological or economic progress but in creating a better, more equitable world. This is ultimately about the human spirit and where we go next; it's about lifting it together and solving the bigger challenges ahead. As Seth Godin suggested, education is no longer about remembering facts but solving problems. Of course, the ingenuity of our species will continue to invent new technologies designed to improve our lives and it is within our education practices that learners, young or old, will gain the insights and skills to enable this. We will always arrive at crossroads where we don't have a map, where we won't know the unintended consequences of our acts. What occurs to me, after all that I saw and heard, is the importance of the teacher, not as an information delivery system, but as a guide and human compass to what is important and ultimately, to what is right.

John Dewey, in his essay 'The Child and the Curriculum' (1902),[24] argues that in the debate about education's purpose there are two distinct views. One, he suggests, holds that the subject matter, or curriculum, is the purpose, furnishing the end and determining the method. The other school of thought, and one that I'm more inclined to support, says:

> The child is the starting point, the center, and the end. His development, his growth, is the ideal. It alone furnishes the standard. To the growth of the child all studies are subservient; they are instruments valued as they serve the needs of growth. Personality, character, is more than subject matter. Not knowledge or information, but self-realisation, is the goal.

Call me old-fashioned, but I wouldn't trust an algorithm to do this.

Thank you for reading.

@GrahamBM

#LearningREimagined

Resources

1 Equinox Learning 2030 Summit
learning2030.org

2 *Stop Stealing Dreams*, Seth Godin
www.sethgodin.com/sg/docs/stopstealingdreamsscreen.pdf

3 www.itu.int/en/ITU-D/Statistics/Documents/publications/mis2013/MIS2013_without_Annex_4.pdf

4 farmerline.org

5 otra-educacion.blogspot.co.uk/2013/06/cuba-and-finland.html

6 1to1schools.net/2012/06/ballpoint-pens-the-ruin-of-education-in-our-country

7 www.oecd.org/countries/singapore/46581101.pdf

8 ibid

9 zhaolearning.com/2012/06/06/test-scores-vs-entrepreneurship-pisa-timss-and-confidence

10 www.essafoundation.co.uk

11 twitter.com/atopiary

12 www.youtube.com/watch?v=0ZJwSjor4hM

13 twitter.com/lulzsec

14 Sebastien James, Review of Education Capital, April 2011, Department of Education, UK; www.education.gov.uk/publications

15 www.theguardian.com/education/2012/oct/02/new-school-building-designs-curve-ban

16 Measure of Academic Progress
www.nwea.org/node/98

17 Ballard & Tighe IPT Oral Proficiency Tests
www.ballard-tighe.com/products/la/iptFamilyTests.asp

18 www.wired.com/2012/11/netflix-data-gamble

19 The Crisis of Democracy, Report on the Governability of Democracies to the Trilateral Commission, published by the New York University Press, 1975
www.trilateral.org/download/doc/crisis_of_democracy.pdf

20 Childcare Minister Elizabeth Truss attacks unruly nurseries
www.theguardian.com/education/2013/apr/22/childcare-minister-elizabeth-truss-nurseries

21 The Rise of Alternative Education in China, CNN
www.cnn.com/2014/03/26/world/asia/china-alternative-education

22 China's students take on tough Gaokao university entrance exam, BBC
www.bbc.co.uk/news/world-asia-china-18349873

23 www.asercentre.org

24 *The Child and the Curriculum*, John Dewey, 1902
www.gutenberg.org/ebooks/29259

But did they realize that they were cheating the children whom they had been paid to teach, and that their failure to turn up for classes could destroy the future of promising

But Dede had other thoughts. Getting angry at this was not going [...]m. Maybe it w[...]e exercise the[...] the day, an[...]